Heinrich von Kleist

the major works of
Heinrich von Kleist
by ROBERT E. HELBLING

A New Directions Book

ACKNOWLEDGMENTS
Excerpts from James Kirkup's translation of *The Prince of Homburg* (Copyright © 1959 by James Kirkup) are reprinted by permission of John Cushman Associates, Inc.

Passages from *The Marquise of O—— and Other Stories,* translated by Martin Greenberg (Copyright © 1960 by Criterion Books, Inc.), are reprinted by permission of Criterion Books, an Intext publisher.

Manufactured in the United States of America
First published clothbound and as New Directions Paperbook 390 in 1975
Published simultaneously in Canada by McClelland & Stewart, Ltd.

Library of Congress Cataloging in Publication Data

Helbling, Robert E
    Heinrich von Kleist.

    (A New Directions Book)
    Includes bibliographical references and index.
    1. Kleist, Heinrich von, 1777–1811—Criticism and interpretation. I. Title.
PT2379.Z5H4   1975   838'.6'09   74–26509
ISBN 0–8112–0563–0
ISBN 0–8112–0564–0 pbk.

New Directions Books are published for James Laughlin
by New Directions Publishing Corporation,
333 Sixth Avenue, New York 10014

Contents

Preface

Over one hundred sixty years after his death at the age of thirty-four, Heinrich von Kleist remains a peculiarly ambivalent figure in world literature, a subject of endless academic debates in Germany, but relatively little known abroad. Yet, those outside of Germany who have read one or two of his *Novellen* or dramas, even in translation, or were fortunate enough to see the celebrated Gérard Philippe in the title role of *The Prince of Homburg* at the *Comédie Française* in the late fifties, have all been struck by the boldness of Kleist's artistic vision and style.

In Germany the secondary literature on Kleist is voluminous, fairly comparable in size to that written on Schiller or even Goethe. Among critics, he has been all things to all people: a romantic, a realist, a Rousseauist, a Prussian nationalist, a Junker *manqué,* a social critic, a political writer, a metaphysical dreamer, an existentialist temperament, a psychoanalytic talent, a Catholic writer *in extremis,* and much more. Maybe it attests to Kleist's greatness, certainly to his uniqueness, that he does not run according to type, that he "is" all these things and yet none in particular.

In recent years his name seems to crop up increasingly in literary circles as a forerunner of the literature of the "grotesque" and "absurd," as a strangely modern and Kafkaesque temperament, a writer of *Novellen* who, ahead of his time, excelled in what might be called "chronicle fiction," while his drama is seen as an early expression of the contemporary concern with the powers and failures of language to "communicate."

In all these debates what is never questioned is Kleist's passionate interest in the problem of human subjectivity, man's intense and spontaneous affirmation of his individuality. In a world in which the center no longer holds—and Kleist experienced in his life and thought the collapse of political institutions and intellectual structures in a most personally agonizing way—the only access to reality for the individual seems to consist in his opening himself up to his own being, no matter what the consequences. But Kleist does not advocate the drugged consciousness of the modern would-be mystic. Nor does he offer any facile psychological massage. On the contrary, he retains throughout his writings an uncompromising, almost cruel, perception of the inescapable realities of the empirical world. The result is a dramatic clash between individual consciousness or "feeling" and a deceptive or unresponsive world, trembling on the verge of the absurd. The redeeming feature in this brutal confrontation is the greater self-possession attained by the hero, or rather heroine, for a majority of Kleist's great but lacerated souls are women—a fact which might be of considerable interest to the modern surveyor of feminist literature.

My study attempts to give a balanced and analytic view of that central theme in Kleist's *Weltanschauung,* its genesis in his thought, and its variations and artistic expression in his major works. In this endeavor I have tried to avoid the urbane Anglo-Saxon predilection for mere psychological or formalistic interpretation on the one hand and the at times speculative, metaphysical tendency of German criticism on the other. But I am indebted to both sides for helping me formulate my own views and insights, which I hope will make

Kleist's works more accessible to the student of German literature as well as to the general English-speaking reader.

The organization of the book should aid in this intent: all analyses contain synopses of the works, and the compact theoretical second section, "The Elusive World of Kleist: Problems of Kleist Criticism," may be read with equal benefit, I believe, before *or* after the discussion of the works, depending on the degree of the reader's acquaintance with the literature on Kleist. For the novice, it might be more helpful to read the discussion of the works first. A brief history of Kleist criticism up to the Second World War, together with an annotated bibliography of newer works and articles, as well as an index, conclude the volume.

All quotes from Kleist's writings are from available English translations of his works and, where no translations exist, I have provided my own (especially from Kleist's epistolary writings and essays). My thanks go to the publishers of the existing translations, who have graciously accorded permission for quotations.

I also wish to thank Professor Kurt F. Reinhardt, who many years ago directed my dissertation on some philosophic aspects of Kant and Kleist and in his seminars and writings greatly stimulated my own thought. Any lapses in my critical approach and penetration are my responsibility, not his.

R. E. H.

A Peripatetic Writer
without a Biography

A Peripatetic Writer without a Biography

For all his contemporary fame and the arduous scholarly research spent on tracing his life and the genesis of his works, Heinrich von Kleist has largely remained, in the words of a recent critic, "a writer without a biography." [1] To be sure, he wrote many letters to his friends and family which have been preserved. But they only allude to, never fully reveal, the personal existential conflicts that held him in their grip and led to his tragic suicide. Though often deeply involved in the business of this world, Kleist never seemed to be wholly of this world. He remained an enigma to himself and his friends, for throughout his short life he was in quest of an elusive certainty about himself and the world that lent his personality a restless, protean quality which defies complete analysis. Even the pictures we possess of him show such a variety of likenesses that in some cases their genuineness must be questioned. A death mask which at times has been said to be Kleist's may be that of another, and the one portrait of undoubted authenticity, made in 1801 after an original miniature, incurred Kleist's own disfavor for its lack of verisimilitude.

Born on October 10 or 18, 1777,[2] in Frankfurt-on-the-Oder into a family of distinguished officers and generals, Kleist at the age of fifteen embarked halfheartedly upon a military career himself and participated in the campaign against the French Revolutionary armies in the Rhineland. He soon came to abhor the life of a soldier and upon his return to Potsdam sought relief from the monotony of garrison life in the pleasures of music. Endowed with an exceptional but untutored talent, he played the clarinet and flute in a quartet of like-minded officers, among them his lifelong friend Rühle von Lilienstern. But consumed by a thirst for knowledge and "truth," Kleist, in the spring of 1799, resigned his commission and entered the University of Frankfurt, then a sleepy provincial institution. In two long letters addressed to von Lilienstern and his former tutor, Christian Ernst Martini—Kleist had lost both parents early in life—he expresses the hope of finding true happiness in virtuous endeavor and intellectual perfection:

. . . if in the process of schooling our judgment, of honing our intellectual acuity through all manner of experiences and studies, we gradually enshrine in our hearts the principles of magnanimity, justice, altruism, steadfastness . . . then we will never be unhappy.[3]

With obvious pride he adds that in the pursuit of this goal he has so far devoted all his energy to the study of mathematics and philosophy, which he considers to be the twin pillars of all knowledge and truth. Within less than one and a half years Kleist managed to absorb, though somewhat hastily, an impressive amount of scientific and mathematical lore and to become engaged to Wilhelmine von Zenge, the daughter of a ranking officer. His letters of that period abound in disquisitions on the necessity of establishing a firm plan of life which would assure continued intellectual progress and happiness. Many of his letters to his fiancée are moralistic treatises designed to teach her the principles of the good life. There are occasional hints of a contained sensuality, but his impulses are deflected by gnawing doubts about his capacity to find fulfillment in life through love. His anxious questioning often produces the youthful pedantries which have unnerved some of his critics. Ostensibly, Kleist was steeped in the eudaemonistic canons of a popular and somewhat outdated phase of Enlightenment thought. But it is obvious from his introspective stance that he was wrestling as much with his own problems as with the principles of an optimistic philosophy. His frequent appeals to reason are prompted not only by an ambition to excel in abstract thinking but also by his intense search for the purpose of his own life. Kleist is agitated by a vital concern, not a mere philosophic problem, yet for some time he tries desperately to understand the one in terms of the other.

Enough of his own anguish pierces through the crust of Enlightenment jargon to reveal the future dramatist. He voices the nagging suspicion that human life might be under the sway of mere irrational chance. A plan of life based on "understanding" and "reason," enacted with a sense of "duty," would be an inner bulwark against the caprice of "fate." Some of the terms he uses are borrowed from professional philosophy, Kantian or "popular," but are made to express the search for his own inner vocation. Yet the molds of a ready-made philosophy could not possibly contain his immense, though vague, aspirations. Soon his letters redound with notes of anguish ostensibly caused by a dark premonition that his striving would never be fully understood by friends and family alike and that he might have to face his destiny in loneliness and terror. He sought refuge from the threat of inner solitude in his attachment to Wilhelmine. Behind the schoolmasterly tone and the naïve zealousness with which he hoped to fashion his fiancée into an exemplar of moral beauty, we can easily discern the struggle of a lonely young man for a fully satisfying union with a woman. He seemed to be aiming at nothing less than the godliness of the "I–Thou" relationship described by Martin Buber more than a century later, which may well lie beyond the ken and experience of most ordinary mortals. The awkwardness of Kleist's attempts to arrive at such a union presents a tragicomic spectacle: a moralizing, inhibited Faust who preaches at a sensible girl seeking no more than a simple domestic happiness unspoiled by eerie pedantries.

Kleist soon began to realize that hackneyed moralistic phrases were incapable of conveying the entire depth of his subjective being and to muse wistfully over the failure of language as a vehicle of true communication. ". . . we lack a means of communication. The only thing we possess—language—is incapable of portraying the soul; it only gives us broken-up fragments . . ." [4] In his letters of November 1800 to March 1801, he resorts increasingly to metaphor and visual imagery to suggest the real nature of his inner experience. The writer in Kleist was in the making before the "Kant crisis" released the suppressed talent. Though immersed in the personal quest for his inner vocation, Kleist at times managed to be refreshingly alert to the problems of the contemporaneous world. With journalistic skill he describes in one letter the scatterbrained agitation of the citizens of Würzburg before the approaching French forces. During a visit to an insane asylum he proves to have astoundingly modern insights into mental therapy when he informs us that many of the patients could be restored to a useful life if only their families were capable of unflagging love, as though he foresaw his own alienation from his family in future years. In other letters, he describes with a traveler's curiosity the customs and idiosyncracies of many German principalities and devotes some attention to the Catholic form of religious worship, which, at this time, he deemed mechanical and devoid of feeling. Although he felt more favorably inclined toward Catholic liturgy and art in later years, he always remained at an inner distance from any organized religion, even that of his own Protestant upbringing. Dogma and ceremonial could no more help him in his quest for selfhood than a philosophic system.

As of August 1800, Kleist had abandoned his studies at Frankfurt, moved to Berlin, and undertaken a mysterious journey to Würzburg in the company of a newly acquired friend, Ludwig von Brockes, who took a fatherly interest in the distraught young man, a few years his junior. He seemed to have kindled in Kleist a certain love of nature, though rather of the academic, Rousseauist variety, and generally tried to help him find his place in life with more ease. What exactly prompted Kleist's abrupt departure from Frankfurt and Berlin has remained largely a matter of conjecture. There seems to be little doubt, however, that a short essay written by Wilhelmine at Kleist's own behest, of which he had apparently seen but the first page, left him in a state of inner agitation. In her dutiful way Wilhelmine had probably expounded the joys of motherhood—the essay has been lost—which might have stirred up some doubts in Kleist about his capacity to satisfy the physical demands made on him in the ideal union of which he was dreaming. The fear of impotence may have had a minor physical cause exaggerated out of proportion by his hypertension, which in turn may have had psychosomatic effects. In any case, Kleist sought relief from his real or imaginary ailment and chanced upon a medical specialist practicing in Würzburg who supposedly cured him.[5] For a fleeting moment he lived in a state of euphoria, anticipating the domestic bliss that might soon be his. He extolled the idyllic notion of living in a country setting surrounded by Wilhelmine's love and edifying books, an ideal which some critics attribute to Rousseau's influence. Kleist himself interpreted the Würzburg journey as a *per aspera ad astra* experience which supposedly enabled him to overcome a crippling neurosis or physical impediment and contemplate the prospect of useful citizenship and fatherhood. It is especially at this moment that he imposed on Wilhelmine his pedantic epistolary exercises on moralistic subjects designed to prepare her better for her future role as mother and spouse.

But it is quite apparent that Kleist was indirectly engaged in another disquieting self-examination. Symptomatically, he did not return to Wilhelmine in Frankfurt but stayed in Berlin. Soon his letters reverberate with strident notes of despair. He saw but a dim future ahead of him. The prospect of accepting government employment filled him with loathing. In one letter, he asks Wilhelmine for a long wait of ten years before she could expect him to settle down in a profession. Or he proposed whimsical projects to her such as a joint move to the French-speaking part of Switzerland, there to teach German, or a venture into France to establish himself as a lecturer on Kantian philosophy. As soon as he had to convert his diffuse yearnings into the practical exigencies of life, he apparently found nothing but impossible projects. At one point, he locked himself in his room for a full week in a desperate attempt to decide upon an irrevocable "plan of life." To no avail. He sensed a total existential crisis approaching. Even the pillars of science and philosophy on which he had intended to build his life began to totter. Though he professed his deep love of knowledge *per se,* he felt but disgust for the mental confinement required by specialized scholarship. It is all too clear that Kleist was not in search of a professional career but an inner vocation. A long and arduous quest still lay ahead of him, and he bitterly complained that he was constantly living in the future rather than in the immediate present. A rupture with his unsatisfactory present had to occur. It came in the form of his much discussed "Kant crisis."

On March 21 and 22, 1801, he wrote two letters to Wilhelmine and his half sister Ulrike in which he announces the total collapse of his inner convictions as a result of having studied the "newest Kantian philosophy." The explanation he offers is perplexing to his biographers, since he gave evidence of being reasonably familiar with the Critical Philosophy seven or eight months, if not a full year, prior to the overt crisis. It is almost impossible to determine exactly which work of Kant or perhaps even Fichte (who considered himself to be a *"Neukantianer"*) should be most closely associated with Kleist's inner gloom. But it is almost certain that the blame he heaped on Kantian philosophy was as much a subrational decoy as a true explanation for his mood of despondency. In his letters addressed to Wilhelmine and Ulrike prior to the Kant crisis he had largely assumed the artificial stance of a spiritual mentor expounding the optimistic canons of the popular philosophy. But the tenor of his inner life was a far cry from the eudaemonism of Enlightenment thought. When the breach between a facile philosophy and his personal anxiety widened, the crisis was inevitable. Although, superficially, it looked as though one philosophy had destroyed another in his inner world, the "newest Kantian philosophy" almost certainly did not create his despair but rather furnished him with the linguistic means to express it. This is not to accuse Kleist of "inauthenticity." If he put up a philosophic smoke screen between himself and the world, it does not mean that he was fully aware of the true nature of his despair beyond knowing that he must listen

8

to the inner voice, no matter what the consequences. In one sense, he took Kantian philosophy seriously just because its undeniable streak of skepticism responded to his mood.

The twentieth century would define Kleist's inner experience more in terms of the existential categories of "anguish," "forlornness," and the like, as was actually done in France,[6] and more recently in Germany.[7] Kantian philosophy is, of course, not foreign to these moods, since in its ethics it stresses so much the need for self-determination in a world of unknowable, albeit postulated, final causes. Kleist himself describes his state of mind in terms which may conjure up the visions of the absurd and the experience of anguish that fill the pages of modern existentialist literature. He speaks of a strange inner tension. He laments his lack of self-possession and bluntly confesses to Wilhelmine that not even her love could fill him with "consciousness," if he were unable to discover what he ought to do. He could not find an ointment for the burning unrest within. All he could recognize was the summons of an inner urge but did not know where it beckoned. Like Raskolnikov and other existential heroes, or antiheroes, he felt acutely the need of defining himself, not merely in thought but also in action, through a significant deed, although his activist yearnings remained couched in moralistic terms. Repeatedly he voiced the dictum that there is an obligation on man "to do something good, absolutely." But his consciousness gobbled up projects as fast as it could produce them. Instead of accomplishing that fully conscious, self-defining deed he longed for, he was carried along by blind forces. At the same time, he used up his modest inheritance and for the rest of his life frequently had to appeal to Ulrike's generosity to help him out of his recurrent financial crises.

Subsequently, a combination of trivial circumstances made him leave Berlin to go to Paris, there to further his studies in mathematics and "science." But again his inner needs remained largely unfulfilled. He was repulsed by the sophistication, worldly glitter, and frivolity of the metropolis and turned away in disgust from the conceits and the scholarly pedantries of its savants. Conversely, his aesthetic and artistic leanings began to reveal themselves more compellingly. Even in Dresden, on his way to Paris, he was enthralled by the paintings in the city's art gallery, especially Raphael's Madonna, and the stirring organ music in the cathedral. In Paris he frequently visited the Louvre—so he assures us—and mused in one letter that the highest aim of art must be to render forcefully one feeling or mood, as though he wished to indict the waste of sensations he perceived in the life around him. Though his introspection might be attributed to the *dépaysement* experienced by a brooding German thrown into the stream of Parisian life, he recorded his disenchantment in accents that reveal the future dramatist. The outer world is a mass of confusion, life is under the spell of irrational chance, and human consciousness, thrown back upon itself, has its reasons and purposes of which the world knows not.

It is in this mood of inner withdrawal, kindled further by his fascination with Rousseauist ideals about the natural life, that he conceived an eccentric plan of settling down as a farmer somewhere in Switzerland, which appalled his fiancée and shocked his family. But Kleist persisted. After a quarrel, he took leave from Ulrike, who had accompanied him to Paris, and arrived in Switzerland to carry out his design. But Switzerland was in political turmoil and suffered increasingly from Napoleon's intervention in her internal affairs. Though he professed to be apolitical, Kleist chafed at the prospect of becoming a French, instead of a Swiss, citizen through the "unsavory tricks of a prestidigitator." He finally decided to rent a house on the charming island of Delosea on the Lake of Thun and began to write frenetically. So far he had kept his attempts at creative writing practically a secret, though in Paris he had tried his hands at a drama, *The Ghonorez Family*, which he finished in modified form under the title *The Schroffenstein Family* in Berne. Here he also conceived the plan for *The Broken Pitcher* and thought about another serious drama, *Peter, the Hermit*. Instead, he started writing an historical play, *Leopold of Austria*, only to give up that idea in favor of *Robert Guiscard*.

Thus a stubborn and vain battle with an ambitious project began that would lead Kleist to the brink of insanity. Apparently guilt-ridden about his failure in life, he attempted to regain his self-respect through instant literary fame. Moods of hope and despair alternated with frightening speed. In one of his letters, encouraged by momentary progress in his writing, he reports that he was wont to climb the Schreckhorn, an Alpine peak of some 12,000 feet, during Sunday church service—a feat as impossible as his ambition to reach the pinnacle of fame in one quick stroke. In a new thrall of despondency he broke his engagement to Wilhelmine, abruptly asking her to write him no more and adding ominously: "I have no other wish than to die." Increasing political tensions and the imminent French invasion of Switzerland forced him back into Germany. His sagging hopes for literary fame were momentarily lifted by Christoph Martin Wieland, the erstwhile leader of the eighteenth-century literary renaissance in Germany, who offered Kleist shelter in his home at Ossmannstedt. Upon listening to Kleist's recital of the *Guiscard* fragment, he was moved to tears and about a year later wrote a well-known encomium on Kleist and his tragedy to one of his acquaintances:

If the minds of Aeschylos, Sophocles, and Shakespeare could be merged to produce a tragedy, they would write something like Kleist's "Death of Guiscard," provided the entire drama corresponds to what he let me hear of it some time ago.[8]

The Schroffenstein Family also received a favorable journalistic review and Kleist outlined his first two *Novellen,* "The Engagement in Santo Domingo" and "The Earthquake in Chile." But, sensing that his fame would largely depend on the completion of *Robert Guiscard,* he could not unfasten his mind from the topic. As though driven by a daemon, he traveled through Switzerland and northern Italy in company of friends, notably Ernst von Pfuel and Ulrike, who were perplexed by his feckless ways. Upon returning to Paris, he burned the *Guiscard* fragment in self-destructive fury "like a sulking child." His admission of defeat throbs with a burning pain assuaged only by a latent pride:

I have now toiled for over five hundred days and nights to win another laurel wreath for our family. But now our patron goddess instructs me that it is enough. She kisses the pearls of sweat from my brow and consoles me: if all her beloved sons endeavored as much as I, our name would surely be inscribed in the heavens.[9]

11

A new inner crisis loomed. From Paris he traveled to St. Omer, there to join the French forces poised to invade England. Apparently he felt that a glorious death in battle, even in the ranks of the despised French, could compensate for the unattainable literary fame. Or, equally plausible, his sense of shame, added to his innate suicidal urge, led him to seek the anonymity of the common soldier's death. The alarmed Pfuel searched for him all over Paris, including the morgue, while Kleist stalked aimlessly around in the French encampment, in danger of being shot as a spy. He was finally located and shipped back to Germany. In Mainz he suffered a complete nervous collapse and had to be cared for by friends, especially Dr. Georg Christian Wedekind, a well-known medical specialist. For eight months he wrote nothing, and no letters reached the outside world to tell of the inner darkness.

After his recovery, he saw himself compelled to seek government employment. In Berlin, however, the King and his adjutant Köckeritz showed little enthusiasm for the hirsute former officer who had contemplated joining the ranks of the enemy, drifted around irresponsibly and, what's more, attempted to produce "rhymes." Through the efforts of a relative, Marie von Kleist, who had become one of his closest friends and enjoyed some influence at the court, he was given a minor post in the Ministry of Finance. After the battle of Jena, Kleist moved to Königsberg, as did the battered remains of the Prussian army, the civil service, and high society along with the King and his court. Bothered by psychosomatic ailments, he toiled resignedly at his job. But his greatest efforts were devoted to his writing. Under the most unfit circumstances he entered upon the most productive period in his literary career. He completed *The Broken Pitcher*, translated and reworked Molière's *Amphitryon* into a subtle metaphysical riddle, sketched out the first drafts of *Penthesilea*, and apparently worked on three *Novellen*, "The Foundling," "The Marquise of O——," and "The Duel." But the strain caused by the conflict of careers did not fail to affect his whole being. His health deteriorated, and he admitted to a state of depression similar to that which had overcome him in St. Omer. His letters of that period are replete with reflections on the transitoriness of life and the limitations of man's rational faculties, while he extols the power of "feeling" in his creative endeavors. He was finally granted an indefinite sick leave, largely through the good offices of Baron von Altenstein, who showed a humane concern for his personal problems.

In the company of two friends, Kleist set out in January 1807 for Dresden, then teeming with literary activity despite Germany's political and military debacles. But a malignant fate again dogged his footsteps. He and his friends were arrested by the French authorities in Berlin under suspicion of spying, shipped unceremoniously into solitary confinement at Fort Joux near Neufchâtel, and then transferred to Châlons-sur-Marne. At times ill-treated and suffering from material deprivations, Kleist managed to keep up his spirits and work feverishly on his *Penthesilea*. Physical imprisonment seemed to afflict him less than the mental confinement of the civil service. Not that he enjoyed his forced retreat from the world, for on his own admission (in a letter of June 7, 1807, to Marie von Kleist) he was intensely attached to it. When he was finally cleared from the charges brought against him and released, he hastened to Dresden.

There he was reunited with some of his former friends and became a close associate of Adam Müller, the political economist, who had been unstinting in his praise of Kleist's art and published his *Amphitryon* while he was still imprisoned in France. Kleist found immediate access to influential circles and on one memorable occasion was literally crowned as poet laureate. Buoyed up by the eulogies heaped on him, he embarked upon daring commercial and literary ventures. With Adam Müller he founded a literary journal, *The Phoebus*, which he felt would ultimately eclipse the prestigious *Horen* consecrated by the combined fame of Goethe and Schiller. He also made preparations to found his own publishing house in collaboration with some of his friends and the financial aid of the ever generous Ulrike. On occasion he seemed to take the literary world of Dresden for the intellectual hub of Germany. Not unlike Robert Guiscard, whose daring scheme to invade Byzantium forms the historic background of his unfinished tragedy, Kleist himself basked in the illusion that his Dresden enterprises could dethrone Goethe's Weimar as the intellectual capital of Germany. These vain hopes may explain the proud tone of the first *Phoebus* issue and Kleist's boldness in publishing in it fragments from his violent and unorthodox *Penthesilea*. But what had begun as the most promising period in his career ended in dismal failure only about one and a half years later. In Weimar, *The Broken Pitcher,* ineptly directed by Goethe and clumsily performed by his actors, received a cool and even hostile reception. And the full printed text of *Penthesilea* elicited no more favorable reactions from the middle-aged Goethe. His classicist tastes were repelled by the tempestuous drama and its author, who reminded him too acutely of the storm and stress of his own younger years. In Dresden, Kleist's business projects encountered insuperable barriers. Even *The Phoebus* had to be sold for lack of enough subscribers, although Kleist produced essays and literary works for it at breakneck speed. He reconstructed from memory the *Robert Guiscard* fragment, wrote and modified *The Kaethchen of Heilbronn,* finished "The Marquise of O——," and began "Michael Kohlhaas," besides composing a number of essays, among them most likely his much discussed *"Über das Marionettentheater"* ("About the Marionette Theater"). Kleist was painfully aware that much of what he wrote might only be appreciated by future generations. Upon the completion of *Penthesilea,* he remarked demurely in a letter to Marie von Kleist that the drama had little chance of being performed in his own lifetime. Yet, he kept on writing. Meanwhile, Germany's military position against Napoleon had worsened. Dresden was threatened and Kleist's own journalistic and commercial ventures came to naught. The inner hurt drove him into a patriotic frenzy bursting out in polemic verse directed against the usurper and ambiguously symbolized in his drama *The Battle of Arminius.* In a sense, Napoleon became the visual image of the cruel fate which stalked his life.

There were, however, some glimmers of hope in the otherwise gloomy course of events. The Burgtheater in Vienna evinced some interest in his dramas, especially *The Kaethchen of Heilbronn.* He even had legitimate reasons for hoping that he might be engaged there as a director and official critic. Journeying to Austria in company of the young historian Christoph Dahlmann, he was an eyewitness to the glorious but futile victory of Archduke Charles over Napoleon at Aspern (May 21, 1809). In Prague, he undertook steps to found a patriotic journal, *Germania*. But as the hopes aroused by the Austrian victory at Aspern were short-lived, so were the new possibilities in Kleist's own life. His exultant political expectations for Germany were destroyed by the Archduke's defeat at Wagram in July, and none of his own journalistic projects came to fruition. It was rumored that Kleist was again seriously ill—mentally and physically—and even that he had died. A cloak of silence covers this period in his life. On the basis of scant and mostly indirect evidence, it can at best be ascertained that he made some peregrinations through various parts of Germany and possibly Austria, only to turn up quite unexpectedly and in apparent good health in Berlin sometime in February 1810. There his last heroic battle with his fate and the chaos of his time was to be staged.

The new beginnings in Berlin augured well. Kleist brought with him the finished manuscript of *The Prince of Homburg*, which he had succeeded in writing during his hectic journeys. There was some hope that the drama might be performed in the private theater of Prince Radziwill. Meanwhile, *The Kaethchen of Heilbronn* was premiered in Vienna before an appreciative, if somewhat befuddled, audience. At the Prussian court, Kleist was allowed to read an encomium on Queen Louise's great courage in times of national calamity—impassioned verses which moved her to tears. He also renewed his friendship with Adam Müller, who had moved to Berlin, and became personally acquainted with Achim von Arnim, Clemens Brentano, and de la Motte-Fouqué, members of the Younger Romantic School. His circle of friends and acquaintances also included Baron von Altenstein, Kleist's former protector at Königsberg and now Minister of Finance, as well as the publishers Reimer and Hitzig, who took a genuine interest in his literary works.

But soon some of his fondest hopes were dashed again. For unknown reasons, the performance of *The Prince of Homburg* at Prince Radziwill's palace, on which Kleist once more had staked his reputation as a dramatist, did not take place, at least there is no convincing evidence that it did. (The play was premiered only ten years after his death at the

Burgtheater in Vienna and, ironically, its production discontinued after the fifth showing at the behest of Archduke Charles, Kleist's erstwhile hero, who feared the work might have demoralizing effects on his troops.) The publisher Cotta, who had promised to print *The Kaethchen of Heilbronn,* reneged on his commitment and, to add insult to injury, August Wilhelm Iffland, the director of the Prussian National Theater, refused to perform the play on his stage. An unsavory quarrel ensued, in which Kleist rather petulantly suggested that Iffland would be delighted to play the central male figure if the docile Kaethchen were a boy. The sudden death of Queen Louise deprived him of a pension which is assumed to have been discreetly supplied under the Queen's name by Kleist's benefactress, friend, and relative, Marie von Kleist, to whom he was now bound by strong emotional ties. Although Reimer published a first volume of Kleist's *Novellen,* including "Michael Kohlhaas," which he had to finish hurriedly in the printing process, as well as *The Kaethchen,* Kleist was once more without visible means of support. Thus he plunged headlong into a new journalistic venture, *Die Berliner Abendblätter,* the first daily newspaper published in Germany.

His brisk reporting of daily events and daring editorials on the political situation made the newspaper an immediate popular success but soon provoked the apprehension of Prussian officials. Kleist was prohibited from printing any political news, and another theater scandal caused largely by his astute and perceptive criticism deprived him of a theater column. Soon thereafter he was not even allowed to print such irrelevant items as police reports. On May 20, 1811, he made an impassioned plea for freedom of the press in a letter addressed to Prince Wilhelm of Prussia, which went largely unnoticed. Like the Michael Kohlhaas of his *Novelle,* Kleist fought not only for himself but an ideal and appealed to many government officials, especially Chancellor von Hardenberg and his councillor Raumer, only to meet with intransigence or evasion. But Kleist was also somewhat naïve in not perceiving that Hardenberg's imperviousness was partly due to the political views held by his contributors, chiefly Adam Müller, who had used the *Abendblätter* to launch virulent attacks upon Hardenberg's financial and other reforms which threatened to encroach upon the privileges of the Prussian

Junkers. In the meantime, Reimer had managed to publish the second volume of Kleist's *Novellen,* including two which had appeared in the *Abendblätter,* namely "The Beggar-woman of Locarno" and "St. Cecilia, or the Power of Music," as well as "The Engagement in Santo Domingo" and "The Foundling," both of which Kleist had written much earlier but for artistic reasons of his own had never found worthy of publication. The modest sales that could be expected from such a publication in times of war and political upheaval could not remotely compensate for the loss of potential income from the *Abendblätter,* which Kleist was forced to discontinue on March 31, 1811.

Political and personal circumstances forced all of his close friends, including Marie von Kleist, to leave the Prussian capital. Impecunious and alone, his store of literary works momentarily exhausted, Kleist felt an icy bleakness invade his life. He sought the company of cultivated women such as Rahel Levin, who offered him sympathy and understanding but was also very much aware of Kleist's inner isolation and the rigor of his manner. "He lived in severity and chasteness," she said of him at one point. Kleist turned his gaze once more toward the prospect of a courageous death on the battlefield. He offered his services to the King and after considerable delay received some encouragement from the responsible government officials. But the increasing precariousness of the Franco-Russian alliance had forced Prussia to seek a *rapprochement* with France, and the thought of fighting on the side of the French filled him with loathing. In his disarray, he sought help from his family, but the meeting with his sisters and relatives at Frankfurt was disastrous. They could not understand their brother's high-strung aspirations, and the atmosphere around the dinner table was filled with silent and overt reproaches. Stung by their reprobation, Kleist complained bitterly that they were not even generous enough to recognize the modest fame he had brought on their house in long years of arduous struggle. His inner alienation from the world progressed with fatal speed. Terrified, he noticed even his love for the arts waning. He had reached the absolute nadir of his life.

In the course of these trials he made the acquaintance of Henrietta Vogel, mother of a child and wife of a minor government official. Suffering from what was most likely a form of cancer, she had already renounced the world. It seemed to Kleist that two kindred souls, whose somber destinies were fatefully joined, had met at a crossroads. He made a suicide pact with her. Estranged from the living, he found companionship among the dying. In his last letters to Ulrike and Marie von Kleist, he allowed himself a last desperate outcry on the suffering of his life. But simultaneously, he was in the grip of a strange, almost hysteric elation and otherworldly joy at the thought of approaching death:

I pray . . . to God; I now feel gratitude toward Him for the most painful and tragic life any human being ever had to live, since He now grants me the most glorious and voluptuous death. [To Marie von Kleist] [10]

And now farewell, may Heaven grant you a death only half as full of joy and ineffable serenity as mine! [To Ulrike] [11]

It is as if Kleist had gained full self-possession in the knowledge of having lived his life according to the dictates of his own inner consciousness, culminating in his self-willed death. For a fleeting moment he seemed to regain the religious fervor of his youth:

Alas, my dear friend, may God call you soon into that better world where we will be able to embrace each other with the love of heavenly beings. [To Marie von Kleist] [12]

On November 21, 1811, at the age of thirty-four, Kleist shot his companion and himself on the shores of the Wannsee near Berlin. The epitaph on the modest tombstone which marked his grave for many years read:

Er lebte, sang und litt
In trüber, schwerer Zeit.
Er suchte hier den Tod
Und fand Unsterblichkeit.

He lived and sang and toiled
in dreary, troublous times.
He sought the gates of death
and found immortal fame.[13]

NOTES

[1] Blöcker, Günter, *Heinrich von Kleist,* Berlin, 1960.

[2] Kleist's own account of his birthday differs from the official birth register of the garrison in Frankfurt.

[3] Helmut Sembdner, ed., *Heinrich von Kleist. dtv Gesamtausgabe,* Munich, 1964, Vol. 5, p. 40, in an essay addressed to Rühle von Lilienstern, March, 1799, entitled: "Essay to find the sure way of happiness and enjoy it peacefully even in the greatest tribulations." This essay shows many parallels to a letter written about the same time to Christian Ernst Martini.

The *dtv Gesamtausgabe* is a critical edition of all of Kleist's works and writings compiled by Helmut Sembdner and published by Deutscher Taschenbuch Verlag GmbH, Munich, in eight volumes (1964 and 1969). It is based largely on an earlier edition of Kleist's works, also done by Helmut Sembdner, and published by Carl Hanser Verlag, Munich, in 1961. Sembdner's is the most authoritative edition of Kleist's writings so far, although a lengthy prolegomena to a new critical edition was recently published by Klaus Kanzog, which will differ in some details from Sembdner's and be brought out over the next few years.

Quotations from Kleist's letters will be directly translated from Sembdner's edition, hereafter referred to as "Sembd."

[4] Sembd., Vol. 6, p. 156.

[5] It has been speculated that Kleist traveled to Würzburg on a secret mission for the Prussian government. But other than the fact that he went under an assumed name, there is little tangible proof for this theory.

[6] For instance, by Alfred Schlagdenhauffen in *L'univers existentiel de Kleist dans le "Prince de Hombourg,"* Paris, 1953.

[7] Heinz Ide, *Der junge Kleist,* Würzburg, 1961.

[8] Christoph Martin Wieland in a letter addressed to Dr. Georg Christian Wedekind in Mainz, April 10, 1804.

[9] Sembd., Vol. 6, pp. 257–58.

[10] Sembd., Vol. 7, pp. 133–34.

[11] Ibid., p. 133.

[12] Ibid., p. 134.

[13] The original of this tombstone can now be found in the court-yard of the Kleist Museum in Frankfurt. The inscription on the present monument, also very modest, is a verse from *The Prince of Homburg:*

> *Nun*
> *O Unsterblichkeit*
> *Bist Du ganz mein!* (l. 1830)

Now, Immortality, thou art all mine!

The Elusive World of Kleist:
Problems of Kleist Criticism

The Kant Crisis

Of the many crises in Kleist's life, his professed disenchantment with Kantian philosophy was probably the most consequential and, for his biographers, certainly the most bewildering. According to his own account, the crisis struck him with sudden force, but not before he had apparently undertaken a protracted, though only intermittent, study of the Critical Philosophy. In two letters sent to Wilhelmine and Ulrike on March 22 and 23, 1801, he explained in almost identical terms the despair that had overcome him in the wake of his reading the "newest Kantian philosophy": [1]

If all men had green glasses instead of their eyes, they would be led to say that all objects they see *are* green. . . . We cannot determine if what we call truth is really truth or whether it only seems so. If the latter is correct, then the truth we are able to gather on this earth will no longer be valid after death—and all our efforts to acquire a patrimony accompanying us to the halls of death are null and void.

Alas, Wilhelmine, if the edge of this thought does not wound your heart, do not mock another whose deepest and most sacred feelings have been struck down by it.

My sole, my highest goal has been destroyed, I no longer have one.[2]

About seventy years later, in his essay on Schopenhauer, Nietzsche was to praise Kleist's very personal reaction to the veiled skepticism of Kant's thought:

Yes, when will men again feel in the natural Kleistian manner, when will they learn again to judge the meaning of a philosophy with their deepest and most sacred feelings? [3]

Although we can perhaps sympathize with Nietzsche's eulogy of Kleist's emotional purity, we remain nevertheless baffled by the philosophic reasons and psychological motives which brought on Kleist's crisis. In his letters from August 1800 to March 1801, direct references to Kant are scant. Yet, we are justified in assuming that he had more than a passing interest in the Critical Philosophy before he suffered his inner collapse. For example, in one letter,[4] Kleist asks his half sister Ulrike to send him a treatise on Kant which he had written sometime earlier. At another time,[5] he muses that he might want to teach the "newest philosophy" in France. At still another point, he takes umbrage at the Kantian concept of "duty." [6] Or he weaves the Kantian notions of "understanding," "judgment," and "reason" into a letter to Wilhelmine [7] to illustrate a pedagogic ideal he wants to impress upon her. The philological problem is not solved by dismissing Kleist as a nascent poetic genius incapable of abstract thinking or a zealous autodidact who erred in the labyrinth of Kant's philosophy before he understood its "true" meaning. Most contemporary Kleist critics are willing to concede that his mental powers ranged effectively over a wide spectrum of knowledge and his grasp of abstract ideas could be thorough and correct despite the short time into which he crowded his formal studies. On several occasions in subsequent years, he discussed with considerable insight certain technical inventions and scientific principles. And his knowledge of mathematics was quite respectable for his time. He also seemed to harbor no illusions about the complexity of

Kant's philosophy and the difficulty of propagating it. At least he knew that it had not yet made a perceptible impact in France—a first thorough French commentary on Kant, written by Charles de Villers, appeared only in 1801.

The question then is which aspect of Kant's philosophy can be directly related to Kleist's crisis or, more specifically, what ideals were shattered in him by the Critical Philosophy. The problem is compounded by factors in Kleist's psychological make-up. These suggest that he used Kant's philosophy as a ready-made foil for his own personal anguish, which he could never entirely conceal behind the borrowed philosophic optimism of his precrisis days.

While in Kleist's time the Leibnitz-Wolffian philosophy was on the wane among the intellectual avant-garde, it still influenced the thinking of the right-minded citizenry and was even taught with a touch of religious fervor at the University of Frankfurt, where Kleist received his academic training. The most prominent element in the popular Enlightenment creed was undoubtedly its belief in the perfectibility of the world and the mind's capacity of grasping the universal teleology through observation and logical deduction. This optimistic mode of thought was underpinned by the notion of a pre-established universal harmony ingeniously expounded in Leibnitz's *Monadology,* which appeared on the literary scene early in the eighteenth century. In ethics these assumptions led to the eudaemonistic dicta that man's virtue is directly proportional to his understanding of the laws governing the universe and that happiness is the inevitable reward for virtue. This rational optimism, known as the *Popularphilosophie,* underwent a resurgence in the later eighteenth century following the posthumous publication of Leibnitz's *New Essays on Human Understanding* in 1765.

In the Germany of the late eighteenth century, Leibnitzian philosophy found an especially strong advocate in Moses Mendelssohn. In various writings, he argued that man's capabilities extend from an appreciation of material utility over a perception of beauty to a direct intellectual intuition of the first principles of truth,[8] and he expounded eloquently the eighteenth-century *idée fixe* of a Great Chain of Being linking one degree of perceptual and substantial perfection to the next [9] in a kind of pre-established harmony. Or the ideal of a teleological science is vividly presented in Hermann Samuel Reimarus's treatises, where it is shown how the perfect suitability of animals to their function entitles the observer to infer the ultimate harmony of all things. But most important for Kleist's own early intellectual quandary were Christoph Martin Wieland's *Sympathien* and the lectures of his tutor at the University of Frankfurt, Christian E. Wünsch.

Wieland's *Sympathien* is a belletristic piece of writing steeped in a good deal of pious sentimentality. He propounds the idea of the mutual attraction of kindred spirits in some pre-existence mysteriously repeated on this earth.[10] Man's vocation or destiny is also fashioned in that other world and is communicated to those whose inner perceptions are attuned to the voice of providence. The ideological background to this jejune brand of Platonism is the notion of a world eternally striving for perfection, in which each individual destiny is meaningfully inserted in an overall plan. The individual's first task is to fathom the goal of his own existence in the light of the general purposiveness of the world. Wieland does not give specific directives how one is to arrive at such blissful certainty, although he sets great store by the values of learning or "education." In a relatively late letter,[11] Kleist admitted that as early as 1793, when he was sixteen years old, Wieland's *Sympathien* had made a strong impression on him.

Some of the facile metaphysics contained in Wieland's tract and similar writings found an academic sanction when Kleist entered the University of Frankfurt, where he came under the influence of Wünsch, the institution's star professor. From all available evidence, Wünsch's *Kosmologische Unterhaltungen* ("Cosmological Musings") became for a while Kleist's *vademecum* from which he derived some of the edifying discourses he addressed to his fiancée. In Wünsch's academic textbook we find the whole stock in trade of the popular philosophy but clothed in the trappings of "experimental physics." Wünsch sings paeans to the beautiful suitability of all things to their pre-established purpose. He is convinced that virtue and happiness are correlated with knowledge and that the successive approximation of man's knowledge to divine omniscience is accompanied by a feeling of pleasure, for the human being realizes in the process of acquiring ever greater knowledge that the operations of his own mind are in essential harmony with the teleological drive of the universe. To all this, Wünsch adds his own Pythagorean version of the Great Chain of Being. The other planets in the universe, he pretends, are inhabited by intelligent beings—many of them more advanced than man—and after death the human soul will forever grow in wisdom as it ascends from sphere to sphere in endless progression.

Even at the time of launching into his academic studies Kleist gave evidence of being affected by dogmatic metaphysics, which could only be reinforced by his subsequent exposure to Wünsch's teachings. In his letters to his former private tutor, Ernst Christian Martini, of March 17 and 19, 1799 which re-echo a youthful treatise that he had addressed to Rühle von Lilienstern under the portentous title *Aufsatz, den sichern Weg des Glücks zu finden und ungestört—auch unter den grössten Drangsalen des Lebens—ihn zu geniessen* ("The Sure Way of Finding Happiness and to Enjoy It Peacefully Even in the Greatest Tribulations"), he describes proudly but overanxiously the articles of his Enlightenment faith. The letter is replete with homilies and precepts borrowed from Homer, Lucretius, Wieland, Goethe, Schiller, and lesser luminaries but centers essentially around his belief in learning and education as a way to the happy life. Mathematics and philosophy he considers as the pillars of all knowledge and truth, and he lauds the ensuing virtue as a sure means to attain happiness.

However, by September 16, 1800,[12] at which date he addresses a lengthy pedagogic discourse to Wilhelmine, it is obvious that some Kantian ideas have made inroads into his thinking, although he is still groping for otherworldly certainties. By all means, the letter is a monument to philosophic eclecticism. Kleist insists on the compelling necessity of investing one's efforts entirely in finding one's personal destiny on earth without losing much thought on man's eternal existence. Neither Epicurean hedonism, he contends, nor the Leibnitzian notion of perfection, not even Kantian ethical voluntarism can bring to light the eternal destiny of man. Then he touches on the philosophy of religion, expressing views that are vaguely akin to Kant's *Religion within the Limits of Reason Alone*. Discounting the importance of external ritual, he identifies religion primarily with morality and the fulfillment of "duty." At this point, despite his earlier censure of Kant's ethics, he proceeds to enhance the notion of duty in a fashion reminiscent of Kant's *Critique of Practical Reason.* The fulfillment of sheer duty with its attendant feeling of reverence invokes the ideas of God and immortality, not as metaphysical certainties but as justifiable hopes. Then he reiterates once more his intention not to become absorbed in otherworldly speculations but to do all he can to find the purpose of his being in the here and now. In the same breath, however, he talks about the great eternal plan of nature in which he hopes to occupy his due place in accord with the divine will.

In summary, he dismisses almost jauntily the optimistic assertion that man can *know* eternal purposes but replaces the lost intellectual certainties with the religious and metaphysical hopes attaching to Kant's moral postulates. However, he chooses to ignore the Kantian emphasis on the autonomy of the moral will and the ensuing metaphysical freedom of man and rather doggedly reiterates his earlier teleological belief that one's personal destiny must and can be found in the light of a universal plan of nature.

The juxtaposition of the letters of March 17 and 19, 1799, and September 16, 1800, shows clearly that over a period of one and a half years Kleist's borrowed Enlightenment creed had gradually become colored by Kantian modes of thought but that neither philosophic system could entirely satisfy his need to find a personal vocation supported by a credible metaphysics. Throughout this period, however, he continues to stress the existence of a universal plan of nature and the necessity of attaining "truth" through "education." Truth and education always seemed to mean more to him than a mere impersonal accumulation of scientific facts. On several occasions he lashed out against the stifling pedantries of specialized scholarship. What he obviously had in mind was the ideal of a *Universalwissenschaft,* a universal science, which would reveal the nexus of universal purposes that endow mechanical laws with ultimate "meaning" and vouchsafe the eternal progress of the spirit.

Kleist's continued anxious questioning of the sum total of

things, however, reveals an ingrained skeptical streak in his make-up which broke loose in the Kant crisis. Still, we remain perplexed by its suddenness and massiveness as well as Kleist's heaping blame on the *"newest"* Kantian philosophy. Prevailing critical opinion has it that Kleist's reading of a specific philosophic work or portions thereof must be considered a trigger-event in the eruption of the crisis rather than the latter being the cumulative effect of his intermittent exposure to Kantianism. Much ingenuity has been expended on attempts to discover just exactly what Kleist meant with his cryptic reference to the "newest" Kantian philosophy and to retrace the steps in his thinking up to the crisis point. The arguments often have the cogency and excitement of a skilled lawyer's address to a jury, but just as often they reveal the advocate's own acuity of mind rather than the "truth."

In essence, one theory purports that Kleist struggled with the tangled arguments of the *Critique of Pure Reason* for a long time before he grasped their true nature. While the scientific phenomenalism of the first two portions of the *Critique* may have given him some pause, so the argument goes, it is only the third part, the "Dialectic," which struck him with full force. It is in the last section of his revolutionary work that Kant denies resolutely the epistemological validity of metaphysics. In its pursuit of grasping ultimate ideas, Kant argues, reason tends to go beyond the mere "understanding" of the empirical world and in so doing creates but a nest of metaphysical illusions. At best, reason can *postulate* the metaphysical ideas of God, immortality, and freedom as a basis for ethical conduct, but it can have no certain knowledge of them.

Kleist's letter of September 16, 1800, briefly discussed above, undoubtedly reflects some rudimentary Kantian notions. He seems partially reconciled to the impossibility of gaining metaphysical knowledge and derives his belief in God and immortality from his practical endeavors on earth, although he spends no effort on exploring the consequences of man's autonomy or metaphysical freedom, which forms the basis of Kant's ethics. Even so, it may be assumed with some degree of plausibility that relatively long before his crisis Kleist had integrated into his own thinking some of the central ideas of the *Critique of Pure Reason*, and also their connection with the *Critique of Practical Reason*, without becoming greatly upset.

One could surmise, therefore, that the crisis was prompted by a new element entering his thought. There is much cogency in a recent theory [13] which claims that Kleist's dilemma was precipitated by his reading of the *Critique of Judgment*, especially the second part, the "Critique of Teleological Judgment." Undoubtedly, Kleist's idea of a true science was of a teleological sort, his pedagogic ideals based on it and the "Critique of Teleological Judgment," of a kind to cut teleological optimism to the quick.

While Kant concedes that one can detect in objects of mathematics a formal or intellectual purposiveness, it is still rather a "purposiveness without purpose." Geometric and mathematical constructs show a kind of internal coherence but do not display some ultimate purpose. The case is more difficult with a product of nature such as an acorn or a blade of grass, which has a kind of innate formative power or purposiveness. But even here, Kant argues, teleological assumptions can at best be heuristic principles of scientific investigation. Finally, he dismisses quite sardonically the notion that the human mind can unequivocally grasp the existence of some extrinsic purposefulness that would hold all things together in a universal, teleological nexus.

It is quite plausible that Kant's destruction of the teleological idea in science had a more shattering effect on Kleist than his earlier reduction of metaphysical knowledge about God and immortality to mere postulates of practical reason. But the first sentence of Kleist's own description of his frightful new insight into the abyss of human ignorance and delusion, cited at the beginning of this chapter, is more reminiscent of the *Critique of Pure Reason* than the "Critique of Teleological Judgment," although in the second sentence where he recapitulates his erstwhile belief destroyed by the new philosophy, teleological notions figure prominently. It must also be conceded that in the "Critique of Teleological Judgment" Kant does not fundamentally change the epistemological position adopted earlier in the *Critique of Pure Reason*. He simply extends and elaborates it to encompass and reduce to its proper function the teleological ideal in science. But this may have been just enough to tip the balance in Kleist's thinking.

On the other hand, there is also some suasive power in Ernst Cassirer's argument [14] to the effect that the cause for Kleist's despair is to be sought not in Kant's philosophy at all but in Fichte's. In fact, Fichte casts even more doubt on the reliability of "pure knowledge" than did Kant, although he is not attempting to say, as some Romantics apparently thought he did, that there is no world of sense but only dream and illusion. Fichte insists, however, that "reality" is not something apart from consciousness. Thus, with respect to "pure knowledge" the world of representations cannot have the reality of a being-in-itself. Yet, since "pure knowledge" can view the world only as if it were a being-in-itself, its representations are indeed illusory, unless one accepts Fichte's philosophic deduction that being and consciousness are fundamentally one.

It may well be that Kleist misunderstood Fichte's basic epistemological position. Indeed, he states in his "Kant letter," "We cannot determine if what we call truth is really truth or whether it only seems [*scheint*] so. . . ." If one assumes that Kantian philosophy was the reason for Kleist's distress, then one must admit that he was flagrantly wrong in equating "illusions" (*Scheine*) with "appearances" (*Erscheinungen*), for Kant makes a clear distinction between mere subjective impressions (*Scheine*) and appearances (*Erscheinungen*). The latter constitute an "objective" world that will sustain scientific propositions. Admittedly, Fichte's philosophy lends itself readily to such misconceptions, and the adjective "newest" in Kleist's reference to Kant's philosophy could *à la rigueur* be applied to Fichte, who indeed considered himself to be a "Neo-Kantian." Moreover, Fichte's *Vocation of Man,* a popularized exposition of his metaphysics, was published early in 1800 and could easily have come to Kleist's attention. Yet, there is no express reference to Fichte in Kleist's letters and writings until January 1808 when, in his ill-fated journal *The Phoebus,* he aimed a polemic attack at the obscurity of Fichte's writings. It must also be upheld, against Cassirer, that Kleist could not have been much concerned with the semantic nuances between *Scheine* and *Erscheinungen* when he revealed his inner disarray to two young women unfamiliar with philosophic jargon.[15]

If Kleist had consciously intended to, he could not have better concealed from us the exact nature of the philosophic reflections contributing to his despair. For the interpretation of Kleist's dramas and *Novellen,* however, it is perhaps of minor importance to know exactly with which work of "Kantian" philosophy to associate his crisis. By all means, his general disillusionment with man's rational powers and the reliability of "appearances" could not remain without repercussions in his works. However, his private anxieties expressed in so many letters were at least of equal importance in the formation of his dramatic world view as was his concern with philosophic abstractions. Very early Kleist glimpsed a world fundamentally other than he anticipated in his philosophic moments.

Particularly striking is the intensity with which he expressed his Enlightenment creed in his early disquisition on happiness. His edifying discourse emits the cracked sound of adolescent pretense. He seems to cling to his creed all the more desperately as he despairs over finding his own calling on earth. His private anxieties break through the glossy surface of philosophic dogma precisely because he insists so much on its truth. Especially revealing is his repeated assertion that happiness is a mere "inner" tranquillity, a state of mind, that can withstand the blows of an awesome fate, as though the world were a threatening rather than a benevolent presence. And "virtue" seems to be more than mere righteousness to him. It is rather peace of mind derived from the comforting knowledge of having found one's personal God-given destiny— a rather impossible ideal. But Kleist insists almost petulantly that man must and can rely on a firm inner disposition in his search for a secure life. In several places he calls "fate" a "tyrant" that plays havoc with outer circumstance and threatens man's inner serenity. In other precrisis letters he praises "feeling" as the only sure guide to peace of mind, even as an arbiter in practical decisions and as a sort of heightened consciousness transcending the limits of mere "understanding."

Kleist's dramatic world is thus a world of oppositions of inner and outer realities, of things felt and things seen or understood. Yet, he could not blithely accept such a world.

Time and again he insisted on the necessity of showing absolute "trust" (*Vertrauen*) in important human relationships. It is as though he attempted to counteract the terrible instability of the world of appearances by an indestructible inner bond, cementing human beings together by the sheer force of their inner feeling. It has long since been recognized that "trust" is one of the foremost motifs in Kleist's works, and its origins can easily be traced to his early letters.

Other tendencies, if only in their incipient form, can be discerned in his precrisis epistles that play a large part in his literary works. Here and there, he voices the fear that he will never be able to "communicate" his true concern to the outside world and must lock it in the deepest recesses of his soul. In other places, he wistfully condemns the whole business of abstract learning and lauds the life of action. These utterances portend the inner isolation of his dramatic characters and their often doomed attempts at finding their personal destinies in frenetic, even hysteric, action.

As one follows the meanderings of Kleist's thought in his letters, it becomes increasingly obvious that it is foolhardy to make apodictic statements about the causes and effects of his inner distress on the basis of ready-made psychological canons or philosophic dogmas. What is certain, however, is the manifest intermingling of borrowed ideas with personal apprehensions prompted largely by his quest for his own vocation in life. As he resigned his army commission and with it an exactly defined professional and social function, the problem of finding his very personal destiny became especially acute. His hope of finding a safe port in an ideal marriage was but a mirage. When he broke his engagement to Wilhelmine he made the same leap into darkness as did Kierkegaard a few decades later, with only his inner urge for authenticity to guide him. But more perhaps than his companion in suffering, Kleist was assailed by the demons of doubt. At least, he always retained a "realistic" sense of the limitations of personal inwardness and the difficulties the individual encounters in seeking to be properly related to himself and his god, or ultimate reality. Symptomatic of his skepticism is the wistful tone of his essay "About the Marionette Theater," written probably in 1806, which constitutes a landmark in Kleist criticism.

NOTES

1 Kleist uses the adjective "newest" in the letter of March 22 to Wilhelmine but not in the one dated a day later, addressed to Ulrike, where he refers merely to the "Kantian philosophy."

2 Sembd., Vol. 6, p. 163, letter to Wilhelmine.

3 Friedrich Nietzsche, "Schopenhauer as Educator" ["*Schopenhauer als Erzieher*"], in *Thoughts Out of Season* [*Unzeitgemässe Betrachtungen*].

4 See letter of August 14, 1800, to Ulrike, Sembd., Vol. 6, p. 52.

5 See letter of November 13, 1800, to Wilhelmine, Sembd., ibid., p. 120.

6 See letter of September 16, 1800, to Wilhelmine, Sembd., Vol. 5, p. 50.

7 See letter of May 30, 1800 to Wilhelmine, Sembd., Vol. 6, pp. 44–45.

8 See Mendelssohn's *Briefe über Empfindungen* ("Letters on Sensations").

9 See Mendelssohn's *Phaedon* and *Morgenstunden oder Vorlesungen über das Dasein Gottes* ("Morning Hours or Lectures on God's Existence").

10 Kleist's *The Kaethchen of Heilbronn,* written in 1807–8, shows traces of Wieland's ideas.

11 See letter of July 29, 1801, to Adolfine von Werdeck, a passing acquaintance and friend, Sembd., Vol. 6, p. 199.

12 See Sembd., Vol. 5, pp. 50–53.

13 See Ludwig Muth in *Kleist und Kant,* Köln, 1954.

14 See Ernst Cassirer in "Heinrich von Kleist und die Kantische Philosophie," *Idee und Gestalt,* Berlin, 1921.

15 Kleist pointed this out himself in a "postcrisis" letter of March 28, 1801, addressed to Wilhelmine.

The Essay "About the Marionette Theater" and the Problem of "Feeling"

Kleist's aesthetic and reflective writings, which increased in number as he became more absorbed in journalistic ventures, do not amount to a fully integrated *Weltanschauung*. But written spontaneously as they were, they help provide some insight into his perception of the world. While they are not encompassing enough to serve as a ready-made crucible for all the complexities of his works, they contain certain themes and motifs that can be readily perceived in both the dramas and *Novellen*. Among his aesthetic and remotely "philosophic" essays, "About the Marionette Theater" (*Über das Marionettentheater*), written in 1810, is easily the best known. Despite its somewhat tenuous comparison between the physical phenomenon of movement in puppets and certain mental phenomena in man, the essay is admittedly fraught with aesthetic and metaphysical allusions and has often tempted the critics to use it as a magic key to unlock the secret of Kleist's world.

Marionettes, Kleist's narrator suggests, have the perfection of spontaneous, unconscious movements because they have only one center of gravity. Their movements are controlled from one point. The puppeteer has control only of this point, and as he moves it in a simple straight line, the limbs follow inevitably and naturally because the figure of the marionette is completely co-ordinated. Symbolically, marionettes represent beings of innocent, pristine nature. They are members of only one world, responding "naturally" and "gracefully" to divine guidance. This is underscored by their apparent weightlessness. They hardly touch the floor; they are not bound to the earth, for they are drawn up from above. They represent a state of grace, a "paradise lost" to man, whose conscious and willful or "free" self-assertions make him "self-conscious." The dancer exemplifies the "fallen state" of man. He is not upheld from above, but rather feels himself bound to the earth and yet must appear weightless in order to perform his feats with apparent ease. He must try consciously to attain "grace." Thus his center of gravity shifts continuously and the effect may be affectation rather than grace:

For you know, affectation is shown when the soul (*Vis motrix*) is at a point other than that of the center of gravity of the movement.[1]

Nevertheless, the dancer still has a "heavenly glimmering"[2] of the paradisaical harmony symbolized in the marionettes, if only indirectly: he *understands* the laws which fasten him to the earth, but his self-willed efforts to defy these very laws are not even remotely conducive to the attainment of genuine grace. He is a creature of two worlds, and no matter how much he understands or "reflects" on his own state, his intellectual faculties are unable to restore unity or wholeness to his soul. To illustrate his point further, Kleist cites the examples of a young man who loses all his innocent charm as he becomes aware of his own reflection in a mirror and of a bear whose instinctive reactions to the feints and thrusts of a swordsman make him a superior defensive artist to a human fencing champion. Kleist arrives at the summary and wistful conclusion that the harmony of paradise lost would be regained only if human consciousness could pass "through the

infinite" and thus become united with the divine again—
obviously a rather difficult feat:

But, as the intersection of two lines, from the one side of a point,
after passing through the infinite, returns suddenly to the other
side; or, the image of a concave mirror after moving into the infinite
appears suddenly again, near and before us; so, when Knowledge
has gone, so to speak, through the infinite, Grace returns again,
appearing at the same time, most purely in the structure of a body
which has either no knowledge, or an infinite knowledge, to wit: in
a marionette or in a God.[3]

Taken by itself, the essay contains several strands of symbolic allusion which are fascinating enough to be briefly outlined. First on the epistemological level, it restates in
emblematic form Kant's insights into the limitations of human
reason, provided one identifies, for the moment, the dancer's
"consciousness" primarily with intellectual faculties. In that
case, the "infinite consciousness" that intrigues Kleist and
eludes the dancer's grasp could be likened to Kant's problematic notion of a direct intellectual perception or intuition
(*intellektuelle Anschauung*), which can be roughly described as
the ideal faculty of immediately apprehending *things-in-them-
selves*. Kant's refutation of this rationalistic dogma leads to
the very heart of his Critical Philosophy. A direct intellectual
perception can be predicated only of the divine mind. The
human mind can rise no higher than pure "concepts of reason" or "principles" that can set forth an ideal at which reason must aim. But no such concept can give knowledge of an
actual or even possible reality. Kleist seems to agree partially
with Kant when he depicts the human mind as irremediably
caught between the absence of consciousness (the marionette)
and an intellectual perception or infinite reason (God).

Second, the essay illustrates what ravages the advent of self-
awareness and self-determination has wrought in the human
person. This theme is connected with the first but has a more
theological orientation. It recapitulates the Garden of Eden
myth. As a result of his acquisition of knowledge, man knows
that he knows; he has become self-centered, capable of self-
determination—more precisely he enjoys freedom. But his
emancipation from direct divine guidance also spells disharmony in his own soul and discord with his Maker and the

universe.[4] Man's consciousness lacks a center of gravity, it is out of kilter with itself and God. It suffers from "original sin." The world and ultimate reality seem to be fundamentally "other" than man's consciousness. There is a hint of the "absurd" breach between man and universe in the essay, although Kleist will not attempt to make of it a virtue, a touchstone for man's humanity, as twentieth century writers such as Camus tend to do.

Third, the essay expresses tersely the chiliastic credo expostulated in certain philosophies of history. This aspect of its symbolism is an extension of the second, for "freedom" can be viewed not only as an inherent element in the conscious life of the individual but also as a corollary in the dialectic unfolding of a kind of cosmic consciousness manifesting itself in the thrust of human history. In the ultimate stages of historic development, so the argument goes, men will come to understand the laws governing the historic process and "freely," thus consciously, submit to its compelling necessities, thereby bringing about a collective "harmony" of men on earth in an ideal "rational state." This secularized paradise would in a sense be a substitute for the unattainable unitive state or harmony of the individual with an infinite consciousness. That the essay's symbolism could be extended to such a philosophy of history seems to be suggested by Kleist himself when he says that the attainment of an "infinite consciousness" by man would constitute the "last chapter in the history of the world."

But the analogies between Kleist's ideal of an infinite consciousness and historic reason with its built-in notions of collective freedom and harmony are at best tenuous. Kleist's final remark in the essay is made in a casual manner and, if he identifies the advent of a higher consciousness with the "last chapter in the history of the world," it does not mean necessarily that he has in mind the future establishment of the ideal State. He might rather be thinking of a world in which each individual is at one with himself in the supreme knowledge of living his very personal destiny in accord with the divine will. This, to him, would be a true "state of grace." Kleist's longing for personal certainties could hardly find satisfaction in the notion of a social utopia on earth. His aspirations always remained highly individualistic. The idea of an historic reason operating on a mythic, collective level unbeknown to the individual is at best a derivative notion of Kleist's "infinite consciousness." His guarded attitude toward the millenarianism of the German philosophy of history is tersely expressed in an essay entitled "Observations on the Course of History" (*Betrachtungen über den Weltlauf*), which appeared in the *Berliner Abendblätter* only a short time after the publication of the *Marionettentheater*. In a few lines, he satirizes unwarranted certainties about a world plan. Although the essay may be the result of a passing fit of skepticism, it nevertheless suggests caution in linking the symbolism of the *Marionettentheater* too closely with the chiliasm of nineteenth-century philosophies of history. When we come to the interpretation of Kleist's works, the idea of a future ideal State may play a role only in his last drama, *The Prince of Homburg,* and then only with many qualifications.

Indeed, throughout his works, Kleist amply illustrates that he has a very subjectivistic notion of an ideal consciousness and that he mourns its absence or the disruptions of it in the inner life of the individual by social exigencies, mistrust, and deceptive appearances. Nevertheless, he longs for a "center of gravity" in man's inner experience—a kind of "graceful" spontaneity or unity in his perception of the self and the world—which would allow him to move through all perils with the assurance of a sleepwalker. As in Kleist's marionette, the center of gravity of the "graceful" individual would be directly acted upon by a divine motive force. By implication, there is a note of mystic immanence in Kleist's pictorial view of a Godlike existence as portrayed in the *Marionettentheater.*

But as most symbolic or allegoric writings, the *Marionettentheater* is hardly a foolproof blueprint for the interpretation of the psychological and existential realities which inform the kind of literary works that Kleist wrote. To begin with, Kleist ascribes "grace" simultaneously to the marionette and to God, namely to that which lacks consciousness altogether and that which is replete with it, by analogy to the zero and the infinite. And in the essay itself he rather skeptically dismisses the possibility of attaining the completeness of a unified consciousness for man. It is therefore questionable whether he would set out to portray in any one instance the full triadic swing from virtually unconscious integrity over inner schism to conscious and absolute self-possession. Yet, gropingly he makes forays into the mystic territory of inner grace only to come back with vastly divergent findings.

The Kaethchen of Heilbronn is guided by a visionary dream of which she is not even fully conscious—she can reveal it only while asleep—and wanders through life with angelic equanimity. Like a marionette, she is guided from above and fulfills her glorious destiny by merely following the spontaneous assertions of her heart. Significantly, the drama has the trappings of a fairy tale. Penthesilea also has a dream, but it comes to her in full consciousness and in the form of a prophecy made by her mother. She seeks its fulfillment with frenetic abandon which leads to tragic illusion in life and is alleviated only by a feeling of inner redemption upon her death. Alkmene, the heroine of *Amphitryon,* must shield her intuitive certainty from contrary sense evidence, as must others, such as the Marquise of O——, and in the process suffers the torments of doubt and deception but lives to see her inwardness extolled by divinity. Then, there are those like Sylvester in *The Schroffenstein Family* who, under extreme stress, lose consciousness as though to seek access to a higher realm through gates of momentary darkness, more precisely through the "nothingness" signified by their fainting spells. In surrendering to an inner summons, all of them seem in one way or another to partake of "grace," to differing degrees and with quite different results.

By all means, the imagery of the *Marionettentheater* suggests that it is the inward-oriented man who is battling close to God's citadel, even if he succumbs to error and weakness. To critics, the figures of the graceful but unconscious marionette and the graceless but conscious dancer also strongly suggest that Kleist glimpses a redemptive quality in those powers of the soul which are at the farthest remove from the fully developed intellect. The idea of the "nonrational" thus becomes identified with the notion of the "nonconscious" of Kleist's essay and, conversely, the "conscious" with the "rational." This inference finds support in Kleist's repeated references in his letters, essays, and literary works as well to the superiority of man's intuitive powers over mere rational processes. For instance, as late as 1810, he declares in his essay "On [the Notion of] Reflection":

Be it known that reflection or deliberation had better set in after than prior to acting. If it enters into play before or at the moment of decision, it only seems to confuse, hamper, and suppress the power necessary to action which flows from the magnificence of feeling. Conversely, it is after the fact that the purpose of man's reflective ability will make itself known, which is to become aware of that which was erroneous and fragile in one's act so as to condition one's feeling for future occurrences.[5]

Then he illustrates the idea with the example of a wrestler who cannot deliberate at length which move to make and which muscles to activate next while engaged in a bout, but must rely on immediate reflex if he is to prevail. Nine years earlier, in a letter to Wilhelmine dated January 11–12, 1801, he expressed a similar idea when he exhorted his fiancée to act according to the promptings of her "feeling."

What transpires in these statements is not necessarily that Kleist denies the relevance of rational processes altogether but that he stresses the role of spontaneity in the human quest for individuality. "Reflection" has its place, but it can at best be an *ex post facto* justification and not a directive agent for one's self-creative acts. Unfortunately for those concerned with semantic precision, Kleist uses throughout his literary and essayistic writings a disconcerting array of terms to denote inner spontaneity, often in a synecdochical manner, such as "soul," "heart," "inwardness," even "consciousness" and, very prominently, the rather portentous "feeling" (*Gefühl*). Similar to the dramatic characters he created, Kleist himself was groping for inner certainties and expressed his insights only in a tentative way, while always remaining a partial mystery to himself. Quite in keeping with the subject matter, his utterances were often impulsive and therefore lacked the semantic precision which dispassionate analysis might afford.

In Kleist criticism, the term "feeling" has gained preponderance and even the status of an indispensable heuristic tool. Some interpreters, influenced no doubt by the image of the marionette, use it to designate a motive force originating in a realm lying beyond "consciousness" and impute the disruptive forces in the life of Kleist's characters to the fallibility of man's sense perceptions and reasoning powers. Some have even gone so far as to ascribe to the Kleistian notion of "feeling" a cognitive function superior to that of reason or understanding. In that case "feeling" and "consciousness"—alias "reason" or "understanding"—are used virtually as antonyms, and the dramatic conflict is seen primarily as a war waged between these two powers in the hero himself. Other critics tend to use the term "feeling" rather in obverse fashion as a synonym for "consciousness," to mean the whole inner vibrato of the soul—its intuitions, dreams, mystic intimations, spontaneous impulses and rational processes as well. If so used, the term "feeling" may cover the whole gamut of inner experiences, from practically unconscious "reflex" to highly conscious "reflection," though it still denotes man's intense subjectivity, his consciousness or "feeling" of self as opposed to a mere perception or understanding of the external world. In that case, the dramatic conflict is seen primarily as a clash between the individual's "inner consciousness" and the world outside.

The two critical attitudes are not irrevocably opposed to each other, for it is clear that a conflict between man's inner world and the surrounding realities will invariably cause discord within the individual, maybe a potentially tragic schism between feeling and reasoning. However, the holistic concept of "feeling" seems to come closer to the existential confrontations the Kleistian hero must endure. He cannot remain entirely self-enclosed but through sobering experiences in the world is led to a point where he must "reflect" on that which seems to constitute his very essence as an individual *hic et nunc*. An original upsurge of practically "unconscious" spontaneity is inevitably followed by greater self-awareness. This experience is expressed movingly by Kleist's perhaps purest heroine, Alkmene:

> I'd rather that the feeling myself
> Which I have had since mother nursed me
> Which tells me that I am Alkmene,
> I'd rather that a Parthian or a Persian seemed this feeling.
> Is this my hand? Is this my breast?
> Is that my image in the mirror!
> He [Amphitryon] should be stranger to me than myself?

If you would take away my eye, I'd hear him still;
Without my ear, I'd feel him; would I not feel,
I still should breathe him; and if you take
My eye, my ear, my touch, my sense of smell,
Leave me my heart; it is the bell I need [6]

. . . .

What is obviously at stake in the Kleistian hero's struggle
with his "feeling" is his subjectivity, which he experiences
intensely. If he fights continually to have a reasonably clear
sense of self, he "feels" that he needs a corner of certainty,
an inner sanctum where he can retire for refuge or refusal—
the refusal to do other than he consents to do, the refusal
to "be" other than he is and wants to be. It seems less important to him to explain the world than to come to terms
with it in the light of his own perception of self. His intense
subjectivity is a sense of the worth of the unique person he
is, and when deceived by the world or erring himself he
still feels that the door to "reality" can be found only by
opening himself up to his own being. Therefore, he battles
not to be a mere social integer, but rather to achieve personal
coherence, to control those forces that threaten to diminish
and fragment him, witness Michael Kohlhaas, and even Penthesilea, who go to their deaths in inner peace, knowing that
through error and deception they have not betrayed their
sense or feeling of self. Even in love, the Kleistian hero's
sense of worth makes him feel that it is denigrating to regard
another's self more important than his own. Kleist's lovers
are peculiarly "self"-centered, which may be the defect of
their virtue. An ideal "I-Thou" relationship never develops,
or at least is never fully depicted. In "The Marquise of O——,"
to single out one instance, we learn much more about the
heroine's sense of hurt caused by her deceiver than her ultimate reconciliation with him. The latter is treated rather
perfunctorily.

However, to the very last, an aura of mystery surrounds
Kleist's major characters. We never quite stop learning or
wondering about them. In an almost phenomenological
sense, Kleist presents them as consistently "self-transcend-
ing" beings. They have a strong feeling *that* they are possessed of a unique personal essence but, upon reflection, they

cannot express exactly *what* that essence is—for in reflecting upon themselves, their true essence is already ahead of themselves. Thus, after sobering and revealing experiences, they feel the tragic necessity of reorienting themselves without losing their *selves* and, overwhelmed, fall into unconsciousness or cryptic silence, accept death, or can utter their wonderment only in such riddlesome exclamations as Alkmene's elaborated "Ach!"—which does not so much conclude her drama as place it on yet another level of existential experience. This inconclusiveness of man's intense search for his subjectivity is one of the very fascinating and at the same time "modern" elements in Kleist's works. It ensues from his notion, pictorially condensed in the *Marionettentheater*, that man should have a "center of gravity" and that the person in search of that center and defending it against all assaults—the person who does and feels what he feels he must—is worthy of our sympathy, even if he errs. He may not arrive at full self-knowledge but has a superior measure of self-possession, precisely because he relies so much on his subjectivity, his center of gravity.

If Kleist was intensely aware of man's need for inner coherence, he also recognized the compelling existence of disruptive forces in the world. As an essentially dramatic temperament, he could not become absorbed in "romantic" speculations about the mystic unity of self and world. A tragic vision resulted wherein, assuredly, man's "feeling" of self figures prominently but in which other elements must also be considered and put into focus.

NOTES

[1] Sembd., Vol. 5, p. 74. (Translation by Cherna Murray "About the Marionette Theatre" in *Life and Letters To-Day*, Vol. 16, No. 8, Summer 1937, pp. 102–3.

[2] In the Prologue to Goethe's *Faust*, Mephistopheles refers mockingly to human reason as a *"Schein des Himmelslichts,"* a "heavenly glimmering."

[3] Sembd., Vol. 5, pp. 77–78; Murray, p. 105.

[4] In his *Conjectural Beginning of Human History*, Kant makes

the startling remark: "The history of nature therefore begins with good for it is the work of God, while the history of freedom begins with wickedness, for it is the work of man." Analogously, the dancer in Kleist's essay no longer moves "naturally"; he is "free" but devoid of "grace." In German, there are two words for "grace" in the sense of "gracefulness" (= *Grazie*) and the theological "grace" (= *Gnade*). The *double-entendre* in the English "grace" facilitates the transition from aesthetic to theological considerations.

[5] Sembd., Vol. 5, p. 70. (My translation—R.E.H.)

[6] *Ibid.*, Vol. 2, p. 124, ll. 1155–66. (Translated by Marion Sonnenfeld, *Amphitryon*, New York, Ungar Paperbacks, 1962, pp. 40–41, ll. 1150–61.)

The Tragic Vision

It would be a serious mistake to reduce Kleist's tragic vision of life merely to his own personality traits, the seemingly pathological withdrawal of his genius into a world of its own reflected in the inward stance of the protagonists in his dramas. He gave the many intellectual crosscurrents of his age a hearing and found them wanting. His tragic sense of reality could not be blunted by theory. Goethe's classical ideal of creative harmony, Schiller's realm of ideas, and the escapist dream of the Romantics were all equally suspect to him. Despite his prolonged interest in philosophy and science, Kleist did not arrive at an abstract *Weltanschauung*. He became the poet of man's fundamental *Welterfahrung*, experience of the world, based upon a sense of reality that broke through the intellectual clutter of an age crumbling from within and without. The result is a tragic vision of human life that is both new and old.

Reduced to its simplest expression, the single most important theme in Kleist's tragic view is the conflict between the "realities" of the world and the individual's inner vision of them. This theme is rendered more complex through the intense search of the Kleistian character for his own being based on his "feeling" of self, often done in defiance of the world. This quest continually hovers on the verge of tragedy, for the contrariness of an inescapable reality threatens time and again to destroy his inner self-assurance. This, in Kleist's mind, is the "fragile constitution of the world," a phrase which he uses repeatedly in his *Novellen*. But in the midst of seeming debacle, the "heroic" individual safeguards the integrity of his soul. While he must go through a tormenting experience of inner schism, he finally seems to arrive at greater self-possession in life or in death. This leads to the often observed basic paradoxes in Kleist's image of man. Though self-assured, man is prone to err, yet through error affirms his subjectivity. This experience is nothing less than a discovery of the truth of his persona through illusion. A fundamental catharsis and reorientation of the self occurs which establishes a different connection between world and individual. This new relation does not necessarily produce a conscious redemptive wisdom but a deepening of the individual's sense of identity experienced in his "feeling." And it is questionable whether Kleist's hero or heroine—if they survive—will find life more livable after their sobering experiences. They might find it more difficult, since they have experienced the fragility of their own self-assurance. Most likely, they will be more wary of their soul's intimations about the realities of the world.

The same could be said of Oedipus, and his last speech before his exile suggests precisely that idea. But Kleist leaves it an open question whether his hero will feel more at home in the world or more alienated from it after the tragic illumination. The final "Ach!" of Alkmene in *Amphitryon*, uttered after her deep inner torment and the revelation of truth, expresses a whole gamut of contradictory emotions and is symptomatic of the "open-ended" character of Kleist's works. So is Homburg's final question in Kleist's last drama: "Is it a dream?" Like the essay on the *Marionettentheater*, most of the author's dramas and Novellen end on a questioning note.

What one can say with certainty, however, is that through disturbing events the Kleistian character profoundly experiences his unique subjectivity, which heretofore had been dormant. The very nature of one's subjectivity can hardly be grasped abstractly and encapsulated in words. It is a matter of inner experience. Therefore, the Kleistian character, in moments of crisis, does not talk much about himself, but intently listens to himself in silence. This, of course, adds to his puzzling qualities. But precisely because a strong upsurge of subjectivity cannot be fully distilled in intellectual categories of thought, he remains as much a mystery to himself as to those around him. This may be the "modern" and somewhat existential element in Kleist's tragic vision.

However, the religious or metaphysical dimension is not banned from Kleist's world. For all their inner solitude and anxiety, his protagonists are not existential heroes moving about in a world bereft of transcendence. Through error and torment they continue to hope for a sanction, if not sanctification, of their innermost sense of life—their feeling—by a power hidden in the awesome and remote regions of godhead. They do not arrive at an explicit profession of faith or lie prostrate before their Judge. Rather, in relying on an inner summons they hope to be properly related not only to themselves but also to God, to be the tools of God as is the marionette in Kleist's essay. Yet, they hardly ever venture to utter even just trembling assertions about God, for they are as much baffled by His ways as by their own. This is tersely expressed by Sylvester in *The Schroffenstein Family:*

> You thinkest me a difficult enigma.
> Console yourself, for God is such to me.[1]

It is rather Kleist himself who invents situations and episodes or describes personal reactions which suggest the divine presence in his characters' lives. In "The Earthquake in Chile" he tells us:

Josepha leaped enthusiastically to her feet and said that the wish to bow her face in the dust before her Maker had never been so strong in her as now, when He had given such proof of His unfathomable and supernal power.[2]

48

Alkmene in *Amphitryon* is visited by a god, though for a long time she refuses to accept even the thought of his compelling presence. Michael Kohlhaas is the object of mysterious visitations by a Gypsy woman looking and acting like his deceased wife—ostensibly a messenger from another world. The very theme of "The Duel" deals with God's strange ways to man. Many more examples could be cited. True, all these manifestations remain cryptic, but they attest to Kleist's habit of looking over his shoulder to the heavens as he maps out the strange destinies of his characters on earth. The backdrop to the existential experiences of his heroes is the *deus absconditus,* the hidden, mysterious but nevertheless omnipotent God of Protestant theology. "There can be no evil spirit ruling the world, he is only incomprehensible," [3] Kleist wrote to his friend Rühle von Lilienstern on August 31, 1806.

It is precisely because Kleist looks at the human quest for inner certainty *sub specie aeternitatis* that he also has a strikingly acute sense of its many ironies. He knows of the metaphysical aspirations of human "feeling," but is equally aware of its historic and finite limitations. This sense is implicit in the *Marionettentheater.* The dancer is, after all, an ironic figure, for he attempts to find "grace" but most often displays affectation, the very opposite of his intention. Similarly, the ingenuous trust of Kleist's characters in their inner vision of self and reality often produces the inverse of their expectations. They commit tragic blunders, not through willful self-assertion, as in Shakespearean tragedy, but by relying naïvely on the promptings of their feeling. Kleist's drama contains its own version of *hamartia,* tragic error. The term for it which he puts in the mouths of some of his characters is the rather untranslatable *Versehen,* suggesting something like "misapprehension" of reality. It also carries the connotation of a mere inadvertence. After her atrocious killing of Achilles, Penthesilea remarks indolently: *"So war es ein Versehen."*—"So—it was a mistake." [4] The term is in one way an ironic understatement of the enormous grief that comes to Kleist's protagonists in the wake of their tragic errors. But in another way it expresses appropriately the nature of their blundering, for in characteristically Kleist-

ian fashion they commit their errors in purity of heart, inno-
cently, in less than conscious, almost somnambulistic, states
of mind—not through conscious aggression. This is another
reason why the dramatic climaxes in Kleist's works are likely
to be an almost silent inner prostration, barely articulated,
rather than forensic bouts between the protagonists, as in
Schiller.

The tragic irony in Kleist's works is heightened by indirect author interference. Kleist manages to have his characters express their self-assurance or lead the action to temporary clarity at the very moment we are subtly made aware
of impending reversals and disasters. In "The Earthquake in
Chile," Donna Elizabeth anxiously whispers something into
the ear of Don Fernando. In *Amphitryon,* the inscription
on the diadem given as a token of love to Alkmene by her
husband miraculously changes from "A" to "J" (for "Jupiter") directly after Alkmene had reasserted her innocence.
Kleist succeeds in introducing a subtle element of doubt
suggesting new inner and outer developments just as his characters utter protestations to the contrary. As in the case of his
own life we are soon made aware through the inner development of his characters and the construction of the plots
that the very thing which appears to be most certain is the
least certain. We then know that a drastic reversal is impending and inevitable.

But unlike Shakespeare's typical hero, the character of the
Kleistian hero is not exclusively his own undoing. It is equally
due to the unfathomable motives of other human beings, the
frail social institutions of man, or even the cryptic manifestations of supernatural powers. From this basic dramatic clash
between "inner" and "outer" world derive all of the corollary
themes found in Kleist's works, such as remnants of a supposedly Rousseauist belief in the natural goodness of the
individual as opposed to the monstrous artificiality of certain social institutions, the tragic shortcomings of mere reason in disentangling the web of confusion enveloping the
world, the impossibility of communicating directly the essence of one's subjective awareness to another human being
equally enclosed in his own inner experience. All of these
themes are expressions of man's "alienation" from a reality
that has become impenetrable and chaotic, a reflection per-

haps of Kleist's own estrangement from the world crystallized in his Kant crisis.

Expressed in traditional dramaturgic parlance, Kleist's dramas and *Novellen* show the conflict between "character" and an inexorable "fate." "Character" denotes in his case the individual's inner "feeling" while "fate" appears in various guises as the deceptive world. Kleist always achieves a subtle balance between these two entities, but in the ensuing dramatic tension, it is clear that his sympathies lie with those individuals who must defend their inner integrity against deceptive appearances. Through outer disarray and inner torment they show a surprising greatness of character bordering on noblesse. If their feeling of self cannot entirely shield them from the deceits and the cruelty of the world, it can at least sustain their sense of human dignity. As to the world, Kleist can only redeem it by suggesting through an occasional miracle, enigmatic supernatural occurrences, reflections put in the minds of his character or, more directly, in his epistolary writings that despite its deceptiveness the world must be governed by a benevolent spirit. "There seems to be no God, and yet there must be a God," would adequately summarize Kleist's metaphysics.

The basic existential insight that man must seek his being through torment and error and largely without immediate divine aid is responsible for the feeling of unrelieved anxiety that pervades Kleist's world. It also colors his notion of "chance" as a manifestation of "fate." In one of his early letters he evinces an almost surrealistic sense of the absurdity of human fate when he relates how the braying of an ass caused his team of horses to shy, overturning the carriage and almost killing him. In reflecting on the event he intimates that human fate does not consist of meaningful incidents suggesting some cosmic design, but of grotesque accidents. No purposeful universal nexus seems to hold man and world together. They exist in baffling juxtaposition as two seemingly unrelated realities. In his first drama, *The Schroffenstein Family,* this sense of absurdity wells forth in a kind of "metaphysical seasickness," as one commentator puts it.

Although Kleist's feeling of the "absurd" is tempered later on by his concern with man's inward search for his destiny, strange coincidences continue to play an important role even in his more adult vision of the world. If Kleist suggests that human life must be viewed *sub specie aeternitatis,* then he does it with daring irony, as in "The Duel," where in the plot itself he shows how misguided are the pretenses under which man-made laws presumably embody the divine will. Conversely, he succeeds in suggesting with similar irony that "chance" may be but the grotesque mask of a higher impenetrable fate. Ever since his Kant crisis, Kleist knew that man can only have limited or relative knowledge of the world, no matter how much he may long for the divine vision.

On the other hand, the phenomenal world is but the outward, visible manifestation of a mysterious *thing-in-itself.* Similarly, irrational chance is but the visible, immediate revelation of an invisible, remote fate. In the drama, this may be more difficult to suggest than in the *Novelle,* for there human life is portrayed through the earthly dialog of the characters—unless the modern dramatist resorts to devices reminiscent of the ancient chorus, as in the Epic Theater or the "play within the play"—while in the *Novelle* the author may allow himself the luxury of a more omniscient viewpoint. However, the very nature of the *Novelle* lends itself to a conversion of mere chance into ominous fate. Without dwelling on character development or psychological motivation, it shows how an event strikes a human life from the outside with sudden force. Its tempo is swift and the action fraught with dramatic tension, for the characters must struggle against the sudden upsurge of hostile powers. Mere coincidence or chance may thus take on the foreboding qualities of tragic fate. And though focusing on the event, the *Novelle* may illumine in quick flashes new aspects of human nature in the midst of catastrophic happenings. Given the respective artistic possibilities of drama and *Novelle,* it is quite understandable that Kleist's dramas dwell more on the inward and the *Novelle* more on the outward fate of man. And his first drama, *The Schroffenstein Family,* is in one sense "immature" precisely because its plot hinges so much on senseless chance happenings overwhelming his characters from without at the expense of their inner depth.

In a world of unrelieved tension and seemingly hostile, irrational forces the Kleistian hero is often overcome by an intense feeling of powerlessness. In Kleist's world, man is hardly the master of his fate, he is at best the captain of his soul, and then only at the cost of great inner stress. He is the chattel of his inner destiny, "condemned" to be himself. Man is in this sense *ohnmächtig*, "powerless." It is not surprising that in Kleist's works *Ohnmacht*, denoting primarily "fainting spell," but also "lack of power," is a recurring motif. The loss of consciousness which frequently afflicts his characters is more than a cheap literary device designed to resolve an otherwise insoluble inner conflict or to relieve the dramatic hero of all responsibility in moments of crisis. The *Ohnmacht* motif is rather a vivid dramatic metaphor suggesting the precariousness and frailty of man's inner consciousness, assailed as it is by disintegrating outer forces, such as the distrust and the baffling actions of others, hostile social codes, or the capriciousness of a daemonic fate. When the discrepancy between the truths produced by his inner perceptions and the contrariness of the outside world becomes too great, the Kleistian hero lapses into a momentary loss of consciousness, symbolized in *Ohnmacht*. In other words, *Ohnmacht* epitomizes the effect of a dramatic clash between inner "truths" and outer "realities"; it·is not mere melodrama.

Ohnmacht, then, serves as a symbolic "gesture" intimating the unfathomable depth of the human soul. As such it is also an extralingual means of expressing the individual's inner solitude. When it occurs, as it most often does, at a dramatic climax, its ominous silence, the sinking of the self into its own depths, suggests the isolation of one consciousness from another and the impossibility of language to communicate the essence of one's most personal inner experience to another human being. The obverse of *Ohnmacht* is the Kleistian hero's longing for mutual trust among human beings engulfed in the same tragic destiny. *Vertrauensprobe,* a test of trust in word and deed, is another key motif in Kleist's works. In his view, the ontological rift that separates one individual from another could only be bridged through absolute trust. Impelled by their own "feeling," his major characters invariably demand such trust of those who play a vital role in their lives. They not only demand trust in what they say and do, but also in what they do *not* say and do *not* do. It is as though they wanted to force others to accept unquestioningly their inner vision of truth and goodness in a frantic attempt to overcome their inner isolation. At times, such trust is forthcoming and is able to cut through a web of illusion and misunderstanding. At other times, however, the demand for absolute trust is thwarted and turns into poisonous distrust giving rise to gnawing self-doubts or exploding into destructive fury.

One cannot help asking how Kleist, the consistent tragedian and great sufferer, could write comedy with such consummate artistry as in *The Broken Pitcher* or create an atmosphere of ironic detachment as in "The Marquise of O——" and other prose writings. Ever since the inception of dramatic festivals by the Greeks, it has, of course, been recognized that the comic is in a sense the obverse of the tragic. Both depict the ludicrous rift between human pretense and reality, the dissonance between aspirations and possibilities, although from a different perspective and in a different social setting. The proximity of the tragic and the comic is portrayed graphically in the image of the dancer in the *Marionettentheater*. Within the context of the essay, the dancer is a caricature of the split consciousness, the loss of innocence and original self-assurance that afflicts man. In comparison with the marionette, the dancer is clumsy. The immediate aesthetic effect of his attempts at being graceful may be comical, but behind the apparent grotesqueness tragedy looms large. The awkwardness and inner division of man can be grimly humorous or passionately tragic. In a letter of October 30, 1807, Kleist shows a striking awareness of the comic inhering in the tragic when the latter is viewed in the perspective of the passing moment with all its compelling immediacy. "How do you feel about the world, i.e., the physiognomy of the moment?" he asks, "I find that there is something comical in the midst of its distortion. It is as though the world suddenly relented in its motion, like an old woman in the middle of a waltz (if she had clung to her partner, she would have been waltzed to death): and you know what effect this has on her partner. I cannot stop laughing when I think about it." [5] A comparison that is more grotesque than funny, one must admit. But, apparently, Kleist intends to suggest that instances which are glimpsed casually and in isolation, as they can be when the world comes to a momentary stop, appear comical, if not grotesque. The same instances, however, would be tragic if seen within the context of the whole, that is, when the entire sweep of human destiny comes into view.

Kleist's vantage point varies, although the fundamental irony he portrays remains the same. At times, his lens zooms in on the comic of isolated occurrences; other times, its field of vision broadens to encompass the universal forces that shape man's destiny. *The Broken Pitcher* is set in the homespun atmosphere of a little Dutch village; its characters are drawn with all their personal idiosyncracies, their fate entangled in the network of their modest daily pursuits. *Penthesilea,* on the other hand, is steeped in a mythological atmosphere; its protagonists are symbols of cultures in conflict while their fate is determined by the existential and metaphysical aspirations concealed in the human soul. *Amphitryon* lies in the ambiguous region between comedy and tragedy, with its focus switching back and forth between the domestic frustrations of the servant couple and the search for truth and self-identity of their masters. In this drama, the comic and the tragic highlight each other in such a way that the salacious Molièresque theme of the seduction of a mortal woman by a philandering god is at the same time a metaphysical mystery symbolizing the problematic nature of man's relationship to God and the divine potential dwelling in pure feeling.

As regards the *Novelle,* its "objective" form lends itself to a portrayal of apparently isolated, though unusual events in the perspective of a portentous fate and with seeming dispassion on the part of the author. In most of Kleist's *Novellen,* the unusual events which constitute their fictional matter suggest tragedy. But in a *Novelle* such as "The Marquise of O——," the theme of the apparent immaculate conception by a blameless woman seeking the unknown father of her unborn child through a newspaper ad has lascivious overtones bordering on cynical humor. In others, such as "Saint Cecilia," an element of the grotesque intrudes itself. The irruption of alien, frightful forces into human destiny encapsulated in the unusual event cannot always be portrayed as the expression of a meaningful fate. Grotesque distortions of human experience may be the result.

And in one sense, the grotesque portrays unfulfilled tragedy, a lack of catharsis provoking agonized laughter mixed with a recognition of horror which may freeze our guffaws into deadly silence. There is in Kleist a tendency toward the daemonic grotesque, even in the dramas such as *The Broken Pitcher* or *The Kaethchen of Heilbronn,* an irruption of the absurd, the chaotic and ominous which disregards the bounds of the prevailing order and thus brings about strange fusions of disparate elements, abrupt and terrifying changes of mood, the incandescence of frightful paradoxes, and the like. The notion of *Versehen*—misapprehension—which plays such a large part in Kleist's view of human life, is itself grotesque, in the sense of "incongruous," when measured against the unspeakable grief that comes to some of Kleist's characters as a result of their misapprehension of reality. But it also highlights the tragic and comic elements that inhere simultaneously in Kleist's artistic vision of man. In the more tragic mode, *Versehen* denotes an innocent, unconscious error followed by grievous consequences; in its comic modulation, however, it rather depicts foiled intrigue, as in the case of the fumbling judge in *The Broken Pitcher.* But it is typical of Kleist's tragic view that most of his characters, with the exception of the protagonists in *The Broken Pitcher, The Battle of Arminius,* perhaps the God Jupiter in *Amphitryon,* and some secondary characters such as Kunigunde in *The Kaethchen of Heilbronn,* are incapable of conscious deception. In the Kleistian world, deception is not placed in the full consciousness of the tragic hero. It is rather built into the very nature of things—the "fragile constitution of the world" —and forever threatens the human quest for certitude. Even when a tragic character embarks upon conscious deception, as is the case with Achilles who intends to submit to Penthesilea under false pretenses, the "intrigue" illustrates the naïveté of the hero's frame of mind, his way of thinking or, more precisely, nonthinking. Intrigue is not an important aspect of the plot in Kleist's works, in contrast to Schiller's drama where the hero's destiny is enmeshed in the political and historic realities of his time. Kleist, though not entirely oblivious of such realities, rather shows the solitary quest of the individual for the wholeness of his being. In this sense, he portrays an "alienated hero" seeking the meaning of his life in loneliness and terror.

NOTES

[1] Sembd., Vol. 1, p. 102, ll. 1212–13. (Translation by Mary J. and Lawrence M. Price, *The Feud of the Schroffensteins,* in *Poet Lore,* Vol. XXVII, No. V, Autumn 1916, p. 507.)

[2] Sembd., Vol. 4, p. 140. (Translated by Martin Greenberg, *The Marquise of O——— and Other Stories,* Criterion Books, 1960; Ungar Paperbacks, 1974, p. 261.)

[3] Sembd., Vol. 7, p. 23. (My translation—R.E.H.)

[4] Sembd., Vol. 2, p. 256, l. 2981. (Translated by Humphrey Trevelyan in *The Classic Theatre,* ed. Eric Bentley, Vol. II, Doubleday Anchor, 1959, p. 416.)

[5] Sembd., Vol. 7, p. 48. (My translation—R.E.H.)

Style and Language

As is apparent from the foregoing chapters, in Kleist's artistic vision of life man is seen struggling for the wholeness of his being against the conflicting claims of rival orders of reality. The world of inner perception or "feeling" thus becomes pitted against the world of sense and understanding. Kleist's innate skepticism, highlighted in the Kant crisis, did not allow him to set great store by man's rational capacities in sorting out the confusing welter of realities impinging on his destiny. But he could never relinquish his hope that in listening to a peremptory inner summons, the responsive individual would live according to the edicts of a higher power and thereby find his true vocation. The search of the inner-directed individual is in a sense a quest for the absolute in his life by way of mysterious intimations rather than apparent fact. One might even go so far as to say that the individual's strength in defending his inner integrity against opposing realities is a manifestation of the divine.

Yet, Kleist is no naïve worshiper of man's inner conscious-ness, for he knows of its fragility and schisms, its deceits and delusions. His brief essays on language and psycholinguistic processes reflect his insights into the plurality of human con-sciousness. Most often he extols the inner illuminations of the soul and laments the inability of reason to convert these immediately into words. It is as if the "reflexes" of the soul could not be fully reproduced by the "reflections" of the mind. Nevertheless, language should be immediate and ca-pable of irradiating the intuitions of the soul. To the very end of his career as a writer, Kleist was poignantly aware of the failure of language to communicate directly the very core of one's being to another person. In his "Letter of One Writer to Another," written as late as January 5, 1811, he all but admits the futility of the whole literary enterprise:

If, in writing I could reach into my breast and literally grasp my thought with my hands and put it in your soul without further ado, then, truthfully, my innermost need would be fulfilled.[1]

Thus Kleist's works are one great battle with language, its weakness and its power. He puts language on the rack to draw from it its last breath, but he also knows how to use its very limitations as a cutting edge for thought.

Quite significant for Kleist's preoccupation with the prob-lem of language is his essay "On the Gradual Formation of Thought in Speaking," probably written in Königsberg around 1805–6, in which he delineates a psycholinguistic theory that elucidates in part the problem of "communica-tion" confronting the protagonists of his dramas.

He distinguishes principally between two different modes of self-expression. First, he shows how language can engender thought and cites as an example Mirabeau, who, in his epoch-making speech in the French National Assembly, let his mind be carried along by the sheer dynamics of language, until he hit upon the notion of the inviolable sovereignty of the people and its representatives. When he arose from his seat upon having heard a messenger read the King's order to dis-band the Assembly, Mirabeau, Kleist maintains, had no clear notion of what he was going to say. But as he confronted the messenger and surrendered himself to his strong inner summons to oppose the order, language—haltingly at first, and then with full rhetorical force—helped him get a hold of his thought. In this case, language is a kind of "thinking out loud," more precisely, a generator of thought.

In his essay, Kleist also stresses the psychological importance of the interlocutor in the speaker's attempt to encapsulate elusive inner perceptions in words. When he labors over an idea in company of his sister, he confesses, a gesture of hers indicating she is about to interrupt him actually spurs him on, "for my inner perception, already greatly exercised, becomes more agitated by this attempt to snatch the conversation away from me and the capacity of my mind is elevated by a notch as in the case of a great general who is pressured by adverse circumstances." [2] Thus Mirabeau, who needs the challenging presence of the King's messenger to arrive at clarity of thought through words.

The episodes depicted suggest the rhetorical stance taken by Kleist's characters. They often seemingly talk into the blue and *at* rather than *with* their interlocutors, in uneven cadences, searching for inner clarity, in quest of their being through language. However, they do not necessarily succeed in "communicating" their vital concern to the other. More often than not the world of their opposite is but an echo chamber for their own subjectivity. Yet at least it serves the purpose of bringing them closer to themselves, even if only for a fleeting moment.

In act one, scene four, of *The Schroffenstein Family*, Rupert, apparently engaged in conversation with his servant, is in truth confronting himself—literally and figuratively. As he gazes at his reflection in the water he suddenly glimpses his own villainy and exclaims:

> A devil's face looked from
> the spring and gazed at me. [3]

—only to elicit a burst of Mephistophelian laughter from his servant. Even more typical of the Kleistian character's sudden self-confrontations at unexpected turns in the dramatic dialogue is the beginning of scene nineteen in *Penthesilea*. The law of the Amazons enjoins that the female warriors

accept as mates whatever prisoners the chances of battle cast
their way. Penthesilea, however, has consciously sought out
Achilles, who has captured her. As the Amazons rush to her
side to free her, she suddenly reveals the promptings of her
own heart and chides the zeal of her subordinates, who can
only conclude that she must have taken leave of her senses:

> THE AMAZONS. Triumph! Triumph! Triumph! Our Queen is
> saved!
>
> PENTHESILEA., *after a pause.*
> Accursèd be this shameful cry of triumph!
> Accursèd every tongue that utters it,
> Accurs'd the servile air on which it swims!
> Was I not his by every use of chivalry,
> By fairest chance of war his lawful prize?
> When man on man makes war—not on the wolf
> Or ravening tiger but on his own kind—
> Show me the law—I say, show me!—which then
> Permits the prisoner who has yielded him
> To be set free again from his captor's bond.
> . . .
>
> THE AMAZONS. What are these words of madness? [4]

In act four, scene four, of *The Prince of Homburg*, the
Prince has received through the intermediary of his beloved,
Natalie, a note from the Elector which leaves the decision
over his destiny in his own hands. As he confronts both
Natalie, who is with him in his prison cell, and the absent
Elector through the latter's message, he gradually arrives at
the recognition of his own responsibility. The scene is marked
by a muted battle with his own thought and Natalie's anxious
entreaties not to sentence himself to death, but climaxes in
Homburg's sudden insight:

> Let him [the Elector] do as he likes.
> I know now that I am doing as I should. [5]

The episode ends on a hopeful note when Natalie declares her
love for him. (Parenthetically, this is one of the rare moments
of pure understanding and full, though not loquacious, com-

munication between two human beings that one can find in Kleist's dramas.)

It is this need of the Kleistian hero to find inner clarity and define himself through dialogue which explains the often noted scarcity of formal monologues in the author's dramas. It may well be that the self-absorbed individual, more so than the more voluble "extrovert" type, needs an outside stimulus to express himself. In Kleist the problem is intensified by the fact that the individual's understanding of himself is never complete; he remains a partial mystery to himself. Therefore, the "I," at pains as it is to know itself fully, needs a partner in order to gain more clarity about itself.

In his essay Kleist recognizes a second mode of communication which is the inverse of the first, namely a situation where language is merely the vehicle of an already well-conceived thought. But contrary to the French adage, Kleist maintains that what has been well perceived inwardly cannot necessarily be well reproduced in linguistic form. As an example he cites the confusion caused in an otherwise bright student by the questions fired at him during an oral examination, an inhibition of verbal expression which may even spread to his examiners. The stressful situation obstructs the free flow of thought. However, from his subsequent observations it becomes clear that Kleist is not thinking so much about the mere regurgitating of impersonal, abstract thought but rather about communicating a kind of inner vision of self. The more specific and individualistic an inner perception, the less easily can it be expressed in the rough-hewn general categories of language. There is an inner language of "feeling," as it were, which cannot be immediately translated into the forms of common understanding, for it is not "we" who know, Kleist asserts, but an inner and very personal mode of being we may experience at a certain given moment—a kind of mystic inner illumination. In his dramas this idea is often illustrated negatively but nonetheless forcefully. Where his characters communicate with seeming ease, far from expressing their "selves," they merely speak in the prevailing matrices of thought of their society. For instance, when Penthesilea attempts to explain to Achilles her personal needs in terms of her country's history, social institutions, and her own upbringing, she suddenly pretends to detect a furtive ironic smile on Achilles' lips. She may have only imagined it. Nevertheless, the episode subtly suggests that her self-expression is sham; it reveals that she conceals her true self behind impersonal modes of thought. It is as if Kleist meant to illustrate that a person is not merely the sum total of his or her past and social conditions, but that there is a transcending stratum of subjectivity, the real "I," which remains self-enclosed, practically incommunicable.

His dramas are thus as much dramas *of* human dialogue, as merely dramas *as* dialogue. Their language is strained to a high pitch of expression which all but illustrates the failure of speech to create genuine communication between the subjective worlds of the protagonists. Relentlessly, Kleist explores the powers and debilities of language as a means of communication. A trademark of his dramatic, and even narrative, technique is a fondness for *Verhör,* probing cross-examination or anxious and suspicious questioning of one character by another. *The Broken Pitcher* is one long cross-examination, although the dialogue rhythm of thrust and parry is mainly exploited for grimly humorous effects. In the more serious dramas, the end result of cross-examination is, ironically, a greater alienation between interrogator and interrogated. In *The Kaethchen of Heilbronn,* for instance, the heroine cannot find out the truth about herself, much less communicate it to others, when she is subjected to a cross-examination in the Vehmic Court. Significantly, the truth transpires only when she is in the throes of a somnambulistic trance and asked about her dream by Count vom Strahl, who in the process also learns the truth about himself. In *The Prince of Homburg,* the terse cross-examination of Homburg by the Elector immediately after the battle, when the latter asks the young firebrand whether he was responsible for a premature cavalry charge, leads not only to a conflict of wills but a serious misjudgment of each other's personalities. Their alienation from each other is alleviated only when both have been forced into a probing self-examination through the intervention of a third party, Natalie. Kleist was aware that cross-examination or interrogation may dredge up what one *did* but hardly what one *is.*[6]

In fact, an element of bitter irony intrudes upon Kleist's treatment of language, especially in the dramas. At times, his dialogues revolve around a single word or name supposed to disclose the truth but only leading to further confusion—a veiled satire directed against a form of totemism based on the professed magic power of words. In one of the early scenes in his first drama, *The Schroffenstein Family,* Jeronimus attempts to extract the truth from Ottokar with the seemingly innocuous "One word, Count Ottokar . . ." (1. 96), only to stumble into greater darkness. More often than not, Kleist conveys the impression that language is bound up with the world of deceptive appearances. It may be a sharp instrument for specious reasoning but is too blunt a tool to cut through the wall of misapprehension separating one human being from another.

Like the reality it tries to encapsulate, language is ambivalent, full of paradox and contradiction. The drama of the dialogue is thus closely wedded to the thematic material. In *The Schroffenstein Family,* every important word spoken gives rise to tragic misconceptions and suspicions. Jupiter's speeches in *Amphitryon* are replete with subtle equivocations, and Alkmene's final enigmatic "Ach!" defies complete interpretation. The welter of emotions into which she is thrust after the disclosure of the mystery could not possibly be fully articulated in human speech. Her final exclamation, fraught with meaning and yet not "saying" anything, epitomizes Kleist's ironic attitude toward the inadequacies of language. *The Broken Pitcher* is to a large extent a comedy of language confusion. In the early scenes of *The Prince of Homburg,* the self-absorption of the Prince cannot be penetrated by even the sharpest military command. *The Battle of Arminius* illustrates among other things how readily language lends itself to conscious deception. The German word for "promise," *Versprechen,* an important element in Arminius' stratagems, is vested with ironic ambiguity. *Versprechen,* besides denoting a "promise," can also mean "a slip of the tongue," an ironic allusion to the forked tongue of the drama's questionable hero. In *Penthesilea,* Kleist's language throbs with the inner dynamics of his tragic characters without ever establishing harmony between them. Misunderstanding and distrust stalk the Kleistian hero, and no matter how much he strains his language, he is unable to overcome his inner isolation. The poetic language of Kleist's drama is thus characterized by its disruption of normal syntax, its elliptic sentences, frequent interjections and particles, unconventional caesuras, vivid metaphors; all linguistic attempts to communicate the uncommunicable.

Aware of the tragic limitations of language, Kleist consistently looked for extralingual means of communication that could adequately express the individual's inner experience. In *The Schroffenstein Family* the two lovers, Agnes and Ottokar, arrive at mutual trust not through language but in spite of it. In a tense and idyllic scene, Ottokar dispels Agnes's terrifying fear that he might poison her, not through entreaty but by resolutely emptying the phial himself. In *The Kaethchen of Heilbronn,* tragedy is averted through wondrous dream visions revealing to the erring hero his true love. In many cases, Kleist completely abandons the attempt to have his characters communicate with each other. He then simply mirrors their inner agitation through such nonverbal means as eloquent silences, telling gestures, or mere physiological reactions—blushing, perspiring, twitching of the lips, and other expressions of stress and inner confusion. In *The Prince of Homburg,* at a crucial moment of decision the Elector is depicted as suddenly *verwirrt,* "bewildered," an unexpected reaction in a seemingly self-assured character that is no less bewildering to the interpreter of the play. Kleist's stage directions are most often an integral part of the drama, although it may be difficult for even the most accomplished actor to call forth a good blush or work up a mighty sweat at the right moment. The frequent fainting spells that afflict his characters belong to the same category of nonverbal manifestations of inner experience. Their eloquent silence suggests the tragic inability of language to express the individual's deepest feelings.

A quite different manifestation of Kleist's battle with language is his obsession with certain verbal patterns and set expressions. Once he had found a pithy formulation or graphic metaphor for some of his thoughts, he exploited it with cloying perseverance. In this sense, Kleist is one of the most persistent self-plagiarists in world literature. It is as though he wanted to exorcise the mysteries of human existence with a series of magic formulas. This habit accounts for the many repetitions and recoveries one finds in his dramas and *Novellen*, with respect both to motifs and imagery. Some of the recurrent metaphors and images have a quasi-parabolic significance, such as the picture of the arch of the city gate whose blocks obey the gravitational pull of the earth and by this very fact stay in place—a symbol perhaps of the precariousness of human existence, subject as it is to the downward pull of despair and death and which yet persists in its mode of being. Or there is the picture of the sturdy oak tree whose very health makes it an easy prey to the fury of a windstorm. Examples are legion and have been carefully collated by painstaking Kleist scholars.[7]

Among the extraverbal means Kleist employs to suggest his characters' inner experience or to give impetus to the plot, the "eloquent object" plays an important role. When human reason and speech fail to attain clarity, inanimate objects, in an almost surrealistic inversion of functions, speak all the more eloquently—for better or for worse. While they belong to the world of deceptive appearances, such objects seem most often to hold the clue to an elusive truth. The glove in *The Prince of Homburg* seemingly confirms the Prince's fondest hopes of glory and love; Peter's little finger in *The Schroffenstein Family*—a lurid and somewhat tasteless dramatic contrivance—is the key that unlocks the truth, although too late. The capsule of the mysterious Gypsy woman in "Michael Kohlhaas" gives the whole plot a new direction. In *The Broken Pitcher*, not only the pitcher but also the periwig hanging in the trellis and the tracks in the snow are silent but eloquent witnesses to Judge Adam's unsavory nocturnal adventure. These "eloquent objects" lend themselves especially well to the artistic form of the *Novelle*, where a certain object or leitmotif may be the central image mirroring or symbolically representing the action.

At first sight, the linguistic form of Kleist's *Novellen* seems to be the very opposite of his dramatic style. He renounces plumbing the depths of his protagonists' soul and adheres to a factual style of reporting mere external events. And yet, his *Novellenstil* is a correlate of the *Dramenstil*: in limiting himself to the description of the manifestly "objective," he indirectly acknowledges the impossibility of faithfully communicating the "subjective," a tragic discovery which his dramas express directly. Conversely, the forward-pressing narrative leading to a climax with the greatest economy of means, the absence of reflective passages, the emphasis on the actions of the characters create the kind of tension which we usually associate with the drama.

In the *Novellen,* Kleist adopts the viewpoint of the non-participating bystander or reporter who sees and records events as they happen. There is no dwelling on psychological analysis, no attempt to see into the characters to divine their motives. Their inner world or "feeling" is virtually passed over or only hinted at in the rapid succession of events. Kleist's narrative technique is thus a skillful exercise in artistic delimitation. He seems to suggest that the interaction of subjective worlds can perhaps only be shown in its objective manifestations, namely in the actions of the characters and a strange concatenation of events. It is especially in Kleist's *Novellenstil* that the philosophically inclined may detect the imprint of Kantianism: the inner truth of persons, their "subjectivity" or, by analogy, the *thing-in-itself,* can only be grasped as objective "appearance," as external action. But it is equally true that the inherent narrative form the *Novelle* can be but a mirror of action, while the dialogue or speech of drama is the action itself.

Yet for all its noncommital objectivity, Kleist's narrative style does not conceal, but rather "reveals." It is as if Kleist wanted to drive home a point or unravel a "truth" with breathless haste. The stylistic means producing this effect are apparent even upon a first reading of the *Novellen.* There is an astounding telescoping of time; climaxes and significant events are drawn together, and all intervening incidents are cursorily passed over. Even the description of the locale of action is most often perfunctory. What remains is sheer action conveyed by an abundance of verbs and particles of motion. On the other hand, "affective" elements such as adjectives are used sparingly, though effectively. In his concern for objectivity Kleist uses indirect discourse with obsessive frequency, a practice which elicited both the dismay and admiration of Thomas Mann: "Kleist succeeds in developing an indirect discourse over twenty-five lines without resorting to a single full stop: in this discourse we find no less than thirteen dependent clauses introduced by *that* and, at the end, a 'briefly, in such a manner . . .'—which, however, fails to pull the sentence up short, but instead gives rise to yet another *that* clause!" Mann is singling out a passage from "The Marquise of O——" which indeed epitomizes this aspect of Kleist's narrative technique. Although the official translation by Martin Greenberg, for good reasons, leaves out the conjunction *that* (*dass* in German), the English version still gives a good idea of the forward rush and the telescoping effect of the sentence:

Letting go the lady's hand, the Count sat down and said that he was forced to be very brief: he had been wounded mortally in the breast and carried to P——; for months there he had despaired of his life; during this time his only thoughts had been for the Marquise; he could not describe the pleasure and the pain that coupled together in his image of her; after his recovery, he had returned to the army, where he had felt a terrible restlessness; more than once he had reached for a pen to pour his heart out to the Colonel and the Marquise; but unexpectedly he was sent to Naples with dispatches; he could not be sure that he wouldn't be sent from there to Constantinople—he might even have to go to St. Petersburg; meanwhile it was impossible for him to go on living any longer without clear understanding about something that was absolutely necessary for his soul's peace; he had not been able to resist taking a few steps in that direction while passing through M——; in short, he cherished the hope of obtaining the Marquise's hand, and he implored them as earnestly as he knew how to give his suit an immediate answer.[9]

However, a subjective interpretative element intrudes upon Kleist's objective narrative through the many interpolations, the involuted syntax for which his prose is justly famous or notorious, as the case may be. The many subordinate clauses linked by conjunctions seem to reveal a kind of logical structure in the apparent meaninglessness of events. Kleist seems to be striving desperately to see "order"—in a sense but another term for "truth" or "reality"—in apparent disorder. Thus the syntax would have the function of interpretative commentary. On the other hand, the many interpolations could serve the purpose of rendering immediately the onrush of a welter of perceptions in mosaiclike fashion. Instead of a logical sequence, a kind of haphazard but "lifelike" juxtaposition of events in time would then ensue. This seems to be especially true in the later prose. No matter what, the prose of Kleist's *Novellen* succeeds in rendering "reality" as "appearance" with the greatest economy of means while avoiding through syntactical versatility the monotony of mere newspaper reporting. But behind his style, one senses the integrity of an artist who has looked at life closely and wishes to render it responsibly. The "unusual event" becomes for Kleist a focal point of man's destiny. His *Novellen* are not born of mere curiosity about strange events but rather of an anxiety-ridden quest to penetrate the riddles of the universal condition of man.

Kleist's prose style is highly compatible with the formal characteristics of the German *Novelle*. Originally, like all storytelling, this narrative form stems from the Orient. In Europe, its history must be traced to the biographical sketches written by twelfth-century troubadours. The most striking examples, however, are found in Boccaccio's collection of charming and often licentious tales, the *Decameron,* written in the fourteenth century. Almost contemporaneously with Boccaccio, Chaucer published his *Canterbury Tales,* while in France and Spain the novella began to flourish only in the sixteenth and seventeenth centuries with the tales of Margaret of Navarre and the *"novelas ejemplares"* of Cervantes. Most of these novellas are "framed" between a prologue and an epilogue, a company—less often a single individual—telling stories from their own experience, centering upon unusual events. In Germany, the genre was established by Goethe and the Romanticists at the end of the eighteenth and beginning of the nineteenth century. While the German writers of *Novellen* go consciously back to Boccaccio, they most often write single stories, not series, and without the framework of a convivial band of storytellers entertaining each other with their unusual tales. The German *Novelle* may have a frame of its own, but quite as often it stands by itself, as is the case with Kleist's work.

The three main features of the German *Novelle* can be

summarized as follows. The plot should revolve around an *unerhörtes Ereignis,* a central event of unusual though not improbable nature. There should be a sudden or unexpected reversal, a *Wendepunkt,* somewhat comparable to the *peripeteia,* the sudden yet logical reversal of the tragic action found in certain Greek tragedies. Finally, the *Novelle* often contains a *Leitmotiv,* a kind of central image, paradox, or dramatic situation which encapsulates the meaning of the action in almost symbolic fashion. However, in most cases, it is nearly impossible to separate these three elements very clearly from each other. They are often merely differing aspects of the same basic happening. The difficulty of analysis simply stems from the fact that the *Novelle* attempts to effect with the greatest economy of means a symbolic condensation of the epic element in life and human destiny through the unusual event. It is obvious, then, that the *Novelle* cannot dwell on lengthy character development and psychological motivation. It rather shows the overwhelming determining power of outer circumstance in human life. Unusual events can thus be presented as "blows of fate" striking man from without and testing, though not developing, the strength of his character.

Kleist is largely responsible for adding a metaphysical element to the German *Novelle.* Hitherto, Goethe, Schiller, and others had used the form primarily to portray an unusual individual destiny against a well-defined social background. The effect was often didactic or slightly humorous. Kleist's *Novellen,* however, are set in a rather vague social and historical milieu, and his heroes are confronted with situations shattering their belief in a world order. Personal solitude, agonized questioning of the sum total of things, or violent and desperate actions are the result of this confrontation between an individual and his strange destiny. The characters must at all costs defend the unity of their inner consciousness against the deceptions and unpredictability—the "fragile constitution"—of the world. And in those moments when they find their inner truth or self-identity, they may reveal a surprising strength of character.

Interwoven into the general metaphysical framework of Kleist's *Novellen* are themes of a more specific nature. A

Rousseauistic type of social critique can be discerned in "The Earthquake in Chile," where arbitrary human laws do harm to the innate goodness of man and only wreak havoc and suffering. In "The Engagement in Santo Domingo," not only the characteristic Kleistian motif of a test of trust but also the theme of racial hatred is prominent. And in "The Marquise of O——," quasi-cynical allusions to the "immaculate conception" are interspersed in the otherwise sympathetic account of a woman's strange, inexplicable pregnancy.

Even though the form of Kleist's *Novellen* is strictly "objective" in the sense that the author refrains from editorializing or interpreting events, Kleist succeeds at times in vesting his stories with a touch of subtle irony, even sarcasm. In "The Earthquake in Chile," he describes the murderous actions of a zealous Christian as being "full of holy cruelty." In "The Duel," he suggests in the plot itself how misguided are the pretenses under which man-made laws presumably embody the divine will. However, in "The Beggarwoman of Locarno," on the surface little more than the briefest of anecdotes, Kleist has completely limited himself to a skeletal narrative line. And yet, the anecdote is capable of evoking a feeling of the utter senselessness of the supernatural forces guiding human destiny. Written late in his career, it seems to be an especially succinct artistic metaphor of a recurrent experience in Kleist's own inner life.

In one sense, the whole of "The Beggarwoman of Locarno" is but an extended version of those trenchant introductory sentences which lend a distinctive touch to all of Kleist's *Novellen*. These opening clauses most often plunge the reader *in medias res* at the height of dramatic tension, thus commanding his undivided attention without further ado. In some cases, as in "The Marquise of O——" or "Michael Kohlhaas," they even summarize the essential features of the plot in sparse, epigrammatic style:

In M——, a large town in northern Italy, the widowed Marquise of O——, a lady of unblemished reputation and the mother of several well-bred children, published the following notice in the newspapers: that, without her knowing how, she was in the family way; that she would like the father of the child she was going to bear to report himself; and that her mind was made up, out of consideration for her people, to marry him.[10]

Toward the middle of the sixteenth century, there lived on the banks of the Havel a horse dealer by the name of Michael Kohlhaas, the son of a schoolmaster, one of the most upright and at the same time one of the most terrible men of his day.[11]

The introductory sentences of Kleist's *Novellen* have been subjected to much critical exegesis. Some show affinities with the form of the chronicle, others seem more akin to newspaper reporting, still others, such as "The Engagement in Santo Domingo" and "The Duel," begin more broadly and approach rather the form of the historic tale. But, undeniably, all the *Novellen* openings exemplify with admirable artistry the difficult and stringent canons which form the basis of the *Novelle*, and culminate in the art of saying the most with the least. Indeed, Kleist's *Novellen* embody this art to the highest degree.

NOTES

[1] Sembd., Vol. 5, p. 79. (My translation—R.E.H.)

[2] Ibid., p. 54. (My translation—R.E.H.)

[3] Sembd., Vol. 1, p. 138, ll. 2228–29. (See the Mary J. and Lawrence M. Price translation in *Poet Lore*, Vol. XXVII, No. V, Autumn 1916, p. 554.)

[4] Sembd., Vol 2, p. 232, ll. 2297–2308. (See Humphrey Trevelyan's translation of *Penthesilea* in *The Classic Theatre*, ed. Eric Bentley, Vol. II, Doubleday Anchor Books, 1959, p. 391.)

[5] Sembd., Vol. 3, p. 271, ll. 1374–75. (See James Kirkup's translation of *The Prince of Homburg* in *The Classic Theatre*, p. 486.)

[6] Camus' *The Stranger* shows similar insights. The "absurdity" of the courtroom scenes springs in great part from the discrepancy between Meursault's own concept of self and the supposedly objective criteria by which he is judged.

[7] See for instance Walter Silz, *Heinrich von Kleist, Studies in His Works and Literary Character*, Chapter V, "Repetitions and Recoveries," Philadelphia University Press, 1961.

[8] Thomas Mann, Preface to *The Marquise of O—— and Other Stories,* translated by Martin Greenberg, Criterion Books, 1960, Ungar Paperbacks, 1974, pp. 14–15.

[9] Sembd., Vol. 4, p. 100; Greenberg translation, p. 48.

[10] Sembd., Vol. 4, p. 94; Greenberg, p. 41.

[11] Sembd., Vol. 4, p. 5; Greenberg, p. 87.

The Major Dramas and Novellen

Introduction

The grouping of Kleist's works will always remain problem-
atical. While the chronology of the dramas can be established with reasonable certainty, the *Novellen* elude such
classification since Kleist's letters do not reveal much about
their genesis and most of them were apparently published
several years or months after they had been written. Thematically, it is equally difficult to establish clear lines of demar-
cation or development running through his works. All of
them are variations of the same basic theme of existential
anxiety. Kleist attempts to counteract the instability of the
world with man's intuitive certainties, though at times only
to show how precarious that inner world itself is. The constitutive elements of this confrontation between individual
and world, as discussed in the previous chapters, can be
found in ever renewed combinations throughout Kleist's writings: the deceptiveness of the world expressed in fateful
chance happenings and an ironic turn of events; the vulner-

ability of human consciousness revealed in its misjudgments of sensory reality and its own illusions; the tormenting and inconclusive inner search for unity with self and the hope for ultimate sanction in a sea of uncertainty; the inescapable demand made upon man to reorient himself in the world through error and suffering; the insistence on absolute trust to overcome the individual's inner isolation; the whole permeated by an unrelieved disquietude about the breach between human consciousness and the world bordering on a sense of the grotesque.

If there is any observable development in Kleist's works, then it consists of a tendency to stress increasingly the moral and social aspects of man's uneven struggle with the world. This trend culminates in *The Prince of Homburg,* where it produces a drama with distinct idealistic overtones, only to revert abruptly to a sense of the grotesque with "St. Cecilia, or the Power of Music."

In the following discussion of Kleist's major works an attempt has been made to group them according to the predominance of one or the other of the various aspects of his portrayal of human existence, with some attention paid to a likely chronology. While the classification is highly tentative, it serves at least heuristic purposes.

The Drama of the Human Will

"Robert Guiscard"

Kleist's losing battle with *Robert Guiscard,* which was to remain a fragment, is a pathetic and well-known chapter in the annals of German literature. He began to write it shortly after the completion of *The Schroffenstein Family.*[1] But it is highly probable that the germinal idea for the unfinished tragedy antedates the inception of his first complete drama. There is also good reason to maintain that the *Guiscard* project was conceived under the influence of literary models such as *Oedipus Rex*[2] and Schiller's *Wallenstein* rather than Kleist's own metaphysical despair, which found a more direct outlet in *Schroffenstein.* Indeed, in a letter to Ulrike of July 3, 1803, he speaks of a "certain invention in the domain of art" (i.e., literature) which he is about to implement—most likely a reference to his *Guiscard* project. From the outset it seemed to be a more cerebral than visceral expression of his creativity

79

and, for this reason, may have failed despite Kleist's stubborn self-investment in it, which is reflected in the dynamics of its language. And since *Robert Guiscard* remained a fragment that Kleist reconstructed only four or five years after he had destroyed the original manuscript,[3] it stands out as a unique feature in the corpus of his works and may well be treated without meticulous regard for chronology.

A cryptic note is added to the history of the *Guiscard* fragment by Wieland's letter to Dr. Wedekind of April 10, 1804, in which he confidently predicted that Kleist's drama, should it ever be finished, would unite the spirit of Aeschylos, Sophocles, and Shakespeare in one single work. Despite its unassailable dramatic and stylistic qualities, the extant fragment leaves one guessing just exactly what Wieland meant. There are, true, the themes of the plague decimating the populace and a hero whose destiny is connected with the disease, as is the case in *Oedipus Rex*. According to one historical source,[4] Robert's actions, like those of Oedipus, were under the spell of an oracle, which presaged that he would find a glorious death in Jerusalem, although Kleist did not weave this motif into his drama, and whether he intended to do so is a moot question. But the dramatic configuration of the fragment does not let us conclude with certainty that the finished drama would have been essentially an "analytic" play whose action consists in unraveling a fateful interlocking of deeds already done that spell the hero's doom. Similarly, it is difficult to read the signs of a fateful hybris into Guiscard's character and political gambits and to let oneself be convinced that the plague about to fell him would be a meaningful punishment or nemesis for his supposed transgressions. What strikes the candid reader most forcefully is the drama's portrayal of a brutal confrontation between a man's indomitable will and an absurd, mechanical "fate," the plague.

Kleist took considerable liberties with the historic sources of his topic, as he did repeatedly in such later works as *Penthesilea, The Battle of Arminius,* "Michael Kohlhaas," and *The Prince of Homburg.* The Normans are encamped before Istanbul,[5] their ranks thinned and their will nearly broken by the ravaging plague. The rumor is spreading that Robert himself has been struck down by the disease. Greatly agitated, his people converge on Guiscard's tent to find out the truth. Robert, the son of Guiscard, and Abälard, Guiscard's nephew, appear. Thirty years earlier, a dynastic strife had deprived Abälard of the succession to the throne. While Guiscard's son is recognized as the rightful heir, the disenfranchised Abälard, who surpasses his rival in qualities of leadership, hopes to recover the crown after Guiscard's death. Robert offends the assembled crowd by brusquely rejecting its demand to be informed of Guiscard's state of health. The wily Abälard, however, tries to win their confidence by brutally disclosing the truth of Guiscard's illness. He also reveals that Guiscard is lending an ear to a conspiracy that would make himself ruler of Istanbul rather than his daughter Helena, the widowed Empress of Greece and betrothed of Abälard. With a superhuman effort Guiscard himself appears, enthusiastically greeted by the crowd, which sees in him their savior. Trying to assuage fears with reassuring words and convivial aplomb, he falters and, visibly exhausted, must sit down on a drum lovingly moved near him by his daughter. As Guiscard strains to listen to the entreaties of the people's spokesman to lead them out of their misery, the fragment ends.

Whatever might have followed this stark opposition of human will and impersonal fate would most likely have been anticlimactic, although Kleist proved repeatedly that he could lift the action of a drama or *Novelle* to new and unexpected heights by introducing new motifs, as in "Michael Kohlhaas," or through sudden reversals of the action, as in "The Marquise of O——," "The Duel," or *The Prince of Homburg*, where illness or mortal woundings are deceptive. After Guiscard had succumbed to the plague, the focus of the action might conceivably have shifted to the rivalry between Robert and Abälard, as was actually done in one attempt to complete the fragment.[6]

But the dramaturgic problems created by the original conception of the play seem almost insuperable. It is questionable whether a nearly faultless hero greatly admired by the fictional society around him, who is absurdly cut down by an amoral force incapable of suggesting the pervasive presence of a higher wisdom, could be a fitting subject for a tragedy in the traditional, Aristotelian sense. Guiscard is not afflicted with Oedipus' initial blindness toward his own errors. He is no victim of deceptive appearances, though, conversely, he valiantly tries to deceive his people about his illness for their own peace of mind. And in his last gesture of fatigue there is an intimation that he knows of the futility of his resistance to a fatal disease.

Nevertheless, on the political plane there is great irony in his fate. Thirty years before Guiscard had let himself be elected to the throne, in violation of the rights of the legitimate successor. But now he upholds the dynastic claims of his own son Robert against Abälard's, despite the latter's greater political acumen. The people are accessories to Guiscard's autocratic ways. They now adhere to the principle of legitimacy, while thirty years earlier they were easily swayed by the sheer force of Guiscard's personality. It has been speculated that at the time of restoring the fragment Kleist had little use for the Rousseauist notion of the sovereignty of the people, with its implied belief in the supremacy of their wisdom. In most of his works Kleist indeed showed little taste for such idealization. At times, as in *Schroffenstein, Guiscard,* and "Michael Kohlhaas," he comes rather close to exposing the masses as an irrational mob; in "The Earthquake in Chile" he actually does so. But the focal point of his works is never on that theme. His portrayal of the people simply attests to his keen awareness of both good and evil bursting forth in their actions.

The real problem in interpreting *Guiscard* is whether a convincing case can be made for a meaningful interrelationship between the hero's political ruse and the plague. It is open to question whether the disease can be interpreted as a symbolic punishment for an inner decay supposedly revealed in Guiscard's political machinations. In *Oedipus Rex* the plague that scourges Thebes does have such symbolic value; significantly, the hero's struggle is not with the disease but with the hidden guilt within. In *Guiscard,* however, the hero must wage a battle with the plague itself. Despite the possible flaw of character suggested through Guiscard's *Machtpolitik,* or power politics, the drama has some of the makings of a contemporary existentialist play or novel, in which suffering is intolerably condensed because it is no longer seen as justified by a moral law of equivalence governing human affairs. In this ruthless opposition of a man's will to the physical decay assailing him, the presence of a third force—an overarching metaphysical or moral structure—can hardly be felt. There is not even a passing reference to the *deus absconditus* whose remote presence Kleist at least suggests, if not postulates, in his other works. Characteristic of the ultimate bleakness is the behavior of Kleist's chorus, i.e., the people, who are in "restless commotion," vacillating between fear of the plague and confidence in the redemptive powers of their leader. They do not embody that *Reflexion* —a heightened sensitivity for the moral governance of the world—with which Schiller endows his chorus in *The Bride of Messina*.

Kleist, who had experienced in his own destiny the turbulence and rapidly changing nature of his time, could not easily jump from realistic observations to a profession of philosophic faith in the meaningfulness of the historic process. This is why he might have found it difficult to confer, through a dramatic ploy, some "higher" significance on Guiscard's struggle, even to suggest in a Shakespearean manner that man is his own undoing, or to portray convincingly the value of historic forces as a kind of "objective correlative" to human actions. At the most one might assert that Kleist's ingrained sense of the ultimate uncertainty of all things human pierced through the surface gloss of literary tradition to depict a world in which man's intentions are defeated by absurd forces.

Thus the whole meaning of the drama must reside in the resoluteness of the hero's personality. What finally transpires most compellingly in Guiscard's agony is the sheer defiant power of his will in an uneven battle with physical decay. He does not have to wing himself up to the demands of an inner moral law triumphing over self-interest and the malice of history. He is no harbinger of a moral "idea" in the Schillerian sense. A historic drama of that sort would have necessitated greater epic broadness and certainly a somewhat wavering hero, as in Schiller's *Wallenstein*. Nor is the hero portrayed from the same inner perspective of "feeling" as are many of Kleist's later heroes and heroines, a vantage point that lends their character more reflective depth. Guiscard is

obviously a *Tatmensch,* a man of action par excellence, although a suppressed reflective tendency is suggested in the
subtle nuances of Kleist's stagecraft. The dramatic highlights
consist of silent gestures—a sudden look of uncertainty on the
hero's face, Helena's furtive moving of the drum, the barely
audible sigh of relief uttered by Guiscard—a technique an-
nouncing ever so slightly the theater of Chekhov, Ibsen, and
Strindberg. But in his desperate and abortive attempt to finish the tragedy, Kleist seems to have been overtaken by his
own inner development, which led him to probe more and
more deeply into the mysteries and ambiguities of man's inner consciousness. The route he will follow is indicated in
the fragment by the impassioned hymnic language that points
toward *Penthesilea* and is in striking contrast to the chilling
theme. Especially in the mass scenes, the language actually
achieves the fervor of an oratorio:

My lord, beloved duke, your cheerful words/return to us a life we
had given up./The tomb to cover you should not exist:/would that
you were immortal, sire, immortal/—immortal as your deeds! 7

In the final analysis it remains a mystery what exactly
Kleist had in mind by the "invention" he meant to embody
in this drama. Was it of a formalistic nature, namely the
telescoping of the dramatic conflict into a few significant
episodes or its division into mere scenes rather than acts,
either of which would have been nothing startlingly new?
Or was it of a more substantive nature, namely an attempt
to extrapolate from the erratic course of history a concept
of a "fate" that entraps the great historic individual and the
passive masses alike? In that case he might have attempted
to insert the form of an analytic play into an actual historic
context, while observing the three unities. The fragment does
not reveal enough of Kleist's intentions to make apodictic
assertions about them. Nevertheless, the result of his battle
with an unwieldly, grandiose idea is a document of remarkable artistic form. But it proved a dangerous *cul-de-sac* in his
career, from which only new and different endeavors could
extricate him.

NOTES

[1] Conjectural date of completion for *Schroffenstein:* March or April 1802. Beginning date for actual work on *Guiscard:* probably May 1802.

[2] There is evidence that during his one-and-a-half-year-long struggle with *Guiscard* Kleist consulted a German translation of *Oedipus Rex* which he borrowed from the Dresden Library in June 1803.

[3] Hans Joachim Kreutzer's argument that Kleist may actually have finished the tragedy in 1807-8 in Dresden remains unconvincing. See Kreutzer, *Die dichterische Entwicklung Heinrichs von Kleist,* pp. 156-57.

[4] Kleist's sources were most likely K.W.F. v. Funck's "Robert Guiscard, Herzog von Apulien und Calabrien," which appeared in 1797 in Schiller's journal *Die Horen,* as well as Schiller's edition of the Byzantine emperor Alexius' life, as described by his daughter and successor Anna Comnena, published in 1790 in the *Collection of Historic Memoirs.* It is in the latter that the prophesy of Guiscard's death in Jerusalem can be found, although, still according to Anna Comnena, Guiscard actually died on the isle of Corfu, where "once upon a time there existed a city by the name of Jerusalem." (In truth Guiscard died on July 17, 1085, of a fever on the nearby isle of Cephalonia.) Funck describes in detail Guiscard's abortive campaign against Byzantium, during which he besieged Durazzo, among other places. His army was severely decimated by disease, and Guiscard himself lay sick on his ship anchored near Byzantium but recovered. At Durazzo he went around the camp giving comfort to the sick, not heeding the danger to his own health.

There is a noticeable parallel to the account of Napoleon's investment of Acre in 1799 during his Egyptian campaign, when the plague broke out among his troupes and the general against all warnings visited the sick.

[5] Kleist combines Funck's description of Guiscard's death in 1085 with his portrayal of the siege of Durazzo in 1081-2.

[6] C. Roessler, "H. v. Kleist's Unfinished Tragedy Robert Guiscard," *Preussische Jahrbücher,* LXV, 1890.

[7] Ll. 449-53 in the original German version. Translation by L. R. Scheuer in *Tulane Drama Review,* Vol. 6, No. 3, March 1962, p. 190.

"Chance" and Evil in a Deceptive World

"The Schroffenstein Family"

Although Kleist's first complete drama is an immediate expression of his own philosophic disenchantment, it is not the product of impulsive haste but went through various stages of careful planning, writing, and recasting. He wrote a scenario for it under the title *The Thierrez Family* and an intermediate version of the complete drama entitled *The Ghonorez Family*, which was published long after his death on the basis of the extant original manuscript. Finally, he reworked the drama under the title *The Schroffenstein Family* and in the process changed its historically vague Spanish background to an equally vague setting in Swabia. The drama is largely of his own invention, owing very little to literary models and nothing to history. It was published in 1803 rather hastily by his friends Ludwig Wieland and Heinrich Gessner and apparently contains some deviations from the manuscript, now lost, which incurred Kleist's displeasure. Premièred as early as 1804 in Graz, it was a moderate success, and if it did not establish Kleist straightway as a major new dramatist, it gave him at least much needed encouragement.

The immediate impact of the drama is that of a gloomy and passionate "tragedy of errors," in which the grim accuracy of chance compounds the effects of human dereliction. It has often been said that the play dramatizes in alternately powerful and naïve fashion the feelings of bitter irony and cynical disgust about the human condition that overcame Kleist in the wake of the Kant crisis. This observation may account for the general mood of the play, but it does not yield a sufficient set of criteria for literary interpretation. Moreover, such oversimplification may give the erroneous impression that the drama is a mere *Lehrstück* or parable for philosophic skepticism. It is decidedly more than a persiflage of human reason, though it is that also. Rather, Kleist transposes into a vivid artistic metaphor that feeling of uncertainty about all certainties which was the end station of his youthful philosophic journey.

Essentially, *The Schroffenstein Family* illustrates that human beings are forever locked in their own subjectivity and upon interacting cause nothing but chaos and destruction. In the process, absurd chance happenings become focal points at which the inability of all the faculties of human consciousness to perceive truth is glaringly revealed. If a tenuous analogy with Kantianism is indeed permissible, it would suggest that the individual's subjective way of perceiving and interpreting the events and people around him is comparable to the predicament of human "consciousness-in-general," which is irremediably entrapped in its own limited mechanism of understanding.

In Kleist's first play chance happenings are not only an acid test for human comprehension, or rather misapprehensions, they also seem to reflect the intrinsic absurdity of the world. "Design" manifests itself only as an evil scheme in the affairs of men, as though a gnostic demon had upset the divine teleology. The insane coincidences that challenge human comprehension are at best a parody of a meaningful fate. Beleaguered by insoluble riddles, human consciousness is strained to the breaking point and in its desire for certainty readily jumps to unwarranted conclusions. In such a world, the stabilizing forces of society lose their effectiveness. Thus, Kleist uses the motif of a hereditary contract with abrasive irony. A product of reason destined to regulate human affairs, the contract brings about the very opposite of its original intentions, namely unalloyed strife. If there is stability in the world, then it is only in the sense that the sum total of evil is unalterably fixed. The mild-mannered Sylvester, for instance, becomes ensnared in error just when his antagonist, Rupert, gains some insight into his self-deception.

The synopsis of Kleist's first work reads like that of a cloak-and-dagger drama. Upon reciting the play to some friends a short time after its completion, he reportedly broke out into guffaws of laughter. But despite this act of self-deprecation he never completely disavowed his youthful drama. While aware of some of its absurdities, he also knew that it was a serious first effort in finding a literary vehicle for his personal artistic vision of the world.

Two branches of a feudal house live in an atmosphere of mutual suspicion because of a hereditary pact which provides that upon the extinction of one line its possessions shall revert to the other. One family has its seat at Rossitz and consists of Count Rupert, his wife, Eustache, their son, Ottokar, and Rupert's natural son, Johann. The other line resides at Warwand and includes Count Sylvester, his wife, Gertrude, their daughter, Agnes, and Sylvester's father, the blind Count Sylvius. Jeronimus, a youth belonging to a third branch, is torn in his allegiance between the two feuding camps. When Rupert discovers his young son Peter slain, and two men from Warwand standing over the body clutching bloody knives, he is quick to conclude that Sylvester is the instigator of the crime. His suspicion is seemingly corroborated by one of the men, whose last word before dying on the rack was Sylvester's name. Jeronimus denounces Sylvester as a murderer. Upon hearing himself thus accused, Sylvester falls into a deep swoon just as his subjects are lynching Rupert's messenger, who had come to declare war. Now convinced of Sylvester's innocence by the latter's sincere anguish, Jeronimus pleads with Rupert to desist from his murderous plans. He encounters only cynical laughter and, upon leaving, meets the same fate as Rupert's messenger at the hands of an enraged populace. Meanwhile, Agnes and Ottokar have fallen in love with each other—the Romeo and Juliet motif is obvious—and in a scene where she accepts a libation from him, fully believing that it contains poison but is proved wrong, the two succeed in banishing the last remnant of fear and mistrust from their relationship.

In structuring these events, and in the portrayal of character, Kleist skillfully handles the interplay of force and counterforce, accusation and counteraccusation. As Sylvester regains consciousness, his wife, Gertrude, whose suspicious nature resembles that of Rupert, imputes the earlier death of their child Philip to Rupert's machinations. But Sylvester has no trouble in showing her that she could have been similarly accused some years before when a newborn nephew died while under her care. In the other camp, Eustache, whose mildness is akin to Sylvester's, implores her husband in vain to prevent Jeronimus' senseless murder. In an earlier ancillary episode, Johann, crazed with unrequited love for Agnes, madly entreats her to slay him with his own dagger. She faints just as Jeronimus appears, who wounds, though does not kill, the apparent assassin. Circumstantial evidence suggests a dark plot hatched by Rupert in the same way that Peter's death seemed to implicate Sylvester. Sometime later, when Sylvester feels compelled by circumstances to resort to violence, Rupert begins to shudder at his own heinous character. In Kleist's early artistic vision good and evil seem to annul each other in an infernal round of events, suggesting a feeling of absurd emptiness.

Meanwhile, Ottokar, searching for a clue to Peter's death, chances upon a witch's kitchen. In a macabre Shakespearean scene the old sorceress Ursula and her daughter are brewing a magic potion containing a child's finger. He learns that Ursula had discovered a drowned boy floating down a forest stream and cut off his little finger to use it as a charm, whereupon two men from Warwand appeared, mutilating the child's hand in like fashion for a similar purpose. Though close to revealing the truth, events take an ironic turn for the worse. Ottokar, aware of his father's fiendish intentions, meets Agnes in a forest cave and convinces her to exchange garments with him, ostensibly to prevent her own murder—an episode much criticized for its lack of taste and its apparent salaciousness. But in the dead of night, the two fathers slay their own children. Ironically, it is the blind Sylvius—a pale imitation of the blind seer Tereisias—who first recognizes their true identities. The sinister Ursula tosses little Peter's severed finger among the wailing parents and discloses the true cause of the child's death. Johann, stalking around in the cave, his reason about to snap, cynically applauds the witch for a job well done:

> Go on, old woman, go!
> Your conjuring hath served you well. Go on!
> For with this pretty trick I'm well content.[1]

Despite a number of absurdities the drama shows the interdependence of "character" and "fate" with some plausibility. "Character" or "consciousness" is tested at "fateful" junctures—the crucial chance events—which catalyze human destinies. Kleist knows that it is in unusual circumstances or crisis situations that innate human propensities are most revealingly tested. In the portrayal of his characters' reactions to riddlesome chance happenings he succeeds in drawing quite subtle differences in behavior patterns, all of which, however, fail in averting tragedy.

Jeronimus, the would-be mediator, hopes to clear up misunderstandings through his reasoning faculties. He is in the best position to do so, since he belongs to a third branch of the clan not caught up in the torrent of suspicion and hatred that saps the strength of the other two families. At first impressed by the justice of Rupert's cause, he soon concludes from Sylvester's reactions to the news of little Peter's death that he is innocent. No man—unless he were an accomplished actor—could evince such genuine grief and, moreover, prepare to face the danger of going to the enemy to talk to him, as does Sylvester, if he were ridden by feelings of guilt. Jeronimus carefully weighs this evidence against the persuasiveness of the confession extracted from Sylvester's servant on the rack and decides in favor of the former. But with some vindictive petulance—possibly stemming from his Kant crisis—Kleist takes pains in exhibiting the debility of reason in coping with a multifaced reality. For, ironically, Jeronimus' reasoning becomes ensnared in its own "logic." When he suggests to Sylvester in a rather incongruous reversal of his own code of ethics that a confession extorted from Johann on the rack would effectively counteract the confession made under torture by Sylvester's servant, Sylvester has no trouble in showing him that on the strength of such "evidence," he, Sylvester, must pass for a murderer. Whereupon, Jeronimus exclaims in disgust:

> A priest might extricate
> Us from this tangle. It's too much for me! [2]

Ultimately Jeronimus, though ideally placed as a potential *raisonneur,* is at best a two-sided mirror of contending assertions and for all his pains in dredging up the truth is but cynically slaughtered.

Far from attempting to sort out "facts," as does Jeronimus, Rupert jumps on them in order to confirm his suspicions and even manipulates events to make them appear what they are not. In a sneering parody of Sylvester's fainting spell, which prevented the latter from forestalling the slaying of Rupert's messenger, he feigns not to have been personally involved in Jeronimus' murder. But Rupert is more than a melodramatic villain. He is a kind of desperado who against the uncertainties of an unstable world puts trust only in his own assertions. In the absence of a perceptible moral world order he dictates his own order to the world he perceives. Therefore, he has no scruples in bending sensory evidence to the sweep of his own sensations and passions. Nevertheless, upon espying his mirror image in a forest stream, he gains a sudden insight into the satanism of his revolt:

> A devil's face looked from
> the spring and gazed at me. [3]

But he persists in his vengeful ways, out of sheer defiance of the world:

> I care
> Not whether God or devil leads her [Agnes's] feet
> Among my snares. Since they have branded me

A murderer beforehand I will prove
Them right.[4]

Rupert, though somewhat naïvely drawn, has some of the
fearful negative attributes of the "metaphysical rebel," who
from despair affirms only himself and treats others as tools.
The result—a radical loss of humanity—is suggested in his
habit of whistling for his servants, who vainly remonstrate
with him not to treat them like dogs.

The mild-mannered Sylvester is the very opposite of Rupert.
He does not actively try to make the world over in his own
image, though he sees it largely through the purifying medium
of his own inner vision. When faced with seemingly objective
and contrary evidence, he does not twist it to his own desires
but seeks refuge in a nonobjective world within. The intuitive
and God-intoxicated type, he hopes to find certainty and
strength in the depth of his consciousness. When recovering
from his faint, he asserts confidently:

> I rejoice
> Because the mind is stronger than I thought
> For if it leaves one for a moment it is
> That it may seek its God, its fount of strength,
> And come again with its heroic powers
> Renewed.[5]

His saintly inwardness affords him psychological insights
into the paranoid fears caused by distrust that his own wife,
Rupert, and others "project" into the world:

> Distrust is like a plague spot on the soul
> That makes all things, however pure and clean,
> Seem to the eye to wear the garb of hell.
> The meaningless, the common things of life,
> Are shrewdly sorted out like tangled yarn
> And knit into a pattern which affrights
> The soul with fearful forms.[6]

It also makes him into a good dialectician, for he repeatedly
refutes with pith not only the suspicions uttered by his wife
but also some of Jeronimus' "logic." But for all its good-

naturedness, Sylvester's intuitional approach to reality remains too solipsistic to deal effectively with the objective world. Inward certainty is one thing, and redemptive action another. In two lines which form a kind of pendant to Rupert's recognition of inner estrangement, Sylvester wearily expresses his own alienation from God and, perhaps, himself:

> You thinkest me a difficult enigma.
> Console yourself, for God is such to me.[7]

Ottokar, Rupert's son, shares some qualities of activism with his father, but he is also endowed with the intuitional faculty that distinguishes Sylvester as well as the reasonableness discernible in Jeronimus. When he first meets Agnes in the wilderness, he intuits rightly that she is Sylvester's daughter. On a hunch, and aided by his reasoning, he discovers that the missing finger on Peter's hand is a clue to the mystery of his death. Like his father, he too attempts to set things aright, according to his preconceived ideas of them. But, youthful lover that he is, he is not under the sway of revengeful passion but rather guided by his desire to see Agnes untainted by the suspicion of murder weighing on her family. Finally, when he exchanges garments with her, he manipulates reality, not unlike his father. But, instead of foiling the murderous intentions of the parents with his stratagem, he only succeeds in intensifying tragedy.

Kleist portrays the genesis of the bond of trust and love between Agnes and Ottokar in a peculiarly ambiguous way. Agnes drinks from the cup offered her by Ottokar in a youthful gesture of defiance, for she is convinced that he is about to poison her. She knows by now that he is the son of the enemy, and she has no reason to disbelieve the rumors of the innate villainy of those of Rossitz. If the episode demonstrates that only absolute trust in the other's motives could redeem the world from error, it does so rather equivocally. Agnes must make the decision in fear and trembling. She is not guided by a strong inner assurance, as are the memorable heroines of Kleist's later works, such as Alkmene, the Marquise of O——, or the Kaethchen of Heilbronn. In keeping with the pessimistic tenor of the drama, Agnes makes her decision in despair, in an almost suicidal mood, for she must choose not only against rational evidence but also in a state of inner uncertainty. She has nothing to rely on but her own defiance of a world in which her love is thwarted. Underneath her despair one might be tempted to detect signs of an existential hope against hope. If this element is there, she does not seem to be much aware of it, for when her fears prove unfounded she reproaches herself for not having trusted Ottokar:

> O Ottokar! I would
> That it were poison so that I might die
> With you. If it is not, I dare not, can
> Not hope to live with you, since I have so
> Ignobly sinned against your soul.[8]

In her case we cannot find the deep probings into "feeling" that distinguish Kleist's treatment of his heroines in the later works. But in her defiant gesture she at least proves to have the mettle of a positive Kleistian character, for she is capable of complete surrender to an inner urge, even if it is a dark impulse of despair.

If the episode does not unequivocally reveal the presence of initial trust in the two lovers, it certainly makes the point that men *should* have trust, for Agnes's daring leap into uncertainty creates sudden hope. The whole episode is an inverted, though positive, example of the ironic contrast of cause and effect, anticipation and realization, that pervades the drama. The apparent certainties which guide the other characters lead to greater confusion, while the initial uncertainty in Agnes's choice helps to dispel untruth. By way of contrast, the saving grace of trust exemplified in the two lovers emerges as a patently missed opportunity on the part of those who believe only their senses, preconceived ideas, or reasoning abilities.

More than simply expostulating a conflict between reasoning—specious or otherwise—and intuition, Kleist illustrates in his first drama the whole dereliction of human consciousness as such. In a world bereft of divine grace, none of the human faculties of mind or soul leads anywhere near truth, which, according to eudaemonistic canons, is a prerequisite to happiness. This thought, central to the *Marionettentheater,* is put in the mouth of Johann, who expresses it with the lucidity of madness:

> SYLVIUS: Pray, take me home, my son.
>
> JOHANN: To happiness? It can't be done. *The door Is barred inside.* Come, come, *we must go on.*[9]

At the end, Johann is not just uttering incoherent nonsense. Rather, with the feverish intensity of one whose reason has been strained to the breaking point, he petulantly spills out a general truth that others will not dare express but nevertheless are made to experience.

In fact, the poetry of Kleist's first play is replete with a gnomic element. In his subsequent works he shows more restraint in using sententious phrases expressing general truths. But the frequency of gnomic lines shows that *The Schroffenstein Family* is very much *Problemdichtung,* i.e., literature concerned with a problem *in abstracto.* It may also attest to Kleist's unavowed desire to emulate a kind of classicist universality as is found in the plays of the mature Goethe. In other ways, too, the drama exhibits some classicist features, such as the often artificial avoidance of short scenes (so popular with Storm and Stress dramatists) or the lyrical exposition, a device which we encounter only in *Guiscard* among Kleist's other dramas. But generally the sententious phrases, if seen from a dramaturgic standpoint, are not a very felicitous means of making a point, since they are rather artificially grafted on the dialogue.

In the plot itself some episodes are equally contrived. The exchange of garments between the two lovers is a clumsy device to create the kind of deception that accentuates tragedy. And Peter's cut-off finger as a clue to hidden entanglements lends itself to cheap punning, at least in German. It is a *Fingerzeig* (pointing with a finger at something), at first understood by none but Ottokar, but then unmistakably made known as such when it is literally tossed in the midst of the two families assembled around the slain bodies of their two children.

On the other hand, the flaws of the plot are compensated by

the poetic fervor of the language and an underlying rhythmic pattern which, independently of the spoken lines, expressed Kleist's acrid skepticism. Although occasionally strained, the language is capable of expressing the inner dynamics of the characters, as in the following short line spoken by Rupert in his moment of despairing insight:

s'ist innerlich
(it is all within) [10]

Normally, the succession of sibilants and the repetition of the high-frequency sound of "i" (in German) would be unpleasantly thin, but in the circumstances the astringent quality of the line pointedly expresses Rupert's inner exhaustion and emptiness, the absence of good in his soul, which according to orthodox Christian theology is the very nature of evil.

The implied ironic pattern underlying the dialogue is vividly exemplified at the very beginning of the drama. When a chorus of youngsters in the church at Rossitz chants that the revenge called forth upon the house of Warwand will reveal God's justice, we begin to wonder. They protest the justice of their cause once too often to be convincing, just as the young Kleist's own asseverations about a moral universe sounded too hollow, precisely for having been repeated with so much desperate insistence.

But what ultimately sustains Kleist's first drama is the young writer's absolutist urge, disabused though it may have been. Only if man could know the ultimate or have certainty about God's ways could he also be properly related to himself and the world and thus avoid tragic error. With a vengeance, Kleist portrays the illusoriness of such a paradisaical harmony on earth. The various powers of man's consciousness are at war with themselves, and the chance happenings that engage human destiny are merely baffling, not meaningful. The result is radical deception and destructive evil. But in contrast to the writers of "Fate" tragedies, such as Zacharias Werner in Germany (1768–1823), who conceived of chance as an occult manifestation of a mechanical fate (tragic things are fated to happen on a certain day, for instance the 24th of February),[11] Kleist gives us a more sophisticated picture of human destiny. Corrupt feelings, such as distrust, erroneous inferences of reason, wrong timing of action, combine with the fortuitousness of events to bring about tragedy in a world gone awry. Redemptive insights are either powerless or occur too late to forestall disaster.

The impression of a world in the clutches of chaos is heightened by Kleist's skeptical treatment of the results of force and counterforce in human relations. The interplay of the negative and positive does not lead to a redeeming synthesis but rather to futility. The drama is carefully constructed on a dialectic principle. Rupert's villainy is counterbalanced by Sylvester's mansuetude; Gertrude's distrustful character countervailed by the goodness of Eustache, Rupert's wife; the maniacal Johann opposed by the reasonable Jeronimus; the murderous plans of the parents counteracted by Ottokar's stratagem—all to no avail. Good and evil simply annul each other, and the impression left is one of nihilism, although the latter was apparently not Kleist's full intention. Through direct and all too audible author interference in the form of gnomic poetry, he suggests that beyond chaos there may be some ultimate meaning, for instance in Sylvester's affirmation that no evil spirit rules the world, only an incomprehensible one, a *deus absconditus*. The dialectic development of his drama points in one direction, Kleist's own wishful thinking in another. But his tentative profession of faith provides little solace in a drama portraying a world gone mad. It almost appears that after having recognized the artificiality of his pre-Kantian faith, Kleist was for a while an "angry young man," if not a metaphysical rebel.

NOTES

1 Sembd., Vol. 1, p. 156. Page 576 in Mary J. and Lawrence M. Price's translation, *The Feud of the Schroffensteins*, in *Poet Lore*, Vol. XXVII, No. V, Autumn 1916. (Throughout this chapter, *thou* and *thee* have been changed to *you* and *thy* to *your*—R.E.H.)

2 Sembd., Vol. I, p. 102; Price, p. 506.

3 Sembd., Vol. I, p. 138; Price, p. 554.

[4] Sembd., Vol. I, p. 139; Price, p. 555.

[5] Sembd., Vol. I, p. 92; Price, p. 495.

[6] Sembd., Vol. I, p. 80; Price, p. 478.

[7] Sembd., Vol. I, p. 102; Price, p. 507.

[8] Sembd., Vol. I, p. 107; Price, p. 514.

[9] Sembd., Vol. I, p. 153; Price, p. 572. (Italics mine—R.E.H.).

[10] Sembd., Vol. I, p. 138; (My own translation—R.E.H.).

[11] *The Twenty-Fourth of February* is the title of Werner's best-known tragedy.

"The Engagement in Santo Domingo"

Opinions on the time of inception of this *Novelle* differ greatly. It is based on the struggle for independence by the mulattoes of Santo Domingo (now Haiti) against the French, which was particularly fierce in the years 1803–4. When Kleist was incarcerated in Fort Joux in 1807 he could not help but be reminded of Toussaint L'Ouverture, the black general from Santo Domingo who had died there as a prisoner four years earlier. In 1805–6, two books on the history and rebellion of the isle of Haiti were published in Germany which, even prior to Kleist's imprisonment, might have kindled his interest in the subject. But the only certain information we have is the actual publication of the *Novelle* at the beginning of 1811 in a journal edited by Kuhn, Kleist's publisher for the *Berliner Abendblätter*, and its inclusion in the second volume of the *Erzählungen*.

Its story line is not as taut as in some of the other *Novellen,* and Kleist's own thought is rather artificially grafted on the plot, especially in the melodramatic ending. This may be due to the historic authenticity of the background material, which Kleist, for once, observed rather scrupulously, possibly also to his prolonged occupation with the topic (provided, of course, that he conceived it around 1806–7). Nevertheless, he succeeds in creating dramatic tension through a cleverly managed intrigue. The *Novelle* contains elements of an "historic tale." It does not start *in medias res* but with a fairly detailed exposition. However, the opening paragraph, through which we learn how an ungrateful Negro servant had killed his white benefactor, immediately suggests the major theme, namely that of "trust" and its abuse. Variations on the same theme can be found in three subsidiary stories woven into the complex plot. There is the story of Babekan, the old mulatto woman, which illustrates with racial overtones the abuse of loving trust—she had been callously abandoned by her white paramour of many years. The inverse—the sacrificial courage of love—is illustrated in the touching episode of Marianne Congrève, who a few years earlier during the French Revolution had saved the hero of the main story, Gustav von der Ried, from being guillotined by withholding his identity from his pursuers even as she herself ascended the scaffold. Finally, in another story within the story, we learn of the deceit perpetrated by a colored girl who, under the pretense of love, lured a white man into her chamber only to infect him with her own deadly disease. The epic background is a world torn by political and racial strife, more specifically Santo Domingo's murderous uprising of 1803 against the white population under General Dessalines, Toussaint L'Ouverture's successor.

At the outbreak of hostilities, a frightful Negro by the equally frightful name of Congo Hoanga had killed his master, a French plantation owner, M. de Villeneuve, although the latter had showered him with gifts as a reward for once having saved his life. Hoanga is now the owner of the plantation and with a band of blacks roams around the countryside, killing off any white refugees who cross his path. In his absence, his common-law wife, Babekan, and her fifteen-year-old daughter, Toni, the offspring of Babekan's betrayed love for a white man, are to lull any white fugitive seeking shelter in their dwelling into a false sense of security until the return of the band, whereupon he would be put to death. In the dead of night, Gustav von der Ried, a Swiss officer in the employ of the French, chances upon the wayside house. With a number of relatives who are hiding nearby, in need of food and drink, he is attempting to reach a port of safety. Toni's almost white complexion assuages his erstwhile fears and fills him with a feeling of trust. While Babekan tries to deploy all her wiles to lure him into a trap, Toni is beginning to have ambivalent feelings about the treachery, falls in love with Gustav, and undertakes to save him and his family from certain death.

The house is soon filled with hectic intrigue and confused emotions, culminating in the furtive betrothal of the refugee and the strange girl during their night of lovemaking. A series of complicated events brings the imminent catastrophe to a head. Upon Hoanga's return, Toni binds the sleeping Gustav to his bed to serve as a decoy and rushes out to call his family to the rescue. In the ensuing skirmish, Gustav, enraged over Toni's apparent betrayal, puts a bullet through her heart. As she expires, she gasps the leitmotif of the story: "You shouldn't have distrusted me!" When he learns the true motive of her stratagem, Gustav blows out his brains. The remainder of the story is a sad epilogue punctuated by a nostalgic burial ceremony for the two misguided lovers. After many vicissitudes, Gustav's relatives finally reach Switzerland.

Thematically, the story is related to one of the central motifs in *The Schroffenstein Family*, namely the bond of trust and love between Ottokar and Agnes that is a ray of hope in the midst of factional strife. As potential mediators between two warring factions, Toni and Gustav are in a similar situation, although, had they lived, their union would have had little more than symbolic value. But the psychological situation of the two lovers in this story is more complex than in the drama. Toni is outwardly an ambiguous person, half white, half mulatto. As the story progresses, we are made aware that she is equally ambivalent in her inner feelings, of which her racial mixture is but an outward sign. Her feigned sympathy for earlier victims is counterbalanced by the sincere revulsion at the new treachery she is asked to commit. As her sham feelings toward the young officer gradually give way to true affection and love she responds hesitatingly, though sensitively, to the inner change.

The girl nodded her head quickly and laughed; and when the stranger jokingly whispered in her ear to ask whether it took a white man to win her favor, she hesitated dreamily for a moment and then, as a charming blush flamed in her sunburned face, suddenly pressed herself against his breast.[1]

We are not quite sure when the turning point is reached, but ultimately her natural ambivalence precipitates the final catastrophe in spite of herself. She now uses treachery against her own kin in the service of a humane cause and her newly found love. Ironically, as must be expected in Kleist's unredeemed universe, the treachery that succeeded in working evil fails in producing good. However, the final catastrophe is not built into the tragic configuration of the plot in an organic way. Gustav shoots Toni after his rescuers have arrived on the scene and to all appearances should have had enough time to clear up the confusion. And the moral sentiment expressed in Toni's last words is perhaps an unjustifiable author interference, a last-minute attempt to endow the mere conflict of wills with a semblance of meaning.

Yet Toni is an engrossing figure precisely because of that all too human ambivalence that forces her to deceive in sincerity. Throughout the story the focus is on her, and contrary to a typical *Novellen* situation her character is as much developed as merely tested. But though she attains purity of feeling as a result of her love for Gustav, she is not quite comparable to Kleist's great heroines, such as Alkmene or the Marquise of O——, who must defend an inborn integrity against deceiving appearances. It is Toni herself who is the deceptive and puzzling element in the intrigue, although, admittedly, she is forced by a host of malevolent circumstances to play this role.

In Kleist's world, conscious deceit on the part of the central character lends itself better to comedy, as in *The Broken Pitcher*. Deception and pure feeling obviously do not mix well. As has been said, we find deceit and intrigue associated mostly with his secondary characters, such as Kunigunde in *The Kaethchen of Heilbronn* and Count F—— in "The Marquise of O——." Where deceit is clearly identifiable in the central character, it produces a less than admirable hero, as in *The Battle of Arminius*. Toni is partially exonerated by her feeling of contrition about her past treacheries. In her inner conversion she is to a small degree akin to a Schillerian heroine, although she acts not from a keen moral sense but from a very personal and spontaneous feeling and remains in this sense a typically Kleistian character.

The problem of a nascent love that must assert itself against deceptive appearances could have been made to revolve around Gustav. But with few exceptions, such as Trota in "The Duel" or Michael Kohlhaas, and then only with qualifications, Kleist reserves the necessary inner strength to withstand a deceptive world for his women protagonists—an unconscious expression perhaps of his own unfulfilled wish for unqualified feminine devotion. Gustav fails the test of absolute trust, and in the end he merely acts petulantly. We come away from the story with the impression that tragic error is as much due to human obtuseness as to fatal coincidence.

If we follow the pat recipe for a genuine *Novelle,* we might ask ourselves which occurrences precisely constitute the unusual, central event and the sudden reversal of the action. The former seems to be indicated in the story title itself, the rather strange betrothal taking place under equally strange circumstances. Most plausibly, the *peripeteia* or *Wendepunkt* occurs when Gustav finds himself roped to his bed, seemingly betrayed by his betrothed. Kleist suggests this himself when he has Toni reflect that she did not want to awaken Gustav for fear of plunging him brutally from his blissful world of dreams into a sordid reality. The leitmotif, on the other hand, is thematic and suggested in the subsidiary stories of love and deceit between people of different races mentioned earlier. These are at least "eloquent episodes," if not symbolic "objects," which at the same time give impetus to the plot, such as the team of horses in "Michael Kohlhaas."

But the recognition of these technical amenities is immaterial to our appreciation of the story. Despite some flaws, "The Engagement in Santo Domingo" shows a series of masterful strokes in creating tension and irony. Toni, the "godsend" in Gustav's eyes, is first an instrument of actual treachery and then of apparent treachery—a kind of double irony. Then, in attempting to avert one crisis she becomes the instrument of greater tragedy. The broad epic material of a murderous uprising is highlighted in terse, individual dramas and in the complex emotions of Toni and Gustav, while their lovemaking is passed over in complete but eloquent silence. Finally, the central theme of frustrated love and destructive revenge links the story to *Penthesilea,* which Kleist wrote largely during his imprisonment in Fort Joux.

NOTES

[1] Sembd., Vol. 4, pp. 157–58; Greenberg, p. 206.

"The Earthquake in Chile"

Although "The Earthquake in Chile" was probably written after "The Engagement in Santo Domingo," [1] it was the earliest of Kleist's *Novellen* to appear in print. As an example of its genre it is of rare excellence. It revolves around an unusual event—the earthquake and its paradoxical effects on human relations. There is a sudden and cruel reversal of the action prompted by an incendiary sermon delivered in the House of the Lord. And one can see in little Philip, the child of illicit love, a symbol of social conflicts erupting into catastrophe, an "objective correlative" of the *Novelle's* somber mood. The whole action is immersed in irony, sometimes bitter, sometimes benign; not only the cathedral scene—the sudden outbreak of mob violence in a place of worship—but most subsidiary episodes contain an ironic or paradoxical element as well. The irony of the action is effectively supported by the large scope given to chance, *Zufall*, that amoral force in the universe, which both abets and defeats human intentions.

A natural catastrophe—the earthquake [2]—saves two lovers, Jeronimo and Josepha, from imminent death. They were to be executed for their illicit love, consummated in the garden of a nunnery. While many of their tormenters find a violent death, they miraculously survive the disaster. But subsequently, as all the survivors publicly rejoice over their rescue, the two sinners are clubbed to death by an angry mob aroused to violence by the cathedral canon's sermon—the sacrificial victims of religious fervor, or "holy cruelty" as Kleist pungently calls it. While the young son of their friend Fernando and his sister-in-law are mistakenly slaughtered along with them, their own son, Philip, the child of sin, is saved. Kleist seems to illustrate that diabolic balance of opposing forces in human life and the universe which leaves us wondering about the existence of some ultimate design. A natural calamity is counterbalanced by feelings of mercy, while a society saved from disaster is swayed by murderous passions. And —irony of ironies—the cathedral, spared by the earthquake, is the site of man's destructive fury.

In the first half of the story we ascend from the holocaust of the earthquake through Dantesque, hallucinatory scenes to an idyl in a peaceful valley—a Garden of Eden painted in lush colors—where the two lovers are reunited and seemingly accepted by society.

They found a marvelous pomegranate tree, with spreading branches full of fragrant fruit; and in its top the nightingale sang its sensual music. Jeronimo sat down with his back against the trunk, with Josepha in his lap and Philip in hers, and his cloak around them all; and there they sat and rested. The checkered light and shade of the tree danced across them and the moon was already paling in the rosy dawn before they fell asleep.[3]

The second half is a steep descent from the euphoria of love and human kindness to the pathos of hatred and death. The ending is like a sudden stillness after a storm. In a homespun scene, Fernando and his wife express their gratitude over the miraculous survival of Philip, whom they will cherish as they would their own son. But the conciliatory ending is rendered enigmatic because it is couched in a triply-hedged hypothesis.

Don Fernando and Donna Elvira took the little stranger for their own child; and when Don Fernando compared Philip with Juan, and the different ways the two had come to him, *it almost seemed to him as if he ought to feel glad.*[4]

In no other of Kleist's *Novellen* are we so suddenly plunged *in medias res.* When the story opens, we witness Jeronimo's attempt to hang himself in his prison cell just as the earthquake strikes with sudden fury. And then the action moves forward from one *Zufall* to the next, as it had done up to that point. It was by sheer luck that Jeronimo had been able to re-establish relations with Josepha in the nunnery. Circumstances must also have been uncommonly propitious to permit him to consummate his love in the convent garden and to allow Josepha's advanced pregnancy to go unnoticed until she collapsed in a sudden reversal of luck during a religious procession, and precisely on the cathedral steps. Further, Jeronimo had no sooner found a rope—"by pure chance"— than the violence of the earthquake saves him from carrying out his design. The pattern is repeated until the final catastrophe, when a chance movement by one of the secondary characters touches off the mob violence in the cathedral. These "minor causes" with their fateful consequences only seem to point up the fundamental irrationality of the universe.

All these chance happenings, despite a wealth of factual detail, lend Kleist's story an air of unreality. This impression is heightened by his consummate artistry in handling "viewpoint." He quickly moves his camera from the objective narrator to the omniscient author or to the inner perception of events by his two protagonists. He maintains no static position but gives us in quick succession snapshots of events as they envelop his characters from without or are recorded by them from within. The rapid and imperceptible change of viewpoint is capable of vesting the often nightmarish quality of inner visions with factual objectivity, and vice versa.

The result is an almost Kafkaesque atmosphere or the hallucinatory aura found in an Ingmar Bergman film. Outward developments and inner processes are recorded with the same apparent detachment. Nothing is explained, events are merely juxtaposed. In the macabre cathedral scene, a naval officer appears and disappears inexplicably; the father and murderer of Jeronimo emerges suddenly and out of nowhere, he is a "voice" that wields a club. And legions of serpentine arms and hands reach out in the semidarkness to do the killing. In the beginning much of the earthquake is seen through Jeronimo's subjective perception in almost surrealistic distortion. To cite one example, a woman passes by who, weighted down by her belongings, almost scrapes the ground with her forehead, two children clinging to her breast. On the other hand, the objectivity of the third-person viewpoint is scrupulously maintained when Kleist has one character whisper something into the ear of another without letting his reader participate in the secret, although in the given circumstances the seemingly trivial gesture takes on a foreboding quality.

The legendary nature of the action often creates the impression of religious myth or conjures up Rousseauist visions of man's natural goodness shattered by social corruption. The child of sin is conceived in purity of feeling. The natural innocence of the two lovers is at first sanctioned by cosmic events, for they find bliss in a "Garden of Eden"—significantly under a pomegranate tree, a symbol associated with Persephone, the Greek goddess of fertility, death, and rebirth—only to be destroyed by the satanic horde in the cathedral. As Fernando fends off his assailants with prodigious strength he is likened to the archangel Michael battling the Prince of Darkness and his minions. But Kleist does not always let the action talk for itself, as it properly should in a myth. More than in any other of his *Novellen* he departs from epic objectivity and injects from the sidelines editorial comments, though unobtrusively and seemingly in passing. He can do so by putting an almost imperceptible distance between himself as the omniscient author and his anonymous narrator, who is placed in the midst of events and records with apparent dispassion the pious sensibilities of the populace. Endowed with a strong moral sense, the narrator is a living conscience and can assume the same role as does the chorus in an Attic tragedy. When the crowd's indignation at the two lovers' transgression turns into sadistic cruelty the sobriety of his style produces vitriolic irony. As the Viceroy commutes Josepha's sentence of being burned at the stake to one of beheading, it is "much to the indignation of the matrons and virgins of Santiago." [5] And: "Windows were rented out along the route the sinner would follow to her execution, roofs were lifted off, and the pious daughters of the city invited all their friends to join them in watching the spectacle offered the divine wrath." [6] The narrator's preference for "matrons and virgins" rather than "women," his apparent identification with their conviction of witnessing an act of "divine wrath," his meticulous description of their eagerness to experience the thrill of an execution, allow Kleist to engage in indirect editorializing on their hypocrisy. No doubt, the author has subtly guided his narrator's pen. But overwhelmed by the enormity of the events he conjures up in the cathedral scene, the author cannot refrain from inserting himself. He accuses the chief rabble-rouser of "holy cruelty" and unabashedly expresses admiration for Fernando, his "divine hero."

Yet the undeniable elements of religious myth and social critique seem secondary to Kleist's anxious questioning of the sum total of things. His basic concern is with the order or lack of order in the world. Social disorders and destructive human passions are but a reflection of universal chaos. It is significant that the abrupt change from the trembling hope which pervades the first part of the story, to the anonymous violence erupting in the second, occurs precisely at the moment when Jeronimo and Josepha seem to trust most ardently the essential goodness of "the spirit that rules the world." The strident discord that follows is an almost cynical satire on their "will to believe." The hope for redemption from the ills of the world through the power of unsullied natural feelings is turned into cruel illusion. By implication, Kleist seems not only to expose the incomprehensibility of design in the universe but also to ask the deeper question whether there is actually any design at all. The ironic ending and the hypothetical form in which Fernando's reconciliation with the world is expressed do little to dispel this impression.

However, the *Novelle* moves not only on a cosmic and religious plane, it also contains an element of secular ethics that might easily be overlooked in the cataclysmic events. Jeronimo and Josepha as well as Fernando embody values of grace and dignity that contrast sharply with the murderous passion of the mob. The two lovers are not necessarily naïve in the sense that they unqualifiedly accept their own dreams of paradisaical happiness as the real nature of the world. But rather they are naïve or courageous in the sense that, upon apprehending danger, they behave "as if" the world were pervaded by a moral order, though at heart they may know that this is not so. Against the express warnings of Donna Elisabeth, one of Fernando's sisters-in-law, whose forebodings are shared by Donna Elvira, Fernando's wife, they go to the cathedral. There is no indication in the narrative that they are blissfully unaware of danger or ignore their precarious place in society. On the contrary, at the first sign of mob violence they are immediately on their guard. And earlier, the narrator is careful to record their feelings of reconciliation with the world in a hypothetical mode. "Josepha felt *as if* she were among the blessed," [7] "the human spirit *seemed* to spring up like a lovely flower," [8] and it was "*as if* the general disaster had united all the survivors into a single family." [9] The many "as if" and similar formulations suggest not only the narrator's own mild skepticism but also a certain level of awareness of the subjectivity of their perceptions in the two protagonists themselves. When yielding to their great joy of having been saved and having found each other, they steal away "lest the secret jubilation in their souls give pain to anyone." [10] They give evidence of recognizing the discrepancy between their own inner experience and the state of the world. This impression is heightened by the fact that the thoughts and perceptions of those who represent the outside world are not registered in the "as if" mode. The owner of a burning building unceremoniously "lynches" an innocent man he takes for a looter. The cathedral canon sees the earthquake as a heavenly punishment visited upon the citizenry for their iniquity and singles out the outrage perpetrated by Jeronimo and Josepha. These people know they are right and do not question their perceptions.

Ironically, the *hybris* or *Versehen* of the two protagonists consists not in callousness or naïveté but rather in their will to believe that their "as if" mode of behavior might actually modify the course of events. They follow an inner summons to offer their gratitude to God and courageously dismiss the concerns for their physical safety, as though life were "some paltry possession one could pick up again a few steps later on," [11] as is stated elsewhere in the story. Their characters are thus tested and proven capable of inner noblesse or strength. Whether there is an element of personal "guilt" in their *Versehen* is a moot question. The tragic accent is rather on the irreconcilability of a lofty feeling with the depravity of the world. To act as if the world were good may be an ethical dictum of personal dignity and grace. But with his usual skepticism Kleist also shows that perhaps more often than not the inner moral imperative cannot remedy but only counterbalance the ills of the world, and then only at the price of death. This thought may be embedded at the end of the *Novelle* in Fernando's reflection on how he acquired little Philip. The noblesse of his own magnificent courage displayed in the cathedral compensates for the tragedy of the death of his own son and the other innocent victims. But there is an undertone of resignation in the triple hypothesis that seems to suggest that the nobility of autonomous moral action is small consolation for the lack of moral order in the world.

The quick pace of "The Earthquake in Chile," the inherent tendency of the genre to test rather than to develop a character through an unusual event, and the cosmic dimensions of the central catastrophe do not allow Kleist much introspective analysis of individual "feeling." The story thus retains a mythic rather than a psychological nature. To be sure, the sentiment of pure love in the two protagonists, though illicit, is obviously condoned, while its sacrificial destruction in a violent rite of religious exorcism is deplored. And a tragic note is struck when we are made aware that the beauty of pure feeling cannot prevail in a chaotic world. But the trembling assertions and tragic illusions of feeling are rarely seen from within the sufferers. It is in the drama *Amphitryon* and the two *Novellen* grouped around it, "The Marquise of O——" and "The Duel," that Kleist will delve more into the individual inner torment of his heroines, although a mythic or legendary quality will never be absent from any of his works.

NOTES

[1] Through some breakdown of communications among Kleist, Rühle von Lilienstern, and the publisher Cotta, the *Novelle* ap-

peared in 1807 in a journal (*Das Morgenblatt*) against Kleist's will. In 1810 it was incorporated in the first volume of Kleist's *Erzählungen*, published by Reimer.

2 Meant is the earthquake of Chile in 1647.

3 Sembd., Vol. 4, p. 136; Greenberg, p. 257.

4 Sembd., Vol. 4, p. 145; Greenberg, p. 267 (the last clause has been changed somewhat to adopt it more closely to the German original and to emphasize the hypothetical nature of the statement).

5 Sembd., Vol. 4, pp. 131–32; Greenberg, p. 252.

6 Sembd., Vol. 4, p. 132; idem.

7 Sembd., Vol. 4, p. 138; Greenberg, p. 259.

8 Idem; idem.

9 Idem; idem.

10 Sembd., Vol. 4, p. 136; Greenberg, p. 257.

11 Sembd., Vol. 4, p. 139; Greenberg, p. 260.

"The Foundling"

It has been surmised that this *Novelle* is one of Kleist's earlier works, conceived sometime in 1805–6, and that it underwent considerable revision before it was finally published in volume two of his *Erzählungen* (1811). But it is equally plausible that he wrote it specifically for the purpose of amplifying the contents of the second tome, for which he apparently accepted a publishing contract before he had composed all of the requisite stories.[1] In any case, *The Foundling* has a plot that lends it a particular distinction among Kleist's works. It does not revolve around a character whose purity of feeling is subjected to severe, even cruel tests. At least none of the three principals is drawn from that angle of perception. Entrapped in an infernal rondo of events, they are rather shown to be inwardly tainted as though infected by a radical evil.

Piachi, a prosperous old merchant living in Rome at the time of the Renaissance, lost his young son during a plague.

In his stead he adopted Nicolo, the very same boy who had infected his own son but, thanks to Piachi's care, recovered from the disease. He showers Nicolo with kindness as though he were his own son, rears him in his business, and makes him sole heir to his estate. Elvire, Piachi's young second wife, seemingly attached to her aging husband, pines away for the love of Colino, a young nobleman who had saved her life years before, and had subsequently died from an injury received in the attempt. Nicolo bears a striking resemblance to the dead Colino. Unscrupulous, he knows how to take advantage of this coincidence and contrives to seduce his benefactor's wife. Caught in the attempt, he has the impudence to invoke his right of legal ownership to Piachi's estate and sends the old man packing, while Elvire, weak in health, dies from the shock of her experience. Piachi, seething with rage, crushes the usurper's skull in a scuffle and calmly surrenders to the authorities. Condemned to hang, he steadfastly refuses absolution, insisting that he wants to pursue his revenge against Nicolo in the deepest pit of hell.

The story goes through several cycles of irony and contains the usual Kleistian motifs of misjudgment, misuse of trust, and chance happenings. The orphan boy Nicolo, infected by the plague, moves Piachi to Christian charity, for which he must pay with his own son's life. And he adopts the orphan only to be brought to ruin by him. At the end the story takes an unexpected new turn when Piachi, not content with having snuffed out Nicolo's life, declares his intent to torture him further in a Dantesque inferno.

All three characters misjudge each other and thus help conjure up calamity. At one point, Elvire literally mistakes Nicolo for the ghost of Colino. Nicolo misinterprets Elvire's devotion to a man long since dead as a sign of her availability. Piachi gauges his adoptive son's character wrongly, although there is enough evidence that Nicolo is unworthy of his trust, and he also seems to underestimate, largely by ignoring them, Elvire's feelings for her departed lover. A diabolic streak of distorted character traits and specious feelings pervades the story from the start. Piachi's wooing of Elvire is done in a businesslike manner. Elvire's nostalgic attachment to her dead lover has a sickly element in it. Nicolo's callousness is alluded to early in the story when, instead of sharing Piachi's sorrow over the death of his son, he cracks open nuts and eats them with relish. As he grows older, he reveals himself more and more to be the parasite and sensualist he is. Caught in a maelstrom of inauthentic feelings, the three must destroy each other. The chance happenings which impel the action forward are but an expression of the dark forces that fix the course of their destinies. It is by coincidence that Nicolo chooses the Genoese costume to go to a ball in which he surprises Elvire, who then is struck for the first time by his astonishing resemblance to the dead Colino. Again as if by chance, Nicolo discovers that his first name is, mysteriously, an anagram of Colino.[2] And Piachi happens to come home earlier than usual just as Nicolo is attempting to seduce the fainting Elvire.

Thematically, this intriguing *Novelle* cannot easily be assigned a proper place within the corpus of Kleist's works. It occupies its own unique position since it does not dwell much on the usual Kleistian theme of foiled inner certainties causing a tragic reorientation of the protagonist in a world of inescapable realities, although this theme could conceivably be read into Piachi's inner experience. In "The Foundling," Kleist seems rather preoccupied with the preponderance of evil in the world manifesting itself in crass self-interest or counterfeit emotions. The logographic play with the two names "Colino" and "Nicolo" and the masquerade which so impresses Elvire suggest that Nicolo is the counterfeit of Colino. In their striking resemblance there is also a hint of the terrifying proximity of good and evil in the world. If Nicolo is the obverse of Colino, his impudence is a travesty of the dead man's courage, his lecherousness a parody of Colino's capacity for love. The most significant element in the story, however, is the enormity of Piachi's wrath, which takes on metaphysical dimensions:

"I don't want to be saved, I want to go down to the lowest pit of hell. I want to find Nicolo again, who won't be in heaven, and take up my revenge again, which I could only satisfy partly here!" And with these words he climbed the ladder and told the hangman to do his duty.[3]

Ultimately, it is directed at evil *per se* rather than an evildoer. Piachi embodies Kleist's outrage—by proxy, to be sure—

toward the prevalence of egotism, sham feelings, and abuse of trust in the world. What cannot be set aright can only be trampled under foot. No redeeming force can be detected in the *Novelle*. Even Elvire's love for her dead hero lacks strength and viability. Piachi is a metaphysical rebel; all he can do is combat evil with evil. But through the immensity of his revenge, the unflinching adherence to his dark purpose, he belongs in that gallery of strong-willed Kleistian heroes, such as Guiscard, Kohlhaas, and Arminius, whose revolt transcends personal interests.

NOTES

1 The early dating of the *Novelle* is based on linguistic and stylistic comparisons with the other *Novellen* or other internal evidence, such as thematic tendencies that are not always convincing, at times rather contrived. On the other hand, those who feel "The Foundling" was written specifically for volume two of the *Erzählungen* must lean heavily on scant evidence drawn from Kleist's letters, especially a brief note to his publisher Reimer of February 17 (?), 1811, discovered only in 1961. But the letter by no means clearly explains which *Novellen* Kleist had already written at the time the contract negotiations were going on. All that can be asserted is that Kleist did not simply pull out from a drawer a bundle of old manuscripts to be refurbished, but most likely had to write some of the *Novellen* from scratch.

2 "Colino" is also the endearing form of "Nicolo," a linguistic peculiarity which may have escaped Kleist's attention.

3 Sembd., Vol. 4, p. 196; Greenberg, p. 247.

The Comedy of Deception

"The Broken Pitcher"

The Broken Pitcher is one of the best-known comedies in the German theater. It seems to belie the prevailing opinion that the brooding depth and single-minded intensity of the German character are a deterrent to the creation of comedy. In many ways, Kleist fits the proverbial description of the German, and yet he produced a comedy that ranks among the best in world literature. However, there is no denying that the very themes and motifs central to his tragedies are equally germane to the spirit of comedy. Innocent error, conscious deception, misunderstanding, the surprise of discovering an unsuspected truth, the apprehensions caused by an oblique and twisted course of events are fertile sources for both tragedy and comedy. All these elements can be found in Kleist's play. But in contrast to the more tragic pieces where innocent error conjures up suffering, the prominent ingredient in *The Broken Pitcher* is the conscious deception perpetrated by the central character, a judge who is unmasked in his own court.

The inception of the drama reaches back to the time of *The Schroffenstein Family* and Kleist's preoccupation with the theme of *Robert Guiscard*. He received the first impulse for it in 1801, while visiting in Berne, from an etching of a courtroom scene done by Le Veau (1782) after a lost painting by Debucourt. During a meeting with his friend Pfuel in Dresden in 1803, the latter expressed some doubts about Kleist's ability to write comedy. Irked by the challenge, he straightway dictated to him the first three scenes from the play which, apparently, was already well conceived in his mind. However, it was completed only in 1806 and premièred on March 2, 1808, in Weimar, under the direction of Goethe, who showed little understanding for its dynamics and was partly to blame for the unsuccessful performance. Since the play is based on a visual impression or a "scene," its ideational content is almost eclipsed by the thrusts and parries of the dialogue and the rich imagery of the language. Nevertheless, Kleist's preoccupation with the radical deceptiveness of the world, which is seen infiltrating human discourse and communication, lends the play thematic and structural unity.

When the play opens, Adam, a judge in a little Dutch village, is nursing a head wound, a wrenched foot, and other minor injuries as he prepares himself for a court session. Frau Marthe is suing Ruprecht, her daughter Eve's fiancé, for having broken a beautiful pitcher, her pride and joy, during a nocturnal fracas in her daughter's chamber. Justice Walter, the circuit judge, who is on an inspection tour, wishes to observe the proceedings. Adam presides over the trial with his bald head uncovered. Much of the comedy is provided by his groping attempts to explain the whereabouts of his wig, the cause of his head wound, the gash in his cheek, the wrenched foot, and his generally woebegone appearance. In an aside, the intimidated Eve assures him that nothing but the damaged earthenware will be discussed. The enraged Ruprecht calls her a slut and tells the court how he had surprised her the night before in company of another man. He had broken in the door to her room, grasped the doorhandle, and struck the intruder over the head just as he was escaping through the window down the trellis in the dark of night. Adam's wig is found hanging in the trellis. And fresh footprints in the snow that seem to be of the living devil himself

—Adam has a clubfoot—lead from Eve's home to the court-house. The discovery of the judge's foiled attempt at seduction is helped along by the cunning remarks of the court clerk Licht, who harbors great professional ambitions. On the basis of a forged document, Adam had tried to coerce Eve into yielding to his advances by threatening to have Ruprecht sent into military service in a distant colony. As Walter closes the session and Ruprecht and Eve become reconciled, Adam is seen bounding over the snow-covered fields.

The structure and irony of Kleist's comedy have at times been compared to similar elements in *Oedipus Rex*. Both plays are "analytical" dramas. The action begins after the fact and consists of the discovery of an ironical truth by way of circumstantial evidence that helps indict the guilty. But in Kleist's play the situation is in some ways the obverse of its counterpart in *Oedipus Rex*. In Sophocles' drama, the hero, deeming himself guiltless, seeks the criminal and finds himself (in more ways than one). In *The Broken Pitcher*, the hero, knowing himself guilty, seeks to implicate the innocent and loses himself in his world of lies. Oedipus' will to discover the truth is reversed in Adam's attempt to conceal the truth. But both strive to absolve themselves from suspicion, though in opposite ways, only to see their guilt brought to light. There are other parallels of a less striking sort. The clubfooted Adam may be reminiscent of Oedipus, the "swellfoot," and in his foreword to the play, Kleist himself suggests that the scheming Licht could be compared to Creon in whose eyes Oedipus' character is suspect from the beginning. There is a hint of an analogy between Circuit Judge Walter's name, which suggests the German verb *walten*, usually associated with *Schicksal*—the *fate* that *rules* the world—and the Delphic oracle that spells out Oedipus' fate. Both are symbols of those ironic forces in the world that foil human designs.

Not content with the irony inherent in the basic plot, Kleist intensifies it through a witty distribution of intentions in the dramatic characters. Two persons must try to hide the same fact, but for opposite reasons, while three others attempt to fathom the same secret but, again, with different purposes in mind. The ensuing confusion is hilarious and is rendered tense by the ample forewarning of the "surprise" ending given to the reader or spectator. The comic effects of the situation are heightened by Kleist's impressive mastery of the language of comedy. *Quid pro quo's,* puns, subtle insinuations, ambiguous statements, intentional or foolish misunderstandings, the art of distortion, caricatural exaggerations, play with insignificant details—the whole stock in trade of comedy is handled with great skill. The author obtains particularly comic effects through a fugal technique of interweaving independent bits of monologue. Instead of engaging in genuine dialogue, the characters at times merely spin out their own thoughts and apprehensions in contrapuntal fashion. The ensuing double and triple monologues can be uproariously funny and point forward toward the contemporary theater of the absurd, where the possibilities of the technique have been fully exploited by such authors as Ionesco. When Judge Walter's servant announces his master's arrival, which has been delayed by a mishap, the sparks of dialogue fly in all directions, only to be extinguished by Light's laconical remark: "It was a misunderstanding":

> LICHT. (to Servant). I hope your lord, the worthy District Judge,
> Has met with no misfortune on his journey?
>
> SERVANT. Oh, well, we capsized in the narrow pass.
>
> ADAM. Ouch! Oh, my foot's all skinned! My boots will not—
>
> LICHT. Well, now in heaven's name! Capsized, you say?
> But still no further harm—?
>
> SERVANT.   Nothing important
> My master sprained his hand a little bit.
> The shaft broke off.
>
> ADAM.   I wish he'd broken his neck!
>
> LICHT. What, sprained his hand! Well, well! Has the smith come?
>
> SERVANT. To mend the shaft, yes.
>
> LICHT.   What?
>
> ADAM.   You mean the doctor.
>
> LICHT. What?
>
> SERVANT.   For the shaft?

ADAM.	Oh, bosh! To bind his hand.

SERVANT. Your servant, sir.—I think these chaps are mad. (Exit.)

LICHT. I meant the smith.

ADAM.	You give yourself away.

LICHT. How so?

ADAM.	You are embarrassed.

LICHT.	What!
(The First Maid enters.)

ADAM.	Hey! Lisa!
What's that you've got?

FIRST MAID.	Why Brunswick sausage, sir.

ADAM. No, that's my guardian stuff.

LICHT.	What, I embarrassed!

ADAM. They should be brought back to the registry.

FIRST MAID. The sausage?

ADAM.	Sausage! Bosh! These wrappers here.

LICHT. It was a misunderstanding.[1]

But such dialogues also have serious overtones, for the difficulty of the individual to "communicate" reflects the isolation of men into islands of pure subjectivity, one of the central themes in all of Kleist's works. This theme is made more explicit, in a near tragic mode, in the quarrel between the two lovers, Eve and Ruprecht. Both know some of the concealed facts but from different viewpoints and can or will not espouse the other's opinion or feeling about the matter. The tension culminates in Eve's demand for absolute trust in the motives of her silence, which her jealous and boorish fiancé is unable to muster. Were the whole action presented from her corner, it would have some of the tragic accents that are found in "The Engagement in Santo Domingo" or *Amphitryon*. Like most of Kleist's heroines, the naïve Eve has such depth of pure feeling that she could never become an agent of conscious deception, though she must engage in temporary dissimulation to protect Ruprecht. In Kleist's plays, real deceitfulness is lodged in the world surrounding the potentially tragic character, and in *The Broken Pitcher*, a comedy centering on foiled trickery, the protagonist is, characteristically, a crafty and yet likable buffoon.

Much of the dynamics of the comedy stems from the undercurrent of conflicting, half-concealed motives eddying around the same event. Both Adam and Eve attempt to cover up the nocturnal encounter, she to protect Ruprecht, he to protect himself. Conversely, Walter, Licht, and Ruprecht desire to uncover the truth, the one in the interest of justice, the other to advance his own career, the third out of sheer jealousy. The vociferous Frau Marthe is interested largely in seeing her property restored. All characters are finely drawn. The comedy derives as much from Kleist's masterful character portrayal as from the situation itself.

Some of the names have symbolic significance. Adam "falls," literally and figuratively, down the trellis into the hell of judgment day held in his own court, where his moral lapse is revealed. Eve is an innocent temptress, perhaps an ironic inversion of her namesake in the Garden of Eden. Some symbol-hunters also find in the very image of the broken pitcher an emblem of her lost innocence. Licht's name is as ambiguous as his character. He sheds light on the affair, though obliquely and in the interest of his own murky ambitions. If Mephistopheles is a metathesis of *Me photo philes* (no friend of light), then the name applies to Licht, at least with tongue-in-cheek irony. Ruprecht may allude to "Knecht Ruprecht," the blustering attendant of St. Nicholas in the popular Christian festival. For all his contriving, Adam is no melodramatic villain. His earthiness, imagination, and genius for lying are reminiscent of Falstaff and arouse more sympathy than revulsion, especially when he is compared with the devious Licht. His voluptuousness does not strike us so much as moral turpitude but rather as a weakness, the obverse of his vital nature. (Kleist's sympathetic treatment of his buffoon may be rooted in a secret admiration for a temperament so unlike his own.) Hence Adam's depravity must be sought above all in his mythomania. He could be likened to the compulsive liars of Dostoevsky's novels, who must fill an inner void with mendacity, were it not, precisely, for Adam's vitality, which distinguishes him from some of Dostoevsky's maudlin fibbers.

In practically all of Kleist's other works up to this point a demonic quality of deception is associated with an extraneous fate that confuses the senses and confounds the innocent. Imperfect, occasionally even complete, sensory evidence ensuing in wrong inferences, unwitting mistakes, or self-deception still play a large part and provide much of the comedy in *The Broken Pitcher*. But the near demonic element is primarily linked with Adam's cozenage, while the world that confronts him is more rational and apt to dredge up the truth and unravel his web of lies. The notion of an extraneous fate has become personified in the "supreme judge" Walter, who represents a world of law and order. At the same time fate has been made literally objective in visible and eloquent things—the broken pitcher, the wig, the doorhandle, the trellis, the clubfoot and its unmistakable tracks in the snow—which conspire to bring about Adam's "fall." For once, objects bespeak rather than becloud the truth. Ironically, Adam lacks the one piece of evidence that could cover up his bald head as well as his lies, namely the wig.

Linked with the importance of circumstantial evidence in piecing together the fragments of truth is the role played by language. As much as Judge Adam, language itself and, through it, the quirks of the characters' consciousness are on trial. Particularly striking is the tendency of all characters to see in some infamous detail the clue to the whole truth, a partial vision which they express with a linguistic gusto hardly matched in any other comedy. A good example is Frau Marthe, who talks up a storm in describing the erstwhile beauty of the broken jug, obviously thinking in her disoriented way that the irrelevant details she enumerates would not only give weight to her arguments, but actually unearth the truth:

> No, all you see, beg pardon, is the pieces;
> The fairest of all jugs is smashed to bits.
> Right here upon this hole, where now there's nothing,
> The states of the United Netherlands
> Were handed over to the Spanish Philip.
> Here in his robes stood Emperor Charles the Fifth;
> Of him all you see standing is his legs.

Here knelt King Philip, and received the crown:
He's in the jug now, all but his backside,
And even that has got a sorry blow.
Two cousins there were weeping—queens they were,
The Queen of France and she of Hungary—
The tears out of their eyes; and when you see
The one still raise the kerchief in her hand,
It is as if she wept at her own fate.[2]

In describing the whereabouts of his missing wig Adam displays an amazing inventiveness expressed in very earthy images:

The wound today and yesterday the wig.
I wore it, powdered white, upon my head,
And with my hat I took it off, my word,
By error when I stepped into the house.
. . . .
                         You, Margret, go
And ask the Verger if he'll lend me his;
Tell him the cat, the dirty pig, had littered
This morning in my wig. All filthied up
It lay beneath my bed, I now recall.[3]

At times, language seems to run away from the speaker, as in Ruprecht's account of his first glimpse of Eve's tryst with a rival, where his eyes and ears are seen to acquire a life of their own:

And then—as I come nearer through the limes
At Martha's, where the rows are closely arched
And gloomy as the minister is at Utrecht,
I hear the creaking of the garden gate.
Well, well! Then Eve is out there still, says I,
And gaily send my eyes to search the place
From where my ears had brought me news of her—
As blind, and on the spot I send them out
A second time, to take a better look,
And rail at them as villainous defamers,
As vile inciters, infamous slanderers,
And send them out a third time, and I think,
Since they have done their duty well, they must
In anger pull themselves out of my head,

And ask for transfer to another service:
It's Eve herself, I know her by her bodice,
And some one else is with her.[4]

The surrealistic visual impact of such imagery need hardly be stressed. But above all, the principals in the debate seize upon the veracity of the detail to obscure, knowingly or not, the truth of the whole, as in the following exchange between Ruprecht and Adam, when the latter unsuccessfully tries to inculpate Lebrecht, Ruprecht's rival, to divert suspicion from himself:

> RUPRECHT. My soul, Judge Adam, let me tell you this,
> The girl [Eve] is not so wrong in what she says,
> For I myself met Lebrecht yesterday
> As he was bound for Utrecht, eight it was,
> And if he got no ride upon a cart,
> Bowlegged as he is, that fellow sure
> Had not yet hobbled back by ten at night.
> It may quite well have been another man.
>
> ADAM. What's that? Bowlegged! Fathead! Why, that chap
> Can shake a leg as well as any man.
> Let me not be two-legged here myself,
> If any shepherd dog of common size
> Won't have to trot to keep abreast of him.[5]

Kleist's skepticism thus breaks through the forensic virtuosity of the drama's language: the more man presumes to be in possession of the truth, the more it eludes him.

Conversely, at unguarded moments the truth pierces through the surface layers of the characters' consciousness to express itself spontaneously in revelatory statements. When Frau Marthe's clan makes its noisy entry into the courtroom, Adam mumbles to himself:

> That Ruprecht! What the deuce! The whole caboodle!
> —They won't accuse me to my very self?[6]

In scene three, he narrates his dream of the previous night, which rather ominously anticipates the disclosure of his guilt in his own court:

> —I dreamt a plaintiff had laid hold of me
> And dragged me to the judge's seat; and I,
> I sat there all the same upon the bench,
> And scolded, skinned and ruffianed me down,
> And sentenced my own neck into the irons.[7]

Half-consciously and compulsively, he keeps condemning himself with stock phrases, such as "I am a lout," which he has used unthinkingly before but now have the ring of ironic truth and genuine self-recrimination. And no matter how much Eve tries to hide the full truth from view to protect Ruprecht, the incorruptibility of her nature is manifest in the directness of her language, which culminates in her disarmingly blunt statements:

> Good land! This judge you mean! He well deserves
> To stand as sinner here before the court—
> —He who could better tell who broke the jug! [8]

> Judge Adam was the man who smashed the jug! [9]

But generally, the element of suspense is maintained by the unexpected twists and turns of the drama's language, which act as retarding factors in the unraveling of the truth, although the latter can easily be pieced together from circumstantial evidence early in the play. The central image—the broken pitcher—is less a symbol of Eve's lost innocence than a metaphor of the drama of language enacted in Kleist's only comedy: after many false starts, the bits and pieces of the dialogue fall into place to assume the shape of truth.

The Broken Pitcher vividly illustrates the reason why Kleist has at times been called a "juridical writer." Most of his stories and dramas revolve around legal, even criminal cases and their appurtenances, such as Peter's death in *The Schroffenstein Family*, the political murder in "The Duel," the Vehmic court in *The Kaethchen of Heilbronn*, Homburg's court-martial, and so forth. The most famous of his legal cases is Michael Kohlhaas's struggle for justice. *The Broken Pitcher* is one long cross-examination, consisting of public interrogations that are genuinely judicial and private probings through which one individual attempts to encounter the other. But in Kleist's unique comedy the problem of law and men's longing for justice is not treated with the same sense of urgency as in "Michael Kohlhaas" or *The Prince of Homburg*. Justice Walter is concerned largely with the honor of the court and therefore imposes a mild penalty upon the wayward Adam. The conciliatory ending is in keeping with the canons of comedy.

It is questionable, however, whether Ruprecht's and Eve's reconciliation can be complete. Ruprecht was unable to live up to her intransigent demand for absolute confidence. He should have relied on her sense of honor, she exclaims at one point, even if he had seen her through the keyhole in company of his archrival, Lebrecht.

> And even if you'd seen me, through the keyhole,
> With Lebrecht, and drinking from the jug.
> You should have thought, my Eve is good and true,
> And all will be explained to do her credit,
> If not in this life, then beyond the grave.
> And when we rise again there'll still be time.[10]

A deep wound has been opened up in her soul. As a result of the sobering experience, she must reorient herself in life. But as in most other such cases, Kleist leaves us guessing whether she will be able to reconcile herself to the new reality. Like the author himself, his characters seem to recognize the inevitability of compromise with life's shortcomings but deplore the necessity of having to do so. His heroines sink into nostalgic silence after the disenchanting discovery. Eve's attitude presupposes a total view of the world that is based on the assumption of the ontological integrity of one's innermost feeling. Ruprecht's failure and the hypocrisy she must display to save his life cause a potentially tragic split in her own. Kleist, however, stays within the confines of comedy, for he depicts only the "physiognomy of the moment," as he called the comical element in life at one point. Therefore, he has Ruprecht reply to Eve's demand for continued trust to the very edge of eternity: "My soul, that takes too long for me, my Eve." [11]

Even in the midst of comedy Kleist felt compelled to introduce the anxiety-ridden motif of *Vertrauensprobe*—a test of trust—based as it is on his conviction that only unqualified trust in the purity of another's motives could overcome the confusions of the world. It is not surprising that he endowed his judge with diabolic traits, since he consciously sows the seeds of distrust. Inverting the usual situation of his dramas, Kleist projected the deceptiveness of the world into a person who is both buffoon and demon, the symbolic expression of an unstable, even grotesque reality.

NOTES

The translation used is Bayard Quincy Morgan's *The Broken Pitcher* (University of North Carolina Studies in the Germanic Languages and Literatures, No. 31), Chapel Hill, University of North Carolina Press, 1961; reprinted, New York, AMS Press Inc., 1966. The verse numbers of Morgan's translation correspond exactly to those of the original German text.

1 Scene 2, ll. 201–18.
2 Scene 7, ll. 646–60.
3 Scene 2, ll. 234–37, 240–44.
4 Scene 7, ll. 899–915.
5 Scene 9, ll. 1222–34.
6 Scene 7, ll. 499–500.
7 Scene 3, ll. 269–73.
8 Scene 9, ll. 1212–14.
9 Scene 11, l. 1893.
10 Scene 8, ll. 1169–74.
11 Scene 8, l. 1175.

The Test of "Feeling"

"Amphitryon"

With *Amphitryon*, written in 1805–6 and published in 1807, Kleist sends the first real depth probe into the wellspring of "feeling." The drama is an adaptation of Molière's celebrated comedy of the same name. Its theme—the seduction of a faithful wife by a philandering god assuming the husband's shape —was well suited to Kleist's preoccupation with the problem of reality and illusion, connected as it is with man's search for self-identity and inner truth. Under Kleist's hands, however, the piquant boudoir farce mocking Amphitryon's cuckoldry turns into a tense drama revolving around Alkmene's purity of feeling. More than any other of Kleist's works, the drama is multileveled. It moves alternately on farcical, psychological, and metaphysical planes and is replete with dialectic sophistication that makes its interpretation and the definition of its genre a frustrating task. Justifiedly, a fascinated Thomas Mann spoke of the drama's "intellectually stimulating oscillation and ambivalence" and even went so far as to assert that

"It is the wittiest, charmingest, the most intellectual, the profoundest and most beautiful theater piece in the world." [1] The central motif of mistaken identity may be a stock situation in a comedy of errors. But Kleist's own disquieting sense of the constant threat posed to man's self-identity by an unstable, illusory world adds a note of near tragic anxiety to the drama. And the detachment with which the proximity of the tragic and the comic is treated seems to partake of tragicomedy, especially in its aesthetic effects upon the spectator or reader. Finally, the mythological topic of the impending birth of a divine child by a mortal woman has given rise, as might be expected, to rather far-flung theological exegeses.

Jupiter in the guise of Amphitryon spends a night with Alkmene, while Mercury, assuming the shape of Amphitryon's servant Sosias, whom he has cowed into abjuring his identity, guards the palace. When the real Amphitryon appears, Alkmene is surprised by his seemingly quick return from the battlefield, scene of his victory over Labdacus. Anxiously questioning each other, they discover that a diadem Amphitryon had taken from Labdacus and was about to give to Alkmene is already in her possession and has mysteriously disappeared from its still sealed and unbroken box. A quarrel ensues that only sharpens the anguish they both feel. In comic modulation their dispute is repeated in a spat between Sosias and his querulous wife, Charis, whose Philistine sense of virtue had been ridiculed the night before by Mercury (alias Sosias). Meanwhile, Alkmene discovers that the diadem given to her bears the initial "J," and not "A" as she had expected. Made aware that another Amphitryon might indeed have visited her the night before, she hastens to see her husband, who reassures her of his love for her. But she does not perceive that she is again in the presence of the god. Though realizing that she might have erred earlier in not distinguishing between Jupiter and Amphitryon, she cannot believe in the possibility of renewed deception. A dialogue ensues (act two, scene five) in which Jupiter attempts to trick her into admitting her personal love for the god but only seems to deepen her feelings for Amphitryon. In the end, we move from the private to the public sphere. In front of the Theban generals and the people Alkmene is made to confront both Amphitryons and berates the wrong man for having deceived her. When Jupiter clears up the mystery by revealing himself in his Olympian might and foretells the birth of a divine child —Hercules—Alkmene can only utter an audible and enigmatic "Ach!" Although it is never expressly said that the child is actually Jupiter's, it must be assumed from the Hercules myth that this is so, and in Kleist's text itself this fact is at least alluded to in Jupiter's mind-boggling explanation to Amphitryon:

> What you, in me, did to yourself will never harm you, as far as I, in my eternal nature, am concerned.[2]

Irony and ambiguity are handled ingeniously through newly invented episodes and bits of dialogue that convert the drama into a subtle *Gedankenspiel*, an intellectual exercise, as Thomas Mann would have it. Since the spectator enjoys the advantage of an omniscient viewpoint—due in equal measure to the notoriety of the Amphitryon myth and Kleist's treatment of it—he can anticipate that the characters' deepest convictions will be the most liable to error. What Amphitryon calls ". . . useless drivel, full of folly, . . . totally bereft of human brain and reason"[3] in reply to his servant Sosias' account of his nocturnal encounter with his double, the god Mercury, turns out to be the truth. An equally ironic effect is obtained when a character unwittingly expresses the truth while thinking that he or she is merely stating an hypothesis or using a figure of speech. Thus Alkmene when she recounts what impression Amphitryon, alias Jupiter, made upon her at their first meeting after his return from battle:

> It was he, Amphitryon, the god's own son!
> It's just that he appeared to me to be exalted,
> And I felt quite like asking him
> Whether he'd just descended from the stars to me.[4]

Or earlier when she recalls their conversation during their night of love: "You said you were a god and whatev'r else/ Came to your head in your exuberant desire."[5] In another place, the misunderstanding between Alkmene and Amphitryon is comically highlighted when Alkmene's wifely concern for Amphitryon's apparent confusion of the senses applies more properly to her than to him. But a serious note is struck when Alkmene asserts, "You [Amphitryon] cannot disturb my inner harmony," [6] just as she is about to discover visible evidence of her possible error.

It is especially in scenes of his own invention that Kleist draws the irony as taut as the situation will allow. In act two, scene four, after Alkmene produces as proof of her faithfulness the diadem which Amphitryon had supposedly given her the night before, she discovers to her dismay the mysterious initial "J" on it. On the comic side, the perplexing event is foreshadowed in the discomfiture of Amphitryon and Sosias, who in their turn must discover that the jewel they were about to offer Alkmene had inexplicably vanished from its box. The pivotal scene, however, is act two, scene five, which is entirely Kleist's own and calls for closer analysis.

Alkmene has come before Amphitryon—in reality, Jupiter—to make amends for her outburst of anger at Amphitryon's suggestion that she might have made love to someone other than himself, but also to obtain reassurance from his lips that he himself had given her the diadem with the initial "J" on it. Since she discovered the strange letter on the jewel, her peace of mind is gone. The situation is witty and ironic but rife with allusions to Alkmene's potential existential tragedy. Jupiter, who poses as Amphitryon, attempts to elicit from her a confession of pure love for the god untinged by her conjugal attachment to her husband. The ensuing dialogue is replete with equivocations, *double-entendres* and exquisite, at times tortuous, mind-teasers. But, generally, the combination of Alkmene's ingenuousness and Jupiter's superior knowledge creates a dialogue that reveals spontaneously the beauty as well as the human limitations of Alkmene's feeling and also elevates the god from the apparent philanderer of the first scenes to a divine power issuing the highest existential demands to man. Jupiter's tone changes from pacifying solicitude over mild threats, teasing banter, impatience, and irritation to stern summons and loving adoration, all in an attempt to make her see and admit the difference between god and man. Her replies disclose a whole gamut of conflicting emotions, from apprehension, even suicidal despair, to newfound equanimity, bewilderment, and trembling expectation. The rapid succession of moods and the frequent modulations of the tone are more than mere comedy or tragedy and, for that matter, tragicomedy could bear. This scene transcends hackneyed literary categories and informs the whole drama with dialectic subtlety. The steadfastness of Alkmene's love for Amphitryon shines forth with undimmed brilliance in the ever deepening labyrinth of thought. But the more Jupiter prods her into declaring her love for god, and the more she eschews his challenge, the more we are also made aware of the metaphysical shortcomings of her love. There is a hint that she reduces the divine Eros or Agape to mere domestic happiness and earthly bliss. Jupiter scolds her for being unable to worship the god at the altar without visualizing the traits of Amphitryon:

> To whom do you address your prayers at his altar?
> Do you suppose it's to the god up there?
> D'you think your captive mind can fathom him?
> D'you think, used to its own dear nest,
> Your feeling's capable of daring such a flight?
> Are you not always lying in the dust
> In adoration of your love, Amphitryon? [7]

Earlier he had launched into an impassioned panegyric of the greatness of the god's power, which manifests itself in all that is:

> Does he exist for you?
> Do you perceive the world which is his handiwork?
> D'you see him in the shimm'ring sunset
> As it moves through the silent bushes?
> D'you hear him in the rushing of the water,
> Or in the splendid singing of the nightingale?
> Does not the mountain speak to you of him in vain,
> Although it points to heaven? Do not the
> Cataracts, dispersing in the rocks, fail in this mission?
> And when up there the sun shines on his temple
> And rung in with the pulsing beat of joy,
> All creatures laud him who is their creator,
> Do you then not descend into the shaft
> That is your heart—to adore your idol? [8]

Dramaturgically, the two passages are not so much a pantheistic manifesto as a challenge to Alkmene to broaden her vision, to emerge from her idyllic retreat. The god's paean echoes a calling whose challenge Kleist felt throughout his life, but from which he was tempted to retreat on occasion, especially when he harbored the thought of settling down as a farmer in Switzerland to find his life's fulfillment in a domestic idyl with Wilhelmine. He made, however, the Kierkegaardian leap into the uncertainty and loneliness of his personal existential and artistic search. An element of Jupiter's summons to Alkmene to lift her sight can also be detected in Kleist's sincere, though pedantic attempts to elevate Wilhelmine's soul to new heights. And the strange feeling of euphoria which Kleist evinced before his death is another expression of his fascination with the infinite. But Kleist's Alkmene experiences above all the Pascalian fear and trembling before the infinite, not the euphoria. Repeatedly, she hesitates to leave the safe moorings of her domestic world to make the leap into unknown regions of thought and inner experience.

The purpose of the dialectic exercises Jupiter inflicts on Alkmene in this scene is undoubtedly to make her see the necessity of reorienting her inner life and at the same time to praise the inviolability of her love for Amphitryon. Two seemingly contradictory intents. But in almost Hegelian fashion, the two lines of thought rise and converge in one of Alkmene's assertions. Pressed by Jupiter to tell him how she would feel if she were really in the arms of the god (which she is) and the real Amphitryon appeared, she answers:

> If you, the god, held me in your embrace,
> And thereupon Amphitryon, my husband, showed himself,
> Then I should be most sad indeed, and wish
> That he would be the god and you
> Would stay Amphitryon for me, just as you are.[9]

Whereupon Jupiter breaks out into an encomium:

> My sweet and worshipped creature!
> In whom I laud myself so full of bliss!
> So totally harmonious to the thought of god,
> In form, proportion, string and sound,
> My hand has not had such success in eons.[10]

Alkmene's hypothetical answer to a seemingly hypothetical question which yet reflects and adumbrates a real situation, indicates for the first time that she has risen to a heightened consciousness of the difference between the human and the divine. She no longer attempts to merge the one in the other for fear of disturbing her peace of mind, although she admits that the very thought of it saddens her. At the same time, however, she has not betrayed her love for Amphitryon. Unquestionably, her answer could have been different in a variety of ways. Had she refused to acknowledge the separate existence of Jupiter and Amphitryon, she would have stubbornly clung to her naïve desire to divinize the human. But had she, under the impress of the moment, admitted that the questioner was god to her and the other merely Amphitryon, she would have done violence to her human love. A precarious synthesis between two conflicting impulses has been achieved. If Alkmene is "the perfect marionette" of Kleist's famed essay, as she has been called by some interpreters, then the description applies only to her erstwhile state of innocence. But in her great scene with Jupiter, it is precisely that primitive state of inner unity which is challenged. She must become aware of differences and yet attain to a higher unity of soul that would encompass, without erasing them as separate entities, the human and the divine, the heart and the intellect, knowledge and love. Her experience reflects the inner journey of mankind from blissful paradisaical ignorance to conscious unity with the world and the infinite as portrayed in Christian chiliasm. What is depicted in Kleist's drama, however, is the anguish of the journey and the challenge of the goal but not necessarily its attainment. Alkmene's final "Ach," uttered when she has gained full knowledge, may express a recognition of the ineluctable presence of the divine summons in human life but also an awareness of man's distance from the ultimate goal. In this respect the drama recreates the wistful *mood* of the essay on the *Marionettentheater*.

But the elegiac tone does not necessarily dominate, for mingled with it is a comic note of scolding which, modulated in various keys, reverberates throughout the drama. The excoriations that the three human principals, Sosias, Amphitryon, and Alkmene, must suffer in their respective encounters with Mercury and Jupiter and between themselves are verbal punishments for their individual *hybris* or *Versehen* and run the gamut of mimetic modes from low to high. All three characters are subject to varying degrees of shortsightedness or blindness about their own persons, their position in the world, or their attitude toward the ultimate. Sosias' person and inner experience are a mirthful parody of the Cartesian *cogito ergo sum*. He is a mere sensory and sensuous being, limited in mental ability and therefore lacking in self-knowledge. But if he readily bargains away his identity when threatened by Mercury, he also dimly perceives the emptiness of his life. For a fleeting moment, the shadow of tragedy darkens the comic mode of the servant scenes:

> Have now the kindness please to tell me
> Since I'm not Sosias, who I am
> For something, you'll admit, I have to be
> . . . .
>   I'll now avoid
> That devil there and go back to the camp,
> Though darkly leers at me this hellish night.[11]

Amphitryon, though not wanting in qualities of devotion and compassion, demonstrates on occasion a boorish possessiveness toward Alkmene—an expression of his social station as king and commander—and has a confining empirical attitude toward reality which excludes belief in things unseen. He must be brought to acknowledge a power higher than himself. And Alkmene's love, as noted above, must be broadened to make room for a vision of the infinite despite the great anguish which the experience entails.

A very serious, if not tragic, note is struck by the compounding of error in Alkmene's intuitional approach to reality. In act two, scene five, at the very moment she recognizes with horror that she may have erred but quickly withdraws into her former world of bliss by imagining herself in Amphitryon's arms, she errs again. Even after she is fully aware that there are two Amphitryons and she had received the god the previous night, she swears—to Jupiter—that she would never again mistake him, Amphitryon, for another. In the final scene, she repeats her error in a more comic mode when she hurls her wifely invective at the wrong man. The recognition of past error does not prevent her from committing new error. When the god earlier all but reveals himself in asking her threateningly "Are you not always lying in the dust/In adoration of your love, Amphitryon?" her intense desire to see her peace of mind restored does not let her hear the sound of divinity in his voice. Her inner life is pure but also self-enclosed. It contains the defect of its own virtue.

In the final scene, where Alkmene is made to confront the two Amphitryons, we descend from the eerie heights of thought reached in act two, scene five, to a more human and near comic level, only to soar again into higher regions as Jupiter ascends toward heaven. Throughout this scene, the edge is taken off potential tragedy by the soothing presence of the god, who praises Alkmene's purity of heart, reinstates Amphitryon in his husbandly rights, but also lifts both of their sights to heaven with the announcement of the impending birth of a divine child. In the light of the dialogue between Alkmene and Jupiter in act two, scene five, Hercules becomes a symbol of man's hope for a future reconciliation between the human and the divine, whose separation is the cause of Alkmene's inner torment. But the religious allusions contained in Jupiter's "annunciation" need not be exploited for a one-sided theological exegesis of the whole drama. Unmistakably, however, the addition of act two, scene five, and some other less significant changes made by Kleist in Molière's text suggest that the work cannot be interpreted as a mere human tragedy or comedy. A metaphysical dimension has been added. The drama delves into the existential anguish caused by man's confrontation with the infinite and is in this sense a serious play with metaphysical ideas. It gains poignancy by the fact that the dramatic conflict is concentrated in the heart of an individual, Alkmene, who is capable of the purest feelings. Kleist seems to say that the challenge of the infinite occurs in the deepest recesses of the individual's soul, and not on the level of abstract reasoning. Only the intuitive form of life is capable of approaching the divine. But had it not been for the baffling metamorphosis of the god, Alkmene's sense perceptions could never have been confused and consequently her self-assured feeling of love never been stirred up by new possibilities of inner experience—a recognition which may vibrate along with other emotions in her final exclamation. Through her sensory errors, Alkmene's inner life has been reoriented away from a past and limited state of harmony toward the contemplation of a new ideal in the future. And through her, Amphitryon's life has been similarly affected. But for each, the experience is both sobering and elevating, *per aspera ad astra.*

The drama has been variously called a comedy, a tragedy, a tragicomedy, a metaphysical mystery, a heterogeneous product of tragic and comic elements, and the like. Though Kleist himself called it a "comedy after Molière," there is reason to question his own judgment in this instance. The emphasis might well be on "after" rather than "comedy." The play is patterned *after* Molière's comedy, but in the process it turned out to be something different. The problem of definition arises from the fact that no two interpreters can agree on a common "viewpoint" in the critical sense. Seen from the vantage point of Alkmene's personal inner experience, the problem of mistaken identity is hardly comical, certainly not in the sense of being laughable. Ironic error portrayed at a depth of perception where it is a vitiation of one's innermost sense of identity and truth verges on the tragic. Repeatedly, Alkmene bares the wound opened up in her soul in moving terms. "If only I could sink into eternal night!" At the end, we are left wondering whether her glimpse of the infinite can effectively assuage the human tragedy in her life. It is equally plausible to see in Amphitryon's inner experience accents of tragedy. Though his sensibilities seem limited by his earthy empiricism, his devotion to his wife is deep and the very center of his own being. More than once does he express fear at the annihilating blow that is about to destroy the core of his existence:

> Oh what a blow has struck you, poor Amphitryon!
> The blow is fatal. I am finished,
> Already buried, and my widow is
> Already wedded to another man.
> What's my decision now? [12]

Yet his trust in Alkmene's innocence remains unshaken, and he reserves his wrath for the audacious impostor. He passes the *Vertrauensprobe:*

> Each of her words is truth itself.
> Gold, ten times purified, is not as genuine.
> Were I to read what light'ning writes at night,

Or, if the voice of thunder called to me,
I should not trust those oracles
As I believe her truthful lips.[13]

When, toward the end, his wife does not immediately recognize his true identity, he is near emotional and physical collapse and sinks into Sosias' arms. Even Jupiter experiences moments of personal tragedy. He craves a personalized love by his creature, man, but can only be the remote object of universal worship mixed with fear and trembling. In his longing for human love there is a subtle allusion to the mystic doctrine of the interdependency of God and Man. When Kleist finally draws out the diffuse pantheistic power in the god, he may be reducing Jupiter's dramaturgic effectiveness, for everything now is He, "the shimm'ring sunset, the rushing of the water, the mountains," and, by implication, Amphitryon and Alkmene would be included. As a pantheistic god, he becomes a symbol of the divine potential in their love. Dramatically, the stress on the pantheistic trait in Jupiter is apt to blunt the edge of tragedy in Alkmene's, Amphitryon's, and his own human experience. Kleist must have felt that for an alleged comedy he had drawn the tragic element too sharply.

Sosias, Amphitryon's servant, cannot fully grasp the near extinction of his identity as possibly tragic. His character lacks the necessary depth of perception since it is narrowly circumscribed by his innate cowardice and gluttony. He, along with his nagging wife, Charis, and the boisterous Mercury, literally provide the comic relief from the tragic tensions developing between Alkmene, Amphitryon, and Jupiter. In almost symmetric parallelism the rollicking servant scenes parody the dramatic conflict on the higher level in such a way as to suggest the potential comedy in tragedy and vice versa. But the tragicomic effects of the drama are not solely due to this contrapuntal technique. In the major action involving the protagonists themselves, comic and tragic elements are intimately merged. In that case the comic element is subtle, but it can be discerned either by inference or in the actual dialogue. When, at the end, Amphitryon recovers from his faint and must surrender to the power of Jupiter, he expresses pride in being soon presented with a divine child. Fatherhood by proxy may be tragic to a duped would-be progenitor, but seen from the outside, it is not devoid of a comic touch. Jupiter, if seen merely as a frivolous adventurer, suffers his own tragicomic dilemma. Since he cannot elicit from Alkmene an unequivocal admission of personal love for himself, he is in a sense a duped seducer, which he recognizes in his glib aside: "Cursed be the mad delusion which lured me here!" [14]

The setbacks the god suffers as a human lover are deftly suggested in the shifts he is forced to make in his dialectic position due to Alkmene's incorruptibility. Through his baffling double identity he seemingly bests her in their debate (act two, scene five). At times, the language he uses applies simultaneously to Jupiter and Amphitryon and at times only to the god. But ultimately, to shore up his position, he must talk as though he were merely Amphitryon. A half truth verging on a lie is hardly a rhetorical trick worthy of a god. To Kleist, conscious misuse of language with the intent to deceive has rather a diabolic element in it, as he illustrates in Judge Adam, the wily hero of *The Broken Pitcher*. When Alkmene asks Jupiter at the beginning of act two, scene five, who had visited her the previous night and he answers candidly "It was I," [15] he deceives without literally lying. He speaks the truth, although the ambiguity of the situation does not make clear to whom the "I" in his statement refers. A little later, Alkmene repeats her question, and this time Jupiter unequivocally utters a truth which could not apply to Amphitryon:

> It was no mortal that appeared to you;
> It was Zeus himself, the wielder of the thunder. [16]

Alkmene, though alerted by doubts, cannot see the contradiction in Jupiter's first and second statements, and she remains deceived. But at the end of their long dialogue the god is compelled to dissimulate, if not abnegate, his divinity by asserting flatly: "I am Amphitryon," [17] which, given the disadvantage of Alkmene's position, borders on perfidy.

In his verbal communications we can thus observe a progressive deterioration of Jupiter's position from subtle equivocation over blunt disclosure to conscious dissimulation. If

Alkmene's vision had to be broadened to glimpse the infinite, her purity of feeling also had to be vindicated. And she is exonerated as much through the irony of Jupiter's rhetorical defeat as in the melodramatic ending where the god praises her faithfulness in front of the assembled Thebans. Kleist found in the myth of Amphitryon a ready-made theme to illustrate the power and weakness of language. It can reveal and conceal. The misunderstandings created by the god's double identity could of course readily be cleared up by him if he chose to do so. But the important fact is that Kleist has constructed dramatic dialogues, especially in act two, scene five, which show that language easily lends itself to concealment when the consciousness of the "other," in this case Alkmene, is enclosed in its own modes of inner perception, an ever-present factor in human "communication."

Ultimately the drama's significance cannot be exhausted in isolating and interrelating the tragic and comic components in the human experience of its protagonists. Taken as a whole, it is an artistic metaphor of Kleist's concern with the challenge of the infinite to the individual's "feeling," occurring in the midst of the world's deceptiveness. To envelop such a recondite thought in an atmosphere of attenuated tragedy and deepened comedy constitutes Kleist's masterful achievement in *Amphitryon*. Whether or not he succeeded in integrating completely the disparate mimetic elements is a matter of personal sensibility and subjective aesthetic response.

NOTES

[1] Thomas Mann, *Gesammelte Werke,* 12 volumes, Vol. 9, "Reden und Aufsätze." Berlin, S. Fischer Verlag, 1960, pp. 208 and 187. The essay was originally a lecture entitled "Kleists *Amphitryon:* Eine Wiedereroberung." ("Kleist's *Amphitryon:* A Reconquest") on the occasion of the 1927 Kleist celebration in Munich. First published under the title "Die grosse Szene in Kleists *Amphitryon*" in the *Vossische Zeitung,* Berlin, October 16, 1927, then in expanded form in *Die Neue Rundschau,* Berlin, 39. Jg., H.6, 1928. First appearance in book form in "Die Forderung des Tages," S. Fischer, Berlin, 1930.

[2] The translation used is by Marion Sonnenfeld, New York,

Ungar Paperbacks, 1962. Sembd., act three, scene two, ll. 2321–22: Sonnenfeld, ll. 2307–8. In Plautus' drama, Mercury as narrator stresses the ridiculous elements of the situation throughout. Alcmena, for instance, gives birth to a miraculous set of twins. Amphitryon's son is ten months old and Jupiter's seven months. In Molière's celebrated version of the Amphitryon myth, Alcmène only makes rare appearances on stage and is not seen reacting to the news that it is Jupiter who is the progenitor of her son. At the end, Mercury wryly remarks that such matters had better not be talked about.

[3] Sembd., act two, scene one, ll. 764–65; Sonnenfeld, ll. 769–70.

[4] Sembd., act two, scene two, l. 873; Sonnenfeld, l. 876.

[5] Sembd., act two, scene four, ll. 1197–1200; Sonnenfeld, ll. 1195–98.

[6] Sembd., act two, scene two, ll. 960–61; Sonnenfeld, ll. 961–62.

[7] Sembd., act two, scene five, ll. 1447–53; Sonnenfeld, ll. 1442–48.

[8] Sembd., act two, scene five, ll. 1421–33; Sonnenfeld, ll. 1417–29.

[9] Sembd., act two, scene five, ll. 1564–68; Sonnenfeld, ll. 1557–61.

[10] Sembd., act two, scene five, ll. 1569-73; Sonnenfeld, ll. 1562–66.

[11] Sembd., act one, scene two, ll. 373–76, 391–93; Sonnenfeld, ll. 376–78, 393–95.

[12] Sembd., act three, scene three, ll. 1779–83; Sonnenfeld, ll. 1767–71.

[13] Sembd., act three, scene two, ll. 2281–86; Sonnenfeld, ll. 2266–72.

[14] Sembd., act two, scene five, l. 1512; Sonnenfeld, l. 1506.

[15] Sembd., act two, scene five, l. 1266; Sonnenfeld, l. 1264.

[16] Sembd., act two, scene five, ll. 1335–36; Sonnenfeld, ll. 1331–32.

[17] Sembd., act two, scene five, l. 1544; Sonnenfeld, l. 1537.

"The Marquise of O——"

Like "The Earthquake in Chile," "The Marquise of O——" begins at the height of action. A noble lady of unblemished reputation, the widowed Marquise of O——, announces in a newspaper ad that unaccountably she has become pregnant and is seeking the sire of the unborn child, whom she intends to marry in order to provide her offspring with a legitimate father. But in contrast to "The Earthquake" the story is largely a recounting of the strange events that lead up to the startling announcement. The subject has undeniably a salacious flavor, which is, however, attenuated by the obvious sincerity of the Marquise, with whom we become acquainted right at the beginning. To her, the fact of having given herself unwittingly to a stranger is a deeply perturbing, if not tragic, experience, as it was to Alkmene, though in different circumstances. Kleist alludes to the double nature of the theme in two contrasting mythological images. At one point, the midwife called in for consultation remarks cynically that many a widow finding herself in the Marquise's predicament had dreamed she was living on "savage islands" and, alluding to the Virgin Mary, adds that miraculous conception had occurred only once in the history of mankind. In another place, the victim is likened to a swan which, covered with dirt thrown by a mischievous boy, silently dives underwater to "rise up pure and shining again."

In this *Novelle,* the "fragile constitution of the world" is apparently due to moral failure in man, more precisely to a seemingly unprincipled male taking advantage of a faultless woman in an unguarded moment. The fact of moral transgression is clearly more in evidence than in Kleist's other works, with the exception of *The Broken Pitcher,* where, however, the moral edge is blunted by the comic treatment of the subject. But even in "The Marquise of O——" the twisting path of human destiny tends to minimize the importance of man's moral responsibility. Human desires and actions are merely aspects of a world caught up in the interplay of seemingly irrational forces and deceptive appearances. Therefore, the emphasis in the story gradually shifts from the moral infraction of the culprit to the inner feeling of the heroine. The major theme is not the crime and punishment of a moral offender but rather the testing of the heroine's strength of feeling in the face of a hostile reality that seems to prove her wrong. In typically Kleistian fashion, the conditions and the outcome of the test are two edged. The Marquise admittedly errs in assuming that she had not erred. Her error consists not so much in her moral offense—she committed it unconsciously, literally in a faint—as in her prolonged refusal to acknowledge man's basically ambivalent nature. She projects the purity of her own feeling into the world for a sufficiently long time to make her *Versehen,* or "misapprehension," near tragic. But when she finally faces up to reality, she does it with a resolution that challenges and even defies the world. Through her misjudgment of reality and the ensuing torment she "has come to know herself," while her life has undergone a fundamental reorientation. Although her inner integrity is vindicated, she emerges from her ordeal with an acute but realistic sense of the basic instability of man's world.

Stylistically, the impression of the world's impermanence

is created by Kleist's customary procedure of describing effects before their causes, of dwelling upon details before we are sufficiently initiated into the overall nexus of things, and of suddenly reversing the course of the action at crucial moments.

After the death of her husband, the Marquise of O—— had gone into seclusion with her two children in the house of her father, garrison commander of a fortified town in northern Italy around the turn of the 19th century. Her quiet life there is soon brutally interrupted by war. Russian troops assail and conquer the fort. In the thick of battle a band of Russian soldiers attempts to abduct and violate her. An enemy officer who appears to her as a godsend—Kleist uses the term "angel"—saves her in the nick of time from assault. She collapses unconscious in his arms. Soon thereafter, eyewitness reports have it that Count F——, her rescuer, has been killed in another battle. The Marquise is greatly saddened by the news but also perturbed by symptoms of a sickness, such as dizzy spells and nausea. Much to her amazement, the Count reappears—he had only been wounded—and surprises her with a frenetic marriage proposal. He is even willing to cut short a secret military mission to southern Italy, thus jeopardizing his future career. The family succeeds in containing his ardor by promising to consider his proposal upon his return. Meanwhile, the Marquise's "illness" has been unmistakably identified as pregnancy. Her mortified parents cannot believe her pleas of innocence. In a melodramatic scene, she is expelled from the house. On her country estate, surrounded by her two children, she reconciles herself to her strange fate and decides to put the ad in the paper. When the Count returns from his mission, she refuses his advances, thinking herself unworthy of him. Through a stratagem of her own, the Marquise's mother is able to convince herself and her husband of her daughter's sincerity, which leads to a lachrymose reconciliation in the Commander's home. A reply to the Marquise's ad is inserted in the paper stating the time when the unknown offender will make his appearance. To the family's dismay, Count F—— calls at the house at the appointed time. The Marquise is mortally offended and rejects him as a veritable "devil." But a marriage ceremony is held anyway, although it is only after many months that the Marquise will fully accept him as her lawful husband.

In contrast to *Amphitryon*,[1] the reader is not initiated into the secret springs of the action right from the beginning. But when we learn of the Marquise's state of health and the Count's pressing marriage proposal we can, of course, divine the mystery, enjoy the same privileged viewpoint as in the earlier drama, and perhaps savor some retrospective ironies. The Marquise had "thanked her savior" and felt "inconsolable regret" at the news of his purported death. As we thumb back a few pages, we also discover that Kleist had indicated with a mere hyphen the stealthy offense of Count F——, a rather simple but effective narrative device reminiscent of the eloquent silence with which he had passed over Toni and Gustav's lovemaking in "The Engagement. . . ."

. . . then, saluting her courteously in French, he offered her his arm and led her, speechless from all she had gone through, to the other wing of the residence, which had not caught fire yet, where she fainted dead away. Here—when her terrified women appeared, he told them to call a doctor; promised them, as he put his hat on, that she would soon recover; and returned to the fray.[2]

Belatedly, we also realize, that the Count's gesture of putting his hat on may be another clue to the mystery. Not surprisingly, further ironies are in store for us. After inserting the ad in the paper, the Marquise is still convinced that the culprit who had so shamelessly taken advantage of her must belong to the lowest order of mankind, and when she refuses the Count's renewed proposal she imagines she is doing it for his sake, since she feels dishonored.

Interwoven with the ironies are the repeated sudden reversals of the action. We go from quiescent seclusion to the violence of warfare, from false rumors to surprising truths, from certain anticipations to upsetting revelations. All of this is a reflection of Kleist's own experience of an unstable world in which the truths we are most certain of are the least certain. The surprising ending, of course, holds no surprise for us. Even if we had not glimpsed the truth earlier, we could deduce from the underlying rhythm of irony and opposites that the offender will not be a low type of man precisely because the Marquise is so sure of it. And even be-

fore we are vaguely initiated into the secret we have an ink-
ling that the Count is not the paragon of virtue he appears
to be.

What may come as a surprise, however, is the Marquise's
violent revulsion at the seemingly happy outcome:

. . . "Go away! Go away! Go away! I was ready for some villain
of a fellow, but not—not—not the devil!" and, walking around
him as if he had the plague, she opened the door and said, "Call
the Colonel!" [3]

But like Alkmene she had suspected the wrong man and
in her disgust must reject the very thing she loves, except
that the irony is lessened in her case since the one she accuses as a "devil" is indeed the offender. Her abhorrence
is two edged. There is no doubt that she is not only mortified by the Count's moral transgression but also deeply
wounded by the inability of her intuitive feeling to discern
the truth. The latter is probably the more disturbing cause
for her inner agitation. But, in the final analysis, the truth
itself is ambivalent. The Marquise is both right and wrong
about it. She erred unconsciously and, therefore, is justified in considering herself unblemished. Yet, in judging the
world from the vantage point of her inner purity she is
wrong. In this sense, her *hamartia* is truly an intellectual
rather than a moral error. The concatenation of outer events
is, of course, conducive to such misapprehension. Conception
occurring during a fainting spell which afflicts the woman in
the midst of a military action is certainly unusual and fraught
with coincidence. Anticipating Freud, one might be tempted
to say that the fainting happened after the fact and served
as a convenient device for blocking out guilt through the
now familiar apparatus of repression. But such lurid suspicions seem far removed from Kleist's mind. He does all
he can to exonerate his Marquise. Through the depth and
steadfastness of her feeling she gives as much a lesson to the
world as the world does to her. If, as a result of her intellectual error, she must reorient herself in the world, the
fictional society around her must also reassess its values and
own up to the purity of her feeling. In one sense, she is the
victor. Kleist seems to suggest just that in the way he describes the Marquise's reconcilation with her father, the stal-

wart representative of the world and its moral codes, whom he portrays in that scene as a whimpering sot—an episode, incidentally, which to modern sensibilities definitely has Freudian overtones in its exaggerated depiction of a father's demonstrative affection for his daughter.

The test that the Marquise must pass is obviously much the same as the dilemma Alkmene must face: how can inner certainty make itself believed in the world when visible evidence and rational inference speak so convincingly against it? The Marquise's pregnancy and the initial "J" on Alkmene's diadem are disquieting proofs, even to the heroines themselves, that they may have erred. And both must confront themselves without the solace of spontaneous trust by those who could sustain them. Though Amphitryon finally professes his belief in Alkmene's innocence, he does so in her absence, and the Marquise's mother only believes her daughter's integrity after she has used a trick to obtain empirical—not intuitive—evidence for it. She feigns that one of their servants confessed to be the furtive seducer, but when she witnesses her daughter's complete bewilderment she is convinced of her inner purity and launches into a eulogy reminiscent of Jupiter's praise of Alkmene:

"I want you to know," her mother continued, "you who are purer than the angels, that there is not a word of truth in anything I said; that my soul is so corrupt that I could not believe in such radiant innocence as yours; and that I needed to play this shameful trick in order to convince myself." [4]

However, the intensely human setting of "The Marquise of O——," the absence of those mysterious divine interventions which occur in *Amphitryon*, "The Duel," and other works of Kleist, give this *Novelle* a quite earthly tone. But in its moving portrayal of the power and demise of human feeling it adumbrates Kleist's great tragedy *Penthesilea*, whose mythological setting by itself evokes both the earthly and metaphysical dimensions of man's inner experience. But before he could finish his tragedy, Kleist was already working on "The Duel," a *Novelle* in which he explores the question of "feeling" and Christian faith in a medieval setting.

NOTES

[1] There are fairly certain indications that "The Marquise of O——" was written at about the same time as *Amphitryon*.

[2] Sembd., Vol. 4, p. 95; Greenberg, p. 43. Greenberg translates "A little while after, when . . ." instead of "Here—when. . . ," which, though stylistically preferable, diminishes our surprise at the retrospective discovery.

[3] Sembd., Vol. 4, p. 128; Greenberg, p. 81.

[4] Sembd., p. 123; Greenberg, p. 75.

"The Duel"

Thematically, "The Duel" with its complicated plot may well be the most ambiguous of Kleist's *Novellen.* As in *The Schroffenstein Family, Amphitryon,* and "The Marquise of O——," factual evidence points in one direction and the inner feeling of the innocent victims in another. But here, the conflict between reason and feeling is compounded by the enigmatic outcome of a trial by combat said to reveal the will of God. In the ordeal, the evildoer is victorious but later dies from a festering disease caused by a paltry wound he received in the combat, while his mortally wounded opponent recovers miraculously. In this *Novelle,* God appears to be as ambiguous, though in a different way, as in "The Earthquake in Chile," where He unleashes a natural catastrophe killing thousands of people in order to save two wayward lovers from certain death, only to have them slaughtered by a horde of religious zealots.

Set at the end of the fourteenth century[1] in southern Germany, the plot of "The Duel" consists of two distinct threads brought together in an alibi offered by a suspected murderer in court. Accused of the assassination of his brother, Count Redbeard admits that the murder weapon, an arrow, is indeed his but insists that he had spent the night of the murder in the castle of Littegarde, a widowed noble lady living far away from the scene of the crime. As evidence he produces a ring which Littegarde had allegedly given him as a token of love. Littegarde, though recognizing the ring as hers, denies the allegations made against her by the unwanted suitor. Driven away and disowned by her family, she seeks refuge with Friedrich of Trota, a friend and protector, who takes up the cudgels for her and challenges Redbeard to a trial by arms. In the combat, Trota slips and is mortally wounded. Littegarde's dishonor seems to be proved beyond doubt, since God had spoken against her through the trial. But Friedrich recovers from his severe wounds, while his practically unharmed opponent slides ever closer toward death. Yet, the law demands that Littegarde and Friedrich be burned at the stake for their perjury before God, despite the strange sequel to the duel. As preparations for the supplice are made, the full truth is revealed. The ring had actually been given to Redbeard in the dark of night by Littegarde's scheming maid. She had succeeded in disguising herself as her mistress and letting herself be seduced by Redbeard, who thought all along that he had made Littegarde's conquest—a somewhat operatic and contrived occurrence reminiscent of the plot of *The Schroffenstein Family*. The ring episode, in casting a pall on Littegarde's honor, had almost eclipsed the original issue of Redbeard's culpability. But now that his alibi has been proved invalid and he is about to die, the contrite Redbeard confesses to the murder of his brother, whom he had had killed by a hired assassin. Littegarde and Friedrich are united in marriage by the Emperor as Redbeard's body burns at the stake in their stead. Afterward, the Emperor affixes an amendment to the statutes governing trial by arms to the effect that an ordeal will immediately reveal truth "only if it be God's will."

It is readily apparent that the focus of the *Novelle* is not so much on the murder of Redbeard's brother as on Littegarde and the strange ways of God to man suggested in the unexpected aftermath of the duel. With obvious irony in mind, Kleist says explicitly at one point in the story that the law of holy combat will infallibly bring the truth to light, when he has actually constructed his plot in such a way as to make the outcome equivocal no matter who wins the duel. For Redbeard is as much convinced of the truth of his statement concerning the ring as are Littegarde and Friedrich of his dishonesty. In this respect, both accused and accuser are equally deceived. Under the circumstances, what is actually called into question is not the truth or untruth of their conflicting beliefs but the validity of the law of holy combat itself. In Kleist, things never are what they seem, the truth supposedly revealed in a trial by arms not exempt. Had Redbeard been worsted in the combat, he would have expiated the murder of his brother, but unbeknown to anyone but himself. Yet, legally, the ordeal was fought over his alibi and the doubt it cast on Littegarde's character, for which he had, in his opinion and the opinion of most observers, tangible and incontrovertible evidence, namely her ring. His defeat would have proved as little as did Friedrich's with respect to the actual events that produced the *corpus delicti*. Although it may be the clue to the mystery, the "eloquent object," in this case the ring, does not necessarily by itself speak the truth, not any more than the trial by arms. In addition to demonstrating once again that circumstantial or sensory evidence is often delusive, Kleist seems to satirize the human pretense under which man-made laws supposedly embody the divine will. This theme he emphasizes when he has the Emperor amend the law of holy combat with the highly ambiguous clause "only if it be God's will," which, in fact, makes a joke of the whole idea of ordeal by arms. Who is to tell when the outcome of a combat is sanctioned by the divine will or not?

The veiled satire is further reinforced by the inexplicable ebbing away of Redbeard's vital forces after the combat. Although hinting that the truth is not what it appears to be, the unexpected reversal of fate does not have the force of law and is therefore devoid of objective validity. It is only when Redbeard confesses, after the circumstances surrounding his attempt at seduction have been brought to light, that reality confutes legality.

On the other hand, one could justifiedly maintain that Kleist illustrates in this *Novelle* the implications of the religious adage "God moves in mysterious ways." The unexpected aftermath to the combat helps disclose the perpetrator of the real crime, while the immediate occasion for the duel, namely Littegarde's honor, only obfuscates the central issue of the murder of Count Redbeard's brother. As some interpreters have remarked, Kleist sees the way to God cluttered with the debris of man-made laws. Yet God cannot be concerned with legalistic problems, Kleist seems to suggest, but rather with ultimate truth. God may be enigmatic, but not necessarily evil, as he chose to point out repeatedly. Sylvester in *The Schroffenstein Family* voiced such a belief openly; we encounter it directly in Kleist's letters, somewhat obliquely in the Gypsy motif in "Michael Kohlhaas," and still less directly, though unmistakably, in other works. Nevertheless, in such *Novellen* as "The Earthquake . . . ," "The Beggarwoman of Locarno," or "St. Cecilia . . . ," the ways of God to man lead to violent death and madness, which only intensifies the impression of bewilderment about God's designs we gain from Kleist's works. The inscrutability of the divine will is apt to evoke profound disquietude, which is illustrated in Littegarde's and even Friedrich's comportment. Nowhere else did Kleist depict so drastically the paralyzing grip of despair as in Littegarde, with the possible exception of Penthesilea at the moment of recovery from madness or the Prince of Homburg at the sight of his grave. Littegarde is not Alkmene. She cannot be. Though, like Alkmene, she knows herself guiltless, God has apparently found her guilty. Convinced of both truths, she passes through the most agonizing experience of inner schism. Faith in things unseen, when things seen and God's own judgment speak so eloquently against it, is more than she can bear. And she is a child of her time, because she does not doubt for a moment the validity of the ordeal by arms, as is evident in the invective she hurls at Friedrich when he visits her in her dank cell:

"Madman! Maniac!" cried Littegarde. "Hasn't God's sacred judgment gone against me? Weren't you beaten by the Count in that fatal duel? Hasn't he vindicated with his arms the truth of what he accused me of before the court?" [2]

She is on the brink of madness. Her inner schism is revealed when she violently rejects Friedrich's attempts at consoling her and in the same breath calls him her "darling":

"Go away!" she cried, recoiling from him on her knees across the straw. "If you don't want me to go mad, don't touch me! You are an abomination to me; the hottest flames are less dreadful to me than you!"

"Oh, Jesus!" Littegarde cried, flinging herself down in a frenzy of terror at his feet and pressing her face to the floor. "Leave the room, my darling, and forget me! . . ."

"All the horrors of hell are pleasanter for me to look at than the love and kindness beaming at me out of the springtime of your face!" [3]

Friedrich, on the other hand, is seemingly endowed with that strength of inner feeling we usually encounter in Kleist's women protagonists rather than the men. But even he must adopt a defensive attitude toward the factual evidence which belies his and Littegarde's inner conviction. He admonishes her in impassioned terms to ". . . rear up the feeling that you have within you like a tower of rock"—a well-known Kleistian phrase—and

"cling to it and never waver, even if the earth below and the heavens above should founder. Let us believe the more intelligible and reasonable of the two ideas that baffle the understanding here, and, rather than thinking you guilty, let us think I won the duel. I fought for you." [4]

Then he pleads with God to "keep [his] own soul from distraction," as if he were trying to suppress his own doubts as much as hers. Generally, Kleist's heroines withstand the adversity of the world in silence and a kind of inward-directed stance, while Friedrich talks almost sanctimoniously, which is hardly a sign of inner assurance. This does not render him unsympathetic or weak, but it reveals a chink in his armor, symbolized in his sudden and inexplicable faltering during the combat. Yet, ultimately, his asseverations triumph over empirical deception, but only after the struggle had twice led him to the brink of despair—upon his defeat in combat and the near death at the stake.

In "The Duel" the problem of "trust" takes on decidedly religious dimensions. In contrast to Gustav and Toni or Agnes and Ottokar, Littegarde and Friedrich have no doubts about the immaculateness of each other's motives or the integrity of their actions. Among her suitors, Friedrich was "the dearest one of all in her eyes," and after her expulsion from her parental home she implicitly trusts his conviction of her innocence, which he in turn expresses movingly:

"Not another word to defend and justify your innocence! There is a voice in my heart that pleads for you more vigorously and convincingly than all your protestations, or even all the legal points and proofs that you will be able to marshal in your defense before the court in Basel." 6

What is obviously tested is their faith or trust in God. And the greater burden of generating faith against the assaults of despair is thrust upon Friedrich. If he nearly falters in his inward certainty, though not visibly in his outer bearing, we cannot blame him. Kleist has contrived a test of faith for his hero which in severity can stand comparison with Abraham's trial. This much at least can be inferred from the general course of events related by the narrator, especially from the scene in Littegarde's cell. Significantly, Kleist passes over in silence their inner journey from their prison to the stake, where, bound and garroted, they fully expect to die—ironically, in an *auto-da-fé*. The artistic canons of the *Novelle* do not allow the writer to describe at length inner states of mind. He can only relate significant episodes which must speak for themselves.

Although the whole plot of "The Duel" amounts to an ironic comment on the religious claims made for human laws, Kleist does not take the reader into his confidence very early in the story, as in *Amphitryon* or *The Broken Pitcher*, to let him savor immediately some pungent ironies. Very much as in *The Schroffenstein Family*, we are for a long time kept in the dark about the real cause of the tragic deceptions.

But by now we are sufficiently familiar with the underlying rhythm in Kleist's works to anticipate perilous and ironic reversals at the very moment strong affirmations to the contrary are being made. We know the accusation leveled against Littegarde is false, since it is supported by so much visual evidence. When Friedrich starts the combat with superior skill, we can assume he will go down to defeat. Or when Littegarde haughtily affirms that Friedrich could not be hurt even if he fought unarmed, we begin to fear for his life. Finally, if all agree that the trial by arms will dredge up the hidden truth, we must anticipate that the truth will only become more obscured.[7]

Thus, what is ultimately on trial is the *deus absconditus* himself. Though the story leads to a relatively happy ending, and Friedrich, after the ill-fated combat, refuses to accuse God of injustice, seeking the reason for the tragic turn of events in his own sins, we are nevertheless left with a sense of disquietude about the reliability of the divine will. This deep sense of the uncertainty of all things, including God, is summarized in the final motto "if it be God's will." The motif of the trial by arms allowed Kleist to illustrate the ambiguity inherent in ultimate reality or God. If, in this instance, God chose to save the innocent and punish the guilty, it may have been a sheer caprice of his will. In other instances, as in "The Earthquake . . . ," he chose to destroy the pure-in-heart. It would be intrepid to say apodictically what the transcendental meaning of Kleist's stories is, especially when they are placed side by side. We come away from reading them with a sense of anxiety and no certainties.

NOTES

[1] The story is probably based on an episode related in Jean Froissart's *Chroniques de France,* which appeared in a new edition in Paris in 1806, and four years later in a German adaptation by one C. Baechler, published in a popular journal. Estimates of the inception and writing of the *Novelle* range from 1806 to 1811.

[2] Sembd., Vol. 4, p. 236; Greenberg, p. 311.

[3] Sembd., Vol. 4, pp. 233–34; Greenberg, p. 308.

[4] Sembd., Vol. 4, p. 236; Greenberg, p. 311.

[5] Sembd., Vol. 4, pp. 236–37; Greenberg, p. 311.

[6] Sembd., Vol. 4, p. 224; Greenberg, p. 298.

[7] At times, there is a suggestion in Kleist's work, as there is in some Greek tragedies, that self-assurance displayed when fate seems to augur well is *hybris*. Only under adverse circumstances does such inner self-reliance become a virtue.

"Penthesilea"

In *Penthesilea*, as in *Amphitryon*, Kleist explores the deepest reaches of human "feeling," but what he perceives is not the translucency of Alkmene's inner world but the chiaroscuro of a soul tragically divided against itself. He began writing the tragedy in 1806 while still in government service in Königsberg, continued to work on it during his imprisonment in France, and finished it in Dresden in 1807. A fragment appeared in the January 1808 issue of the *Phoebus*, and the whole work was published in book form by Cotta late in the same year. The drama does not merely reflect the depressions and euphorias of these years in Kleist's life but encompasses in fact "the whole suffering and brilliance of my soul," as he declared in a letter addressed to Marie von Kleist in the autumn of 1807. The word *Schmerz*, "suffering," illegibly written in Kleist's hand, has at times been deciphered as *Schmutz*, notably by his latest editor, Helmut Sembdner. If *Schmutz* is translated literally as "dirt," filth," or "smut," we arrive at a wrong, or rigidly puritan, perspective on the psychological and undeniably sexual aspects of the drama. *Schmutz*—if this is the correct rendition of the word—had perhaps be better understood figuratively as "blemish," "tarnish," or "darkness," especially when we consider its counterpart in Kleist's statement, namely "brilliance." The drama uncovers those dark and self-destructive forces in the human psyche which threatened Kleist all his life and finally triumphed over his strongest life-affirming urges. In this sense, *Penthesilea* may well be Kleist's most psychological and autobiographical work, although its mythological framework and symbolic quality lend it the metaphysical significance we have come to associate with his works.

Since Kleist was interested primarily in the conflict waged in Penthesilea's soul, he paid little attention to the orthodox version of the legend and changed its plot substantially. Most important, it is not Achilles who kills the Amazon in combat, only to be smitten by love for his dying victim, but Penthesilea who literally slaughters the Greek in a fit of madness provoked by misunderstood love. The action takes place on a battlefield near Troy. As allies of the Trojans, the Amazons have poured forth to wage war upon the Greeks encamped around the city. Ares, their god, has commanded the female warrior tribe to set out on its periodic conquests. In order to perpetuate their tribe, every Amazon will live in temporary union with the opponent she chances to capture in battle. But Penthesilea, the Amazon Queen, violates the sacred tradition of her country by dismissing the law of Tanais, the founder of the state, which obligates her to take whomsoever the fortunes of war cast her way. Earlier, her dying mother, Otrera, had already expressed the dark premonition that Penthesilea will seek out for herself the most glorious of heroes, Achilles. Upon being worsted by him in combat and overcome by grief and shame, she falls into a swoon. When she regains consciousness, Achilles leaves her with the impression that he had been vanquished by her before she lost consciousness. She declares her love for him but is soon apprised of her error when the retreating Amazons reveal to her that she is really Achilles' captive. Her Amazon pride resurges, and she girds herself anew for battle. Achilles, whose erstwhile frivolousness has given way to stronger feelings of love, devises a stratagem which will afford her the triumph of leading him as a captive to her homeland for the hymeneal feast of roses according to the tradition of her tribe. Only lightly armed, he challenges her to another duel in which he intends to feign defeat. But Penthesilea senses in his challenge only an outrageous mockery of her most sacred feelings, for he must know that she is too weak to vie with him in combat. Flushed with madness, she calls down the vengeance of the furies upon him. Listening only to her outraged feelings, she turns into a fury herself, assembles an array of war machinery and bloodhounds, and sets upon the unsuspecting Achilles. After piercing his throat with an arrow, she buries her teeth in his body. When she recovers from her madness, she listens in despair and disbelief to the account of her monstrous deed and declares herself free from the law of the Amazons. She calls upon her heart to send forth a powerful, destructive feeling and dies by the sheer force of her grief but seemingly reconciled with her tragic destiny.

Penthesilea represents a crucial phase in Kleist's struggle with the problem of feeling. The spontaneous thrust in Penthesilea is partially vindicated and yet leads to an hysterically destructive end. Tragedy seems to emanate as much from the heroine's own inner demon as from an extraneous, diabolic fate. More than in any other work, Kleist casts serious doubt on the ontological integrity of man's inner certainties. In the earlier works, if there was doubt in his mind about the power of feeling to retain its unity, he transposed this apprehension precisely into the very notion of a malevolent fate assailing man's inner world from without. Only sporadically did he suggest that his heroes might suffer from an inner division, when he showed them to be momentarily "confused" or hesitant. It is symptomatic of Kleist's boldness in baring his own inner discord that he did not portray the conflict from the vantage point of Achilles, which would be conceivable, but from the depth of Penthesilea's soul. Were it not for a streak of frivolous gallantry in his character, Achilles would in one sense be the typical Kleistian hero who walks unawares into catastrophe caused by a world misjudging his intentions. Toward the end, his naïve trust in Penthesilea's feeling and understanding verges on the ingenuousness we observed in Alkmene, though it is no match for the inner destructive force that drives Penthesilea to madness.

But Penthesilea's psychological drama has its external aspects that cannot be entirely ignored. It shows her torn between her loyalty to the Amazon State and the peremptory demands of her own individuality. Her inner schism is projected outward into her double role as a woman and a warrior. This contest is rendered more poignant by the clash of two incompatible cultures occurring in the war between Amazons and Greeks. The external phase of the problem, which for the sake of analysis may be abstracted from the heroine's own inner experience of it, is resolved in favor of the claims of individuality or personal feeling. Just before Penthesilea's death, the emblem of Tanais falls crashing to the ground, symbolizing the collapse of a pernicious and unnatural social order.

The external aspect of the conflict in Penthesilea's life has given rise to various symbolic exegeses. A Catholic interpreter, Friedrich Braig,[1] sees in her a kind of sacrificial lamb who through her intuitive certainty, which he likens to the divine guidance operating in Kleist's marionette, atones for the evil, self-willed, and rational idea that produced the Amazon nation. This theological formula is based on the premise that the Scythians, before the invasion by the Ethiopians, lived in the paradisaical harmony of a precultural state. They were robbed of their natural grace through the recklessness of the invaders, which heightened their awareness of good and evil. The unnatural law the Amazons give to themselves after having killed the usurpers is an ill-fated attempt at recovering the lost harmony. The uncomprehending Achilles repeats unconsciously the act of "original sin" by accentuating in Penthesilea the schism between divine nature and human rationality. But through her self-sacrifice, Penthesilea restores original spontaneity or divine grace to her "fallen" people. It takes considerable imagination to arrive at such an interpretation.

More down to earth is Hans M. Wolff's [2] view, based on Rousseauist political theories. From this point of view the Amazon law is considered to be virtually the result of a social contract. Abandoning the free state they had attained after the massacre of their oppressors, the Amazons acquiesced in the interest of the general welfare to accept freely the chains of government. Though depriving themselves of the individual sovereignty they enjoyed in their natural state, they remain free, for they owe no allegiance to a law imposed from without by a foreign power but surrender their individual rights to a central authority in accordance with their own will and rational insight. The Amazon does not obey the law of the State because she "must" but because she "knows." The supreme ruler, however, is bound by the general will and may be displaced if necessary. At one point, the High Priestess in fact disenfranchises Penthesilea from her responsibilities, since her pursuit of Achilles is motivated by personal love and not by reason of State. The genesis of the State of Tanais would thus correspond to Rousseau's idealized depiction of the birth of nations. Its culmination is the *"aliénation totale de chaque associé,"* an ideal which is undoubtedly materialized in the Amazon law. Thus it is possible to maintain with Wolff that Kleist depicts in *Penthesilea* the struggle that ensues when subjective feeling becomes entangled not with an imperfect social order, as in *The Schroffenstein Family,* but with the demands of an ideal State. (Though one must hold against Wolff that Rousseau hardly suggested a depersonalization of love between man and woman as a necessary corollary to the curtailment of the private sphere of life in the interest of the general welfare!) Kleist's conclusion, according to Wolff, is that even a social organism which does justice to the loftiest requirements of reason is pernicious, since it breaks up the natural harmony of the individual soul. Penthesilea is certainly the proper instrument to redress the balance. Not unlike Anouilh's Antigone, she is an *"enragée d'authenticité"* whose actions are guided only by the invincible imperative of the indwelling personal law. In this sense, her feeling triumphs over the world, even if it means her death. But aside from being somewhat farfetched, such theories which claim to exhaust the problem by concentrating merely on its external phase must slight Achilles' dramaturgic function in the play and ignore entirely the psychoanalytic dimension in the portrayal of Penthesilea's character.

The internal phase of the problem is more complex than the external and is in itself two pronged. There is the familiar Kleistian conflict between intuitive and sensory apprehension of reality, which dooms Penthesilea's encounter with Achilles. But there is also the subconscious struggle in Penthesilea's psyche between life affirmation and death wish, which in its turn obscures both her intuitive and sensory grasp of reality. In Achilles' challenge to another combat she does not "feel" his real intention, and when he approaches her, she does not even "see" that he is practically unarmed. She will be prone to accuse an unjust world, fate, or god of destroying the false "realities" created by the subconscious conflict of her torn soul. This is part of the tragic irony in the play, for there is ample evidence that in many ways Penthesilea is her own destroying angel.

Achilles is intimately connected with Penthesilea's inner conflict. He is obviously the object of her love; a love through which she hopes to assuage forever her inner strife and satisfy her yearning for self-fulfillment. He represents to her the absolute, if in "absolute" we see something like inner unity and a state of harmony with the world which would hopefully ensue from glimpsing one's ultimate personal destiny. In an inversion of roles, Penthesilea makes the same intransigent demands upon the unsuspecting Achilles as Kleist himself had made upon Wilhelmine von Zenge, his erstwhile fiancée. Achilles, naïvely unaware of Penthesilea's transcendent aspirations, becomes the instrument as well as the victim of the tragic ironies of fate. Through him Kleist introduces that element of outer deception we know from his earlier works. Thus inner destiny and outer fate become enmeshed through a series of tragic and ironic misapprehensions. Seen from Achilles' vantage point, the ironies ensue largely from his not knowing what side of Penthesilea's complex personality he should appeal to, the woman or the Amazon. When he first enters her camp, unarmed, after having defeated her, he is willing to submit to the strength of her love, though still rather in the manner of an adventurous gallant, which is suggested in the way he approaches the Amazons in Penthesilea's retinue:

> You, blue-eyed beauty, sure it is not you
> That would unleash the dogs on me to tear me?
> Nor you whose glory is your silk-soft locks? [3]

Penthesilea, however, is still under the sway of the Amazon law and wants his admission of defeat, suffered on the battle-field, before she can give free rein to her feelings of love. This, in fact, does happen, but only in her imagination. Encouraged by her faithful consort Prothoe, who justifiedly fears for her sanity if she were to know the truth, Penthesilea deludes herself into thinking that she is the victor. Ironically, it is only in her illusory world that she fulfills her mother's prophecy that she would put the crown of roses on Achilles' head. But as Achilles' passing feeling for her develops into a more enduring love he is willing to make concessions to her Amazon nature and the laws of her State. We reach the peak of irony when he challenges her a second time to combat, intending to let himself be defeated, for he does the right thing at the wrong time. Meanwhile, Penthesilea has completely renounced her Amazon nature and wants to live only for her love. In her newly weakened condition, she can think only of the blasphemous lack of feeling or "understand-ing" revealed in Achilles' challenge and will be driven by her thwarted love to extreme violence.

> He, he who knows I am too weak by far,
> He sends this challenge, Prothoe, to me?
> My faithful breast here moves him not a whit
> Till he has crushed and split it with his spear?
> Did all I whispered to him touch his ear
> Only with the empty music of the voice?
> Has he forgot the temple midst the oaks?
> Was it a block of stone my hand did crown? [4]

It could also be argued that although being deceived about the real motives of Achilles' action, she senses in him an in-capacity for total surrender in love, for up to that point he had indeed done or said little really loving to her. But it is important to note that Kleist introduces a change of heart in Achilles when Penthesilea's own inner development leads her in the opposite direction. The fact that his feelings for Pen-thesilea have deepened is unquestionably made clear in the words he addresses to his companion Diomede:

> This wondrous woman,
> Half Fury, half goddess, she loves me; I—

What care I for the Grecian women? I swear,
By Hades! By the Styx!—I love her too! [5]

One could speculate here on the depth of Kleist's disillusionment with the world. He expressed in his letters more than once a romantic feeling of nostalgia about the transience of all phenomena. Expressed philosophically, even the *a priori* form of "time" through which we perceive the world is deceptive. Time is beyond our grasp as is the real nature of the causes at work in the universe. While Penthesilea misjudges the cause or motive of Achilles' action, he misjudges the time of her inner conversion. Man has no reliable, stable vantage point from which to judge the "other." "All is flux." The Heraclitean dictum takes on dramatic force in Kleist's *Penthesilea*. It is perhaps the ultimate consequence of the veiled skepticism inherent in Kant's Critical Philosophy.

In contrast to other works of Kleist, where misunderstandings usually ensue from the characters' lack of concession to outer reality, Achilles' misjudgment arises precisely from acceding to it. For he discovers and begins to respect the cause of Penthesilea's inner conflict. But Kleist gives irony a new and subtle twist. Though correct, we must repeat, Achilles' intuition comes at the wrong time and thereby is all the more ironic. In one sense, he was right, in another, wrong. Understanding is one thing, time another. Kleist's romantic effusions about the mystery of time found a way into the ironic structure of his most autobiographical play.

But even more than the ironic miscues that seal the two protagonists' tragic destinies, it is Penthesilea's frame of mind which arouses our concern. From the beginning she shows signs of a suicidal urge reminiscent of Kleist's own constant flirting with the idea of self-willed death. Penthesilea seeks death as much as life. In an inversion of irony, fate ultimately provides her with a cause for self-destruction, thereby accomplishing what she herself had willed to do all along, at least in the semiconscious regions of her mind. This psychoanalytic element in the portrayal of her character may account for her seemingly implausible end, if only in emblematic transposition. She literally wills herself to death by conjuring up a powerful and destructive feeling. Her manner of death both symbolizes and climaxes her inward journey toward suicide, which runs the gamut from awareness of inner discord to self-destructive actions. Early in the play she admits,

> And still my heart is discord and defiance [6]

a statement that would be unthinkable coming from one of Kleist's "pure" heroines, such as Alkmene or the Marquise. She also seems to have a dark premonition that the immensity of her feeling could never be satisfied by anything human or earthly and will sweep her toward destruction:

> Cursed be the heart that knows not wise restraint! [7]

The women around her have similar insights into her inner disarray. Prothoe tries repeatedly to shield her from outside reality by catering to her inner illusions, and at one point the High Priestess declares disapprovingly,

> Though nothing holds her, no fate binds her here,
> Only her infatuate heart!

when she is interrupted by Prothoe with the portentous statement:

> *That* is her fate! [8]

In the ninth scene, when Penthesilea has failed in her first attempt to capture Achilles, she falls completely under the spell of her inner torment. Rambling incoherently, she vows to impose her will upon the world, even if she has to "lift Ida on top of Ossa" and capture Helios, the sun god, himself. But then, looking into her reflection in a nearby river she imagines she sees Achilles at her feet and with womanly abandon implores him to take her, but is saved by her attendants from throwing herself into the swift waters.

> Oh, foolish me!
> Why, there he is below me! Take me! I come—! [9]

The first part of the action culminates thus in her suicide attempt; then comes her defeat at the hands of Achilles, followed by the idyllic interlude in scenes fourteen and fifteen, where she finds self-fulfillment in her illusion and, finally, the ultimate catastrophe. Although the drama is not divided into acts, it does have a discernible tripartite structure: first the story of Penthesilea's failure, then the interlude of illusory happiness, followed by the account of the fatal misunderstanding between Penthesilea and Achilles.

Even in her illusive happiness, acting as in an hypnotic trance, Penthesilea bares the death wish locked in her soul,

> Never was I half so ripe for death as now [10]

after Prothoe had exclaimed aghast:

> I see joy is no less your bane than sorrow;
> No matter which, it straight will make you mad.[11]

In the fifteenth scene there is a short episode of singular evocative power. Penthesilea suddenly interrupts her impassioned account of her country's history to ask Achilles why he is smiling. Achilles, who probably never smiled, professes not to have done so and finds a convenient excuse to satisfy her.

PENTHESILEA. . . . .
Stops short and looks at him.
Why do you smile?

ACHILLES. Who? I?

PENTHESILEA. Did you not smile? It seemed so.

ACHILLES. My thoughts had strayed. Forgive me. I was wond'ring
If you were not come down to me from the moon.[12]

She seems by all means to have become suddenly aware of the irony, even condescension, in Achilles, who cannot fully grasp the significance of the Amazon experience in her life. The whole "as if" character of her idyllic union with Achilles is illuminated in a quick flash of psychological insight. For Penthesilea knows subrationally that the whole idyl is illusory. This insight provokes the sad smile at herself which she apparently projects upon Achilles. In her trancelike state of happiness the truth suddenly erupts but is quickly brushed aside, as is the supposed smile on Achilles' lips. In her delusion Penthesilea is not quite deluded. When the hurtful truth is revealed, it is therefore not surprising to see that Penthesilea accepts it with relative calm, as though she had indeed known it in the semiconscious fringes of her mind all along. Although there is a pathetic tug of war between her and Achilles, each imploring the other to follow one another, she does not fall into a faint as we would expect the typical Kleistian heroine to do when outer reality suddenly proves to be the very opposite of her inner certainty. Instead, she now voices openly her wish to die:

> No! I must bury me in endless night! [13]

Then comes the nemesis, Achilles' fateful challenge, and the drama takes its appallingly savage turn. The changes of mood in that third part of the play are as extreme as can be found anywhere in dramatic literature. Penthesilea's passive resignation erupts into destructive fury. Her frustrated search for inner unity through love, most often carried out on a Platonic, metaphysical level, inverts itself into orgiastic madness. The Dionysian note was darkly sounded earlier in the play (l. 1230) when Penthesilea in a thrall of bitter disillusionment suddenly exclaimed "O Aphrodite!" When she comes to after her atrocious killing of Achilles, she lapses again into a strangely quiescent mood, and the sexual overtones of her action die away in a few somber echoes:

> So—it was a mistake. Kissing—biting—
> Where is the difference? When we truly love
> It's easy to do one when we mean the other.[14]

Then the last eruption of despair when she calls death upon herself and falls lifeless to the ground. But her last words, overwhelming in their simplicity, "Now, it is good," suggest that finally she has found inner peace, albeit in utter isolation. The drama closes on an almost religious note of inner redemption. It may be said that Penthesilea's tragically frustrated earthly love finds its fulfillment in a *Liebestod* that points beyond the phenomenal world.

The metaphysical thrust and symbolic quality of the whole play must indeed be underscored again and again, otherwise the titanic proportions of many scenes and images seem absurd and Penthesilea's love little more than maenadic fury or self-centered madness.

The impulse for an otherworldly quest is given in the very premises of the Amazon notion of love. In order to protect their State from renewed dominion by foreign oppressors, the Amazons must reduce their defeated enemies to mere ritual instruments. But in their encounter with men they not only serve the purpose of perpetuating their race; they also seek a vicarious union with their god, the protector of their personal integrity. A divine element is thus supposed to enter into their union with men. Penthesilea, more than any other Amazon, experiences the inner summons of a divinely sanctioned selfhood which she projects onto her pursuit of Achilles. Her search for ontological perfection contains its own *hybris,* for it blinds her to the limitations of the *hic et nunc,* where the divine is inevitably tainted by the earthly. Her *hybris* is followed, however, by the tragic recognition or redemptive vision that her search may lead to fulfillment only beyond death. The peacefulness of her final moments seems to augur an otherworldly perfection. Earlier, in a thrall of euphoria, she intimated that her love was indeed not of this earth when she exclaimed:

> Let my poor heart
> Like a dirt-dabbled, happy child, sink deep
> One wondrous moment in the stream of joy.
> With every splash in those exultant waves
> A stain is washed from my sad, sinful breast.
> They flee at last, the dread Eumenides;
> *I feel the approach of godlike presences*
> And I would join my voice to their happy choir.[15]

But we cannot be quite sure whether in her final mood of apparent serenity Penthesilea has "regained paradise." Kleist never gives us the comfort of such apodictic certainty. Her literally self-willed death is as ambivalent as was her life. It betokens her self-destructive fury as much as her search for fulfillment, the frustrations of earthly love as much as the promise of transcendence. If Kleist intended to suggest a religious idea of salvation, then one cannot quite ward off the feeling of a Kafkaesque paradox expressed in Penthesilea's frenzied quest: there is no god, but there must be a god. The specter of Kleist's own death arises again before our eyes. *Penthesilea* seems indeed to be his own funeral dirge.

The superhuman dimensions of the play are forcefully sustained in its imagery.[16] The most telling set of images deals with the notions of height and depth. At one point (second scene) Achilles, pursued by Penthesilea, crashes with his chariot at the edge of a precipice and nearly plunges to his death. In order to attain her prey, Penthesilea tries to scale the vertical cliff—on horseback!—only to tumble down again from her dizzying height.

> As though to deepest Tartarus she were bent,
> ....
> —And neither breaks her neck nor nothing learns,
> But only girds herself again to climb.[17]

No doubt, the incident must be viewed symbolically; a literal reading would only yield nonsense. The scene obviously presages the deathly relationship between Achilles and Penthesilea and is a dramatic visual condensation of her transcendent aspirations. Often, Achilles is associated with the sun god Helios, dwelling in unattainable heights. In the ninth scene, Penthesilea, still trembling from the defeat suffered at the hands of Achilles, talks about him and the sun as if they were one and the same:

> Too high! I know, too high!
> Far off, in flame-rings unapproachable,
> He circles sporting round my longing heart.[18]

There are also frequent references to light and dark, images that reflect the chiaroscuro of Penthesilea's inner psychological state. In fact, she herself is never bathed in light as is Achilles, but rather hovers over him like the shadow of death:

> Help! O Zeus!
> Beside him now she rides. Her shadow, see,
> Vast as a giant in the morning sun,
> Now strikes him! [19]

In one instance, her very thoughts are said to have "emerged from eternal night."

Other groups of images capture the essence of violence and passion that runs through the play. Penthesilea is likened to a panther, a "foaming-jawed hyena," a she-wolf, or lioness, while Achilles' alacrity is compared to the swiftness and strength of a Persian horse. Pictures of the chase and the harvest, reflecting Penthesilea's mad pursuit of her goal, alternate in swift succession, and elemental natural forces—thunder, lightning, torrents—erupt to suggest the intervention of the gods in the human conflict.

In general, all these images set the atmosphere and create the impression of dynamic action. But derived as they are from Greek mythology, they also attest to Kleist's fascination with the form and circumstance of Greek tragedy. In *Guiscard* he had vainly attempted to reconcile Attic and modern tragedy, and in *The Broken Pitcher* he openly acknowledged his indebtedness to *Oedipus Rex*, while the theme of *Penthesilea* allowed him to use effectively the trappings of Greek mythology. In spirit *Penthesilea* alternates between the illusion of serenity and impulsive violence. In this, the play foreshadows Nietzsche's view of Greek culture expressed in *The Birth of Tragedy*, in which the Apollonian forces of calm and restraint are seen constantly challenged by unbridled Dionysian passions.

NOTES

[1] In *Heinrich von Kleist*, München, C. H. Beck'sche Verlagsbuchhandlung, 1925.

[2] In *Heinrich von Kleist Die Geschichte seines Schaffens*, Bern, Francke Verlag, 1954.

[3] (Quotes from *Penthesilea* are taken from Humphrey Trevelyan's English version of the play (1959), contained in *The Classic Theatre*, ed. Eric Bentley, Vol. II, Doubleday Anchor, 1959.) Sembd., Vol. 2, p. 205, ll. 1430–32; Trevelyan, p. 361.

[4] Sembd., Vol. 2, p. 235, ll. 2382–91; Trevelyan, p. 394.

[5] Sembd., Vol. 2, p. 238, ll. 2457–59; Trevelyan, p. 397.

[6] Sembd., Vol. 2, p. 181, l. 680; Trevelyan, p. 336. (Trevelyan

translates, "hatred and defiance." The German *Widerspruch* can be rendered as "discord" as well as "defiance"; *Trotz* as "defiance" rather than "hatred." For the sake of meter, I have inverted the order of appearance of the two terms as compared with the German text.—R.E.H.)

7 Sembd., Vol. 2, p. 182, l. 720; Trevelyan, p. 337.

8 Sembd., Vol. 2, p. 200, ll. 1280–82; Trevelyan, p. 355.

9 Sembd., Vol. 2, p. 203, ll. 1387–88; Trevelyan, p. 359.

10 Sembd., Vol. 2, p. 214, l. 1682; Trevelyan, p. 370.

11 Sembd., Vol. 2, p. 213, ll. 1665–66; Trevelyan, p. 370.

12 Sembd., Vol. 2, p. 224, ll. 2028–32; Trevelyan, pp. 381–82.

13 Sembd., Vol. 2, p. 234, l. 2351; Trevelyan, p. 392.

14 Sembd., Vol. 2, p. 256, ll. 2981–83; Trevelyan, p. 416.

15 Sembd., Vol. 2, p. 213, ll. 1674–81; Trevelyan, p. 370.

16 A full treatment of the imagery in *Penthesilea* can be found in "The Imagery in Kleist's *Penthesilea*," by Denys Dyer in *Publications of the English Goethe Society*, Vol. 31, 1961, pp. 1–23. The few examples given here have been largely suggested by Mr. Dyer's article.

17 Sembd., Vol. 2, p. 170, ll. 327, 329–30; Trevelyan, p. 324.

18 Sembd., Vol. 2, p. 201, ll. 1341–43; Trevelyan, p. 357.

19 Sembd., Vol. 2, p. 173, ll. 418–21; Trevelyan, p. 327.

"The Kaethchen of Heilbronn"

The Kaethchen of Heilbronn, written in 1807–8 soon after the completion of *Penthesilea,* is Kleist's excursion into the land of the fairy tale. In this drama he allowed himself to dream his own dream, to find an imaginary fulfillment of his personal need for a strong, abiding feeling that would guide man unerringly toward his destiny. Kleist was very lucid about the drama's function as a wish-fulfillment dream. Shortly before his death, in a letter addressed to Marie von Kleist (May 1811), he describes a last upsurge of youthful ecstasy within him, which he likens to the rapture he had experienced in writing *The Kaethchen.* His only regret, he continues, is that he had not let himself be fully carried away by his dream vision but had listened to the advice of well-meaning friends about stagecraft, historical background, and character portrayal, which he holds responsible for some of the drama's shortcomings.

However, Kleist also introduced elements of grotesquery

and parody, which makes us surmise that he felt the need of putting himself at a certain distance from his own fantasy.[1] As a matter of fact, in his last works we can observe in Kleist a progressive detachment from his own and his hero's dream visions. In *Penthesilea*, Kleist's own involvement in his heroine's inner perceptions is still very much apparent, though (or precisely, because) her dream world is shattered, conjuring up the kind of tragedy which mirrors Kleist's own suffering. *The Kaethchen* is Kleist's dream vision, but the slight hint of personal detachment contained in its grotesqueries points toward significant developments in his last two great works. In "Michael Kohlhaas," the "Gypsy episode," introduced somewhat belatedly in the story, is one of Kleist's own dream fantasies, but its meaning is obscured by many ambiguities; while in *The Prince of Homburg*, Kleist is capable of so much distance from his hero's somnambulistic fancies that Homburg is at first an almost comic figure, though at the end of the play his subjectivity, after it has undergone a catharsis, is exonerated. As he journeyed toward his own death, Kleist treated the difficulty of reconciling subjective visions and objective realities with increasing subtlety and detachment, even though he never fully relinquished his unfulfilled hopes for the ultimate triumph of man's subjective nature.

Contained in a letter to the publisher von Collin (December 8, 1808) is Kleist's famous statement to the effect that *The Kaethchen* and *Penthesilea* belong together like the plus and the minus in algebra. What he meant to suggest is obviously the fact that the two dramas are opposite expressions of the same "magnitude"—absolute commitment to an inner summons—which in Penthesilea produces her destructive fury and in Kaethchen her winning forbearance. Though Penthesilea and Kaethchen have much in common, the worlds they live in are diametric opposites affecting them in vastly different ways. They both experience the reality of the "other," their beloved, through a predetermined inner vision. Their love does not spring suddenly from an unexpected encounter but rather from the fact that the beloved corresponds to an already formed inner image of him. In this sense, the "other" is but an extension of their own inner consciousness. They have known of the impending encounter all along. Penthesilea trusts Otrera's prophecy about her love for Achilles, and Kaethchen can rely on a dream vision in which the man she will love, Count Wetter vom Strahl, appeared to her. And for both, their love is not an end in itself. It is a means through which they can experience the fullness of their own being. (Kleist had vainly tried to attain such self-fulfillment in his relationship with Wilhelmine von Zenge.) Existentially, their love is self-centered. It is as much a longing for absolute personal fulfillment as a devotion to the other person. Dramatically, this is evident in the fact that their counterparts, Achilles and vom Strahl, are practically absorbed by their own—i.e., Penthesilea's and Kaethchen's—strong feelings and, at times, seem to be mere appurtenances of their consciousness. This does not mean that Kaethchen and Penthesilea are not capable of "giving," especially Kaethchen, whose self-effacement seems almost pathological, when compared with the peremptory demands of Penthesilea's Amazon nature. But for both, what is at stake is the ultimate meaning of their human existence. Kaethchen finds it in her extreme submissiveness; Penthesilea attempts to find it in her active conquest of Achilles, only to discover it in her lonely death. It is Kaethchen's great fortune—a fate Kleist dreamed of for himself—that her inner vision is actually the expression of a higher reality, a Platonic-Christian realm of truth pervading the sensory world and revealing itself in supernatural manifestations which assure Kaethchen's happiness on earth. Penthesilea's aspirations, on the other hand, are cruelly thwarted by the world of the senses and lead to her tragic death.

Kaethchen, a girl of common birth, inexplicably sacrifices herself in unflagging service to a young nobleman, Count Wetter vom Strahl, who does not want her devotion. Reprimanded and threatened by everyone, including the Count, she can only rely on a strong inner conviction that she must do what she does. In various actions which involve, among others, vom Strahl's scheming bride-to-be Kunigunde, we soon realize that Kaethchen enjoys the special protection of heavenly powers, who intervene on her behalf directly and indirectly at critical moments. We gradually discover how it had been prophesied to her that she would marry a certain knight who, accompanied by an angel, actually appeared to her in a dream. When it is disclosed that Count Wetter vom Strahl had had the same vision the same night, we realize that the marriage between the two had already been made in heaven. All that is needed for their happiness on earth is the removal of some social barriers. In due course, we learn that Kaethchen is actually of noble birth, an offspring, though illegitimate, of the Emperor himself. She is made Princess of Swabia, and the marriage, divinely decreed, is celebrated on earth.

Even a skeletal outline of the plot shows how in this drama the visionary and supernatural bring about a unity between inner and outer world. Wieland's theories of otherworldly affinities guiding the human search for happiness in this life, described in his *Sympathien,* and G. H. Schubert's [2] theories on the lucidity of human perceptions in somnambulistic states provided Kleist with a matrix for his own dream. Kaethchen's inner summons is the expression of a supernatural calling, and in act four, scene two, (the "elderbush scene") she recounts to vom Strahl, while in a somnambulistic trance, the dream that directs her actions. Although the dream turns out to be no mere fantasy, since it mysteriously parallels vom Strahl's own vision, Kaethchen could not fully recall it or grasp its significance in a waking state. The truth is concealed in the darker regions of consciousness and can be dredged up only through an inner vision made possible by a kind of self-hypnosis. Were it not for some of its occult qualities—the simultaneous occurrence of the same dream in two persons destined for each other—the whole episode would disclose therapeutic insights of a rather modern sort.

Related to Kleist's romantic version of "depth psychology" are certain bits of dialogue where the truth of inner states of mind is revealed on a semiconscious and pantomimic rather than fully articulated plane. Although this has to do with Kleist's sense of extraverbal communication, the ensuing psycholinguistic insights are no doubt germane to the pathology of dreams. At one point, vom Strahl, angered by Kaethchen's pursuit of him, reaches for his whip and threatens her. But then his feelings change to tenderness and, espying the whip in a near hypnotic trance, he exclaims:

> What means this horse-whip here?
> . . . .
> Have I a pack of dogs here, needing scourging? [3]

The act of repression has done its job, and the more dialogue and action become incongruous, the more his true feelings —the characteristic ambiguities of love—are unveiled. The analytically minded will be tempted to read sadomasochistic tendencies into such scenes and in this instance perhaps invoke Nietzsche's notorious saying: "You are going to women? Don't forget your whip." [4] At least we are justified in saying that Kleist's dream vision is punctuated with jarring psychological accents, which, however, may be attributed to the parodistic tendencies we can detect in the play.

As in all of his dramas, Kleist introduces "eloquent objects" that add momentum to the action. As we would expect, in Kaethchen's fairy-tale world they do not confuse reality but rather confute the misconceptions about her social status. The Emperor learns of a medallion in her possession which he had given to her mother after his gallant adventure years before. There is also a birthmark on the nape of her neck which vom Strahl, since his dream vision, associates with the Emperor's daughter and discovers on Kaethchen in the "elderbush scene." The realist in Kleist knew that if dreams are to become "truth" the sensory world must be made to conform with the inner vision.

But the drama is not without the typical Kleistian elements of disillusionment and deception, though, in keeping with the nature of a fairy tale, Kleist stops short of their possible tragic or near tragic implications. When Count vom Strahl comes to realize that what he had taken for the genuine inner and outer beauty of Kunigunde is but artifice, he is greatly disturbed by the ease with which he fell prey to deceptive appearances:

> Now, Thou Almighty Heaven, this soul of mine,
> It is not worthy to be called a soul!
> The scale is false by which it measures things
> That earth puts up at auction. Hideous evil
> Is what I bought instead of gentle splendor!
> Wretch! whither shall I fly to flee myself? [5]

While his momentary dismay does not have the depth of Alkmene's sorrow, it belongs to the same category of unsettling inner experiences. And Kunigunde's artfulness in using cosmetics and other beauty aids to conceal her hideous physical appearance partakes of the grotesque. It elicits our cynical guffaws, which, however, soon congeal into embarrassed silence. Her person, as one of her former disabused suitors remarks, is a combination of all sorts of foreign parts:

> . . . She is a piece of mosaic, put together from all the three kingdoms of nature. Her teeth belong to a girl in Munich, her hair was ordered from France, the healthy glow of her cheeks comes from the mines of Hungary, and the graceful figure which you admire in her she owes to a shirt that a smith made for her out of Swedish steel. Do you understand? [6]

With a stretch of the imagination we can visualize her as a grotesque, surrealistic jumble of heterogeneous objects that somehow suggests a human form. In portraying her, Kleist went beyond mere caricature or comic exaggeration but indulged in the kind of parodistic distortion which produces, visually at least, a grotesque effect. She may not be the embodiment of an unknown "It," an alien, even diabolic, world threatening our own.[7] But she is certainly more than a necessary figure in a traditional love triangle. She is also a grotesque symbol of the world's radical deceptiveness, which clouds the senses and attacks the perceptions of the heart and the intellect. In a drama in which Kleist let his positive imagination roam freely in a realm of dreams he could also assign, with relative impunity, the whole mendacity of the world to a nightmarish, sybilline creature. The man of action, which is Wetter vom Strahl—and at times he seems to be capable of little else—watches Kunigunde's world of deception with naïve horror. But he recovers quickly from the shock and is soon caught up again in Kaethchen's world of light. In accord with the happy mood of the play Strahl's glimpse of grotesque chaos is but a furtive appearance.

We find a less ominous parody in Kleist's excessive use of the trappings of the traditional *Ritterschauspiel*—a drama of chivalry—a rather questionable mixture of fashionable ingredients, such as knights, angels, spirits, and witches, a

Vehmic Court,[8] the difference in social status of the two lovers, the long-hidden noble birth of Kaethchen, a cuckolded father happy to have reared the daughter of an emperor, and the black-and-white texture of the whole drama. Although some of these elements may have been suggested to him by his friends, it is as though Kleist indulged in a clearsighted, if tongue-in-cheek, parody of his own frustrated dreams. Only in such an unreal world as is portrayed in *Kaethchen*, he seems to suggest, could his cult of inner assurance and self-fulfillment flourish. But despite his copious use of devices that suggest parody, Kleist succeeded in giving us a tender portrayal of a young girl in search of her destiny with nothing to support her but her inner visions, whose ultimate significance she never fully grasps but nevertheless firmly believes in.

NOTES

[1] The French adaptation of the play, *L'Ordalie ou la petite Catherine de Heilbronn*, done by Jean Anouilh and premièred on September 30, 1966, in the Theatre Montparnasse-Gaston Baty, gave rise to considerable controversy. Jean Dutourd reproached Anouilh for having emphasized the "comic" aspects of the drama, while Gabriel Marcel insisted that the denounced "grotesqueries" effectively recreated the spirit of the original.

[2] G. H. Schubert, a contemporary of Kleist in Dresden, became famous for his lectures and treatises on the "Nocturnal Aspect of the Natural Sciences," which contained theories on somnambulism much in vogue at the time. In addition to Schubert and Wieland, the drama may owe something to Goethe's *Goetz of Berlichingen* (the Vehmic Court scene) and perhaps also to German adaptations of English folk ballads, such as "Child Waters" done by Bürger and von Eschenburg.

[3] Sembd., Vol. 3, p. 64, ll. 1841 and 1843, act three, scene six, p. 305 in F. E. Pierce's translation of *The Kaethchen of Heilbronn*, in *Fiction and Fantasy of German Romance: Selections from the German Romantic Authors, 1790–1830, in English Translation*, New York, Oxford University Press, 1927.

[4] Friedrich Nietzsche in *Thus Spake Zarathustra*, "About Little Old and Young Women."

⁵ Sembd., Vol. 3, pp. 94–95, ll. 2993–98, act five, scene six; Pierce, p. 335.

⁶ Sembd., ibid., p. 93, ll. 2563–71, act five, scene three; Pierce, pp. 333–34. The play is a mixture of prose and poetry. But Kleist is careful in using poetry exclusively in the dialogues between Kaethchen and vom Strahl.

⁷ A reference is made here to Wolfgang Kayser's theories of the grotesque expounded in *The Grotesque in Art and Literature,* wherein he stresses the irruption of an unknown "It," an alien, chaotic world, into our own, which is presumably encapsulated in the grotesque structures found in certain forms of art and literature.

⁸ The play opens with a Vehmic Court scene in which Theobald Friedeborn, Kaethchen's father, accuses Count Wetter vom Strahl of witchcraft in having put a spell on his daughter. Vehmic Courts —*Vehmgerichte* in German—were institutions executing rough popular justice, or what was thought to be justice, which flourished in times of unsettled political conditions or threatened anarchy. The practice was known in Germany from 1150 to 1568 and was especially widespread in Westphalia (Heilbronn, however, is in Swabia).

The "Patriotic" Outburst

"The Battle of Arminius"

This drama, based on the battle of the Teutoburger Wald in 9 A.D., in which the Germanic tribes turned the tide of Roman aggression, is ostensibly a polemic written against Napoleon. It no doubt grew out of Kleist's patriotic mood. But the time of its inception and some peculiar features in its chief characters, plot, and diction make it as much another way station in Kleist's spiritual autobiography as a mere patriotic outburst. *The Battle of Arminius* transcends its historical confines and points toward Kleist's own metaphysical aspirations. It may not only be the fear of political repression that made the drama unpalatable to his contemporaries but also, and in no less degree, some of the pathological excesses of human emotions which Kleist allowed himself to portray in it.

As early as 1801 there is ample evidence in his letters that Kleist held no brief for Napoleon. But even after Prussia's collapse in 1806 and during his imprisonment in France, Kleist's animosity toward the conqueror did not erupt into invective or open rebellion. Prussia's defeat in 1806 coincided with his own resignation from government service and his renewed decision to live exclusively for his literary calling. In Dresden he became entirely absorbed in his personal plans and literary ambitions, above all in the *Phoebus* project. He even had reasons to hope that he would be commissioned to publish the *Code Napoléon* in German. In August 1808, writing to Ulrike, he deplores the fact that the turn of political events will ruin his peaceful activities as a writer and publisher. When all his plans failed and at the same time a new national sentiment was awakened in Prussia and Austria, Kleist's own aspirations found a vicarious outlet in the widespread hope for liberation from the foreign yoke. At this point, Kleist needed a concrete goal to give meaning to his life. The visible plight of Germany moved him more than any abstract notion could, such as the idea of history and its ultimate goal that so preoccupied the speculative minds of his friend Adam Müller as well as Fichte and Hegel. He apparently wrote *The Battle of Arminius* in a state of extreme excitement and, as was his habit, overstated the case for his hero in the direction of his own vision of human destiny.

Kleist's Arminius is as much a metaphysical rebel as a national liberator. In his delirious self-affirmation he revolts as much against human bondage as against the power of the Romans. He is not bent on territorial conquest, the prospect of overlordship in Germany is of no moment to him. On the contrary, he is willing to give up all his possessions, even his sons, if only he be allowed to triumph over the enemy in a "free" death. And the enemy is not only around but also within him—the doubts that threaten to enslave him by disturbing the certainty of his inner feeling. He will hear nothing of the generosity and human worth of some Romans, for it would weaken his single-minded resolve. "Do not confuse my feeling," he exclaims at one point when his allies entreat him to let clemency prevail toward a truly noble Roman. Arminius seeks his own personal destiny, even if it be in death, which he invites. The liberation of his country is but the outward sign of his inner quest. He wants to affirm himself, "bound to no one but my own God," in a lonely search for his ultimate destiny.

The basic plot of *The Battle of Arminius* is relatively simple. But in addition to Arminius' ambivalent character, the play contains some strange episodic materials, a humane representative of Roman might in the person of Varus, cryptic political utterances by the hero, as well as a puzzling motto by Kleist himself—elements that cannot be ignored in the interpretation of the drama.

Arminius, using all the wiles at his disposal, succeeds in welding the warring Germanic tribes into a loose amphictyony to repulse the advancing Romans. In a clandestine message to Marbod, his rival for supremacy in Germany, he promises to yield the crown to him if he joins with him, Arminius, in the fight against the invaders. As a token of his sincerity he leaves his two adolescent sons with Marbod as hostages. Marbod, impressed by Arminius' daring gamble, enters into a secret military union with him and the other German princes. Under a treaty with Arminius, the Roman legions, led by Varus and unaware of Arminius' secret dealings, enter his lands with the express purpose of aiding him in his fight against Marbod. But they are lured into the morass of the Teutoburger Wald, where in the dark of night they are crushed from all sides by the combined forces of the Germans. In the final scene, the unification of the German lands under an elected ruler is foretold, and Arminius at Marbod's suggestion is made temporary overlord.

Kleist enlarges the basic historical plot of the destruction of Varus' army with episodic material of a gruesome kind which many Kleist critics would he had left unwritten. There is Hally, a girl raped by a Roman soldier and killed by her own father to save her from living forever in shame, whose body, at Arminius' behest, is hacked up and sent to all the German tribes to arouse their wrath at Roman iniquity. Worse, perhaps, is the episode depicting the death of the Roman legate, Ventidius. Having become enamored with Thusnelda, Arminius' wife, he incurred her implacable hatred with a frivolous joke he played on her. Under false pretenses he snipped a lock from her blonde hair and sent it to the Roman Empress with the vague promise that upon the ultimate defeat of the Germans at the hands of the Romans, Thusnelda's hair might be shorn and, as a wig, adorn the Empress's head. Thusnelda lures him into a pit and watches in horrified glee how he is mauled to death by a hungry she-bear. Though after her ferocious deed she falls into a fit of near madness, we cannot absolve her as we could Penthesilea, since her feelings for Ventidius were hardly more enduring than his for her. In fact, both she and Arminius have no scruples in exploiting the attraction she exerts on Ventidius for the purpose of lulling the Roman officials into a false sense of security.

Arminius puts on the mask of duplicity seemingly without any moral compunctions. Nothing can deflect him from his way, his *dike* or "justice." However, in the light of Kleist's metaphysical preoccupations it is questionable whether the play is an apologia for political expedience committed in the name of the country. We may come closer to the truth if we see in Arminius' dissimulations an inverted expression of Kleist's peculiar sensitivity to the deceitfulness of the world. Arminius acts toward the world as the world is wont to act toward man—amorally and deceptively. Hence in his "patriotic" play, the usual roles of hero and world are inverted. While in most other works, the world is radically deceptive, here it is the hero who deceives the world and achieves his purpose.

Several Kleist interpreters have rightly pointed out that Arminius does not have a real antagonist in the play. His military counterpart, Varus, is drawn with peculiarly sympathetic strokes. If he is the picture of the ruthless conqueror, then Kleist would have harbored particularly generous feelings toward Napoleon, which we can hardly assume. On the other hand, Varus, if the play is to be interpreted as a *drame à clef,* could be the literary counterpart of some French commander such as General Clarke, the French governor of Berlin, through whose offices Kleist was finally released from imprisonment in France in 1807. In that case, Napoleon's correlate in the play would be the Emperor Augustus, who is not directly inserted in the action. No matter whether such analogies are pertinent or not, Varus is portrayed as urbane, firm, and endowed with a tragic sense of life which makes him face death with courage but also with a feeling of loathing for Arminius' truculence. Kleist obviously could not condemn a man whose destiny mirrored the fate of man in general. His latent sympathy for the unwitting victims of a deceptive world is responsible for the human warmth that irradiates Varus' character, while there is seemingly a streak of cynicism in his portrayal of Arminius.

But the apparent cynicism may not stem solely from Kleist's awareness of the radical deceptiveness of the world. It may in equal measure be due to his candid recognition that a national liberator, not unlike Machiavelli's "ideal" Prince, would have to be cunning, ruthless, and not afraid of dirtying his hands if he were to achieve his goal. In contrast to the Swiss in Schiller's *William Tell,* who are idealized as a "people of brothers," a family held together by the law of love, Kleist saw his Teutons as so many quarreling "hordes"—in his stage directions he does not even accord them the more civilized name of "tribes." By implication, Kleist seems to look askance at the Rousseauist idealization of man's prepolitical state. He may perhaps be suggesting that although the achievement of statehood is admittedly a *sine qua non* in man's journey toward civilization, it will not occur without laying bare man's bestiality. In that case one can hardly maintain that he extols the State as a *ne plus ultra* which automatically bestows a moral sanction on Arminius' guile. Though always in quest of certainties or absolutes, Kleist also queried them, only to acknowledge that none were to be had except in death. The State is no exception. Hence Arminius' distinct longing for death which he utters in the midst of his political scheming:

> If only when my time has come
> on a landmark 'neath the shady oaktree
> surrounded by the last of friends
> I am allowed to die a hero [1]

The realist in Kleist knew that the political and moral are often separated by a deep chasm. And if he portrayed political reality it does not mean that he postulated it as an ideal. Behind the struggle for national independence, Kleist envisaged, ever so furtively, the transcendent idea of a world government reminiscent of Kant's central notion in *Eternal Peace,* a dim hope which he puts in the mouth of Arminius himself:

If ever be the songs of bards fulfilled
and mankind held together by one royal scepter,
a German could fulfill the task,
a Briton, Gaul, or what you will

. . . .

Eventually it will come to this [2]

This unworldly idea leaves Arminius' peers blinking in disbelief, not unlike Zarathustra's audience in the prologue to
Nietzsche's work, and has no less puzzled some of Kleist's
interpreters who find it incompatible with the seemingly fierce
nationalist thrust of the play. The author obviously intends
to create in the audience the same critical distance from the
political machinations of his hero as he himself is capable
of. He is not asking us essentially to condition ourselves to
the brutal shocks he must deal out but to see clearly the rift
between ideal and reality. His "ideal" audience does not consist of storm troopers but thinking men distraught over the
political realities they must witness. In this light, the distich
Kleist puts as a motto at the beginning of his play takes on
ominous significance:

Woe unto you, my Fatherland! Though faithful in my poet's
heart to you, I'm not allowed to strike my lyre in your praise.[3]

To a degree, the vague hope for an ultimate world government uttered by Arminius exonerates him as a hero. He at
least has a vision which transcends the grim necessities of
the moment. In his own way, he is both "upright and terrible" to the extreme, as is Michael Kohlhaas. And when he
calls the best among the Romans the "worst," he may express more than mere apprehension that their magnanimity
could slacken the zeal of his Germans. He may indeed express the insight that the political supremacy of the enemy
is not necessarily based on moral superiority. Political and
military success may be morally undeserved and the magnanimity of the conqueror toward the victim cringing at his feet
too facile a virtue to detract from the Germans' struggle for
freedom. Behind the obfuscations of his words and actions,
Arminius may see clearly the deeper issues at stake.

The recognition of Arminius' less heinous personal motives
can also throw light on the symbolic meaning of the Thusnelda episode, a significance which it obviously has. Drama-

turgically the episode is extraneous, at best parallel, to the principal action. It does not influence or alter the course of the main events. But it puts into sharp relief the political problem. Significantly, Thusnelda does not battle for her children, as a mother would, when they are offered as hostages in a political gambit. Kleist does not pursue this motif which in itself could yield the stuff for absorbing drama highlighting the conflict between the private and political spheres of life and would no doubt invest the title action with a new element. In one short and rather incongruous scene, Kleist has Thusnelda ask for her two sons, who never appear, and from there on she acts as though they did not exist. We never see her in company of her children, and she never again mentions them with a word, let alone pines over their absence. Kleist rather has her assume a public role, even a cosmopolitan stance, when he lets her plead for clemency toward Ventidius, whom she trusts as a human being, Roman or not. When her trust is made light of by the very man she meant to save, she rails as much at her own illusions as at his betrayal. She turns, by proxy, into a murderous she-bear. Her descent into bestiality is a symbolic re-enactment of man's animal nature in war.

Kleist, more so than Fichte, the Schlegels, and Goethe, knew something of the brutal craft of war and even seemed to anticipate the moral dilemmas of modern guerrilla tactics engulfing the whole population, which can hardly be embellished with patriotic sentiments. In the same vein of thought, the Hally episode is a chilling parody of the grandiose type of patriotism. Traditionally, the motif of the princess violated by an enemy soldier calls for her noble, even self-willed death, as for instance in *Appius and Verginia,* the *Rape of Lucrece* and, immediately before Kleist's play, Wieland's fragment of an *Arminius* epic (which Kleist may or may not have known). Hally, however, a mute victim incapable of expressing in lofty hexameters grief over her lost virginity, as does Wieland's heroine, is literally butchered. She does not collapse in a tragic gesture but merely "keels over," whereupon her body is mutilated and grotesquely displayed to kindle hatred among the Germans about the supposed Roman atrocities. Some contemporary theorists of the grotesque, which plays such an important role again in twentieth-century literature, insist that the definition of the term must be restricted to the human sphere and applied when man through force of circumstance has become dehumanized, his body turned into a mere thing (as for instance corpses piled up in concentration camps awaiting transformation into chemical products or the dried skin of a body crushed by tanks, which finds a new use as a banner for a group of partisans [4]). Kleist seems to anticipate such morbid phenomena. Nevertheless the Hally episode, parody or not, is fraught with pathological elements hardly exonerated by literary parallels.

The Battle of Arminius is not Kleist's best effort. Thusnelda, a combination of huntress, seductress, intriguer, mother, and submissive wife, adorned with blue eyes and blonde Germanic locks, is not the kind of pure heroine we encounter in most of Kleist's works. Although he tried to endow her with traits of ingenuousness and unspoiled, natural grace, the attempt failed. Seductive wiles, even if they can be explained away with reference to Arminius' political gambit, are hardly compatible with Kleist's ideal of womanhood. Besides, the Ventidius and Hally episodes have sadomasochistic overtones that detract from their symbolic function. There are redeeming features, such as the metaphysical thrust in the hero and his cosmopolitan ideal, however timidly expressed, which transcend the crude realities of the day he must deal with. Kleist's obvious awareness of the radical immorality of war could potentially attenuate the pathological excesses he portrays. But it is couched in a symbolic superstructure that does not translate itself into the dramatic impact of the play. In its immediacy the drama comes dangerously close to a patriotic tract glorifying the State as a moral absolute. It is only in "Michael Kohlhaas" and eventually in *The Prince of Homburg* that Kleist was able to find more viable artistic metaphors to portray the role of the State in man's destiny.

NOTES

[1] Sembd., Vol. 3, p. 133, ll. 357–60. (To my knowledge, no English translations exist of *Die Hermannsschlacht*. The few translations

given in this chapter are my own. They merely attempt to render the spirit and meaning, but not the meter, of the original lines.— R.E.H.)

[2] *Ibid.*, ll. 308–10 and 315.

[3] *Ibid.*, p. 123.

[4] See, for instance, Arnold Heidsieck, *Das Groteske und das Absurde im Modernen Drama*, Stuttgart, 1969.

The Search for Justice

"Michael Kohlhaas"

While *Penthesilea* sums up earlier tendencies in Kleist's works, it also marks the point of a new departure. Penthesilea combines Guiscard's strength of will with Alkmene's depth of feeling. But in the treatment of Penthesilea's character new insights into the wellsprings of human actions are revealed that add a psychoanalytic dimension to the play. Penthesilea's death wish causes a severe inner schism which may be as responsible for her tragic errors as are the deceptive appearances of the outside world. By contrast, the counterpart of *Penthesilea, The Kaethchen of Heilbronn,* in which happiness ensues from the unassailable inner unity of the heroine, is essentially a fairy tale. Further, in *Penthesilea* the severe conflict between the individual and the State that becomes the dramatic focus in "Michael Kohlhaas" and *The Prince of Homburg* announces itself at least as a subsidiary theme. As a result of the author's sharpened vision of man's divided self, Kleist's last two works deal with the dramatic tension between the individual and the State from the vantage point of an individualistic sense of justice which exhibits as many ambiguities as Penthesilea's inner world. In keeping with the artistic canons of the *Novelle*, however, Kohlhaas's inner struggles are not directly revealed in dialogue but only sketched in bold descriptive strokes or intimated in his erratic actions. To compound the problematic character of the individual's sense of justice (*Rechtsgefühl*), the objective reality with which it clashes, namely the State's jurisdiction, is highly equivocal in itself. Hence, the solution of the conflict seems to be a precarious legalistic compromise, were it not for a supernatural element, introduced in an *ad hoc* fashion, that tips the balance rather in favor of Kohlhaas's individualistic self-assertion. In the process, Kleist gives an agonizing and searching appraisal of the problem of justice in a chaotic world. The ultimate impression we gain from the complex *Novelle* is that of a world pervaded by bureaucratic indifference and anonymous injustice unleashing the demons of fear, resentment, and personal violence—a quite modern theme.

The *Novelle* went through an arduous process of development, which accounts for its length and complicated plot that severely tax the traditionally terse form of the genre. It was probably begun in 1805 when Kleist was a Prussian government employee. A fragment was published in 1808 in Kleist's ill-starred *Phoebus,* but the finished product appeared only in 1810 in the first volume of his *Erzählungen.* Compared with the fragment, the final version contains many changes and additions. The action is set more definitely in history—place, time, and persons are clearly identified—although its historical authenticity is minimal. (Kleist had worked on his idea of the topic before he consulted the relevant historical source, a sixteenth-century chronicle written by Peter Hafftiz.) In concept, the *Novelle* turned out far broader than the fragment lets us surmise. It is no longer a mere moral tale after the manner of Boccaccio but embodies some of the epic dimensions of an historical novel. At times, the background threatens to engulf the foreground material. Finally, the introduction of a new motif with the Gypsy episode shifts the focus of the action toward supernatural happenings that evoke their own train of metaphysical echoes.

The Gypsy incident creates the impression of an afterthought —it is narrated primarily in flashbacks—but it is not necessarily a foreign body in the *Novelle*'s texture, though admittedly it changes the original direction of the plot.

Michael Kohlhaas is a prosperous and respected horse dealer living in Brandenburg and owning some property in Dresden, the capital of Saxony. One day as he is taking some horses to market, he is harassed by the henchmen of a certain Junker von Tronka with some unheard-of transit formalities which he is not prepared to meet. Leaving a team of horses behind as security under the supervision of a faithful servant, Herse, Kohlhaas undertakes to clear the matter with Saxon authorities. But he is treated as a thin-skinned troublemaker, and his appeal is summarily rejected by various magistrates in both Saxony and Brandenburg. Meanwhile, his servant and the horses have been cruelly mistreated on Tronka's lands. As he prepares to take the law into his own hands, Kohlhaas's loyal wife, Elisabeth, attempts to intervene in his behalf through a personal audience before the ruler of Brandenburg. There she is accidentally wounded by a guard and dies without having accomplished her mission.

Kohlhaas now embarks upon violent revenge. In search of the elusive Junker, he burns down the latter's castle, assembles a band of marauders, and ravages the Saxon countryside. The erstwhile righteous citizen has become the scourge of the country and sees himself as a representative of the Archangel Michael on earth, called upon to restore justice in the world. Only Martin Luther's intervention prevents further bloodshed. In a dramatic interview, Luther chastises Kohlhaas for his wantonness but, convinced of the legality of his demands, promises to help him. Through his influence, the Elector of Saxony grants Kohlhaas safe passage to Dresden to defend his cause in court and gives him a rather ambiguous promise of amnesty for his past deeds. As "fate" would have it, Kohlhaas becomes implicated in events that are not of his doing, an act of mob violence on a public square and a plot hatched by one of his former henchmen, Nagelschmidt, a scoundrel and derelict. Kohlhaas is sentenced to be tortured and quartered. But the Brandenburg authorities intervene, he is extradited to Berlin, and his case referred to the Imperial Court. Ultimately, he is condemned to die on the scaffold, while Tronka receives a prison term and is forced to restore Kohlhaas's horses to their former health and to pay indemnities. However, this is not made known until we have learned of a new and surprising development involving Kohlhaas and the Elector of Saxony personally.

On the day after Elisabeth's death, Kohlhaas happened to be present at festivities given in honor of the Electors of Brandenburg and Saxony in a border town. An old Gypsy woman bearing a surprising resemblance to Kohlhaas's dead wife was plying her trade as a soothsayer when all three men, Kohlhaas and the two princes, chanced upon her. She predicted future happiness for the House of Brandenburg but wrote down an apparently sinister prophecy about the House of Saxony's future, which she handed not to the Saxon ruler but to Kohlhaas, who quickly disappeared in the crowd. Later on, as Kohlhaas is being transferred to Brandenburg, the Elector detects by chance a mysterious capsule around the captive's neck. When he learns how it got there and that it contains the Gypsy's prophecy, he faints and subsequently becomes subject to a nervous illness. He deploys many wiles to delay Kohlhaas's trial in Brandenburg in order to gain possession of the capsule, even promising him life and liberty in exchange for it. But his attempts are foiled, largely by the reappearing Gypsy woman who warns Kohlhaas of the Elector's designs, especially in a last note mysteriously signed "Lisbeth." As Kohlhaas steps up to the scaffold, he triumphantly swallows the paper contained in the capsule under the incredulous gaze of the Saxon Elector, who is standing incognito in the waiting crowd. After the execution, the Elector lingers on in a life of frustration and sickness, while Kohlhaas's two sons are to be knighted in recognition of their father's desperate fight for justice.

The story is not so much concerned with the problem of _who_ is right and _who_ is wrong in the struggle between Kohlhaas and Tronka as it is with the difficulty of establishing generally _what_ is right and _what_ is wrong. Its universal appeal stems precisely from the many ambiguities Kleist puts into Kohlhaas's own motives and those of his antagonists. The plot does not simply revolve around an unusual event encapsulating a neat morality lesson, though the central legal dispute over the team of horses, unusual in its dire consequences, is not lost sight of. The story poses the problem of the possibility or impossibility of absolute justice in the world and presents the conflict *per se* rather than a pat solution.

There is an absolutist urge in Kohlhaas which, however, is tinged with many impurities. His sense of justice is keen, but it is contaminated by a need for personal revenge and by an innate streak of vanity in his character. For a long time, Kohlhaas suffers from an unclarity of purpose in his own mind with regard to his battle for justice. He is not fully aware whether he is fighting for his own or a universal right. There are indications early in the story that he is indeed as much interested in restoring order for others as for himself. But after hearing of Herse's mistreatment at the hands of Tronka's servants, he wants to "claim public justice for himself," Kleist tells us rather ambiguously. At times, it is not even clear whether Kohlhaas knows if he is rebelling against the moral obtuseness of a Junker and his cohorts or, more generally, against the blatant injustices and undeserved suffering sanctioned by the world order itself. It is upon the death of his wife that Kohlhaas unleashes his cruel revenge against Tronka. But her death was admittedly due to the action of an overzealous guard—to "police brutality"—and not to the machinations of his antagonists. Lisbeth is a victim of those baleful chance happenings that are man's fate, she is not martyred by the callous injustice of Kohlhaas's personal enemies. The pathetic episode of his wife's death serves to lift Kohlhaas's revolt to a metaphysical level. This is made amply clear in subsequent events, though it may not be clear in his own mind. The immensity of his revolt is precisely the reason why his mind is in danger of snapping. Kleist knows that it is not far from a sense of setting things aright to messianic pretense. He lets Kohlhaas's longing for universal justice reach megalomaniac, even paranoid, proportions. Kohlhaas proclaims himself

"a viceroy of the Archangel Michael, come to punish with fire and sword, for the wickedness into which the whole world was sunk, all those who should take the side of the Junker in this quarrel." [1]

Ostensibly bent upon restoring order in the world he surrounds himself with grandiose pomp. This is the kind of parody which would not need the direct author interference Kleist allows himself freely in this story. He suggests that Kohlhaas suffers from a peculiar *Verrückung*, madness. In German, the pejorative *Verrückung* is etymologically close to the mystic *Entrückung*, transfiguration. Irony ensues, for Kohlhaas has, in fact, been transfigured but rather in the sense of grotesque distortion. In addition, the plot hatched by Nagelschmidt, Kohlhaas's sidekick, who turns out to be the immediate cause of his downfall, represents another travesty of Kohlhaas's sense of justice.

The heavens seem to share Kleist's insights into Kohlhaas's disturbed soul. They usually respond negatively, though never clearly, to Kohlhaas's challenge. At least, they emit angry warning signals at his excesses and at times foil his destructive urge. When he is about to lay low a convent, a "huge lightning bolt" strikes the ground he treads on and a sudden gush of heavy rain thwarts his incendiary designs. Again, when he sets fire to Leipzig a timely rain "which fell from heaven" prevents excessive damage. But, conversely, upon setting Wittenberg in flames a third time, a gusty wind helps Kohlhaas to burn down the city. The heavens are as ambiguous in their utterings as are Kohlhaas's motives in his fight for justice.

Paradoxically, Kohlhaas becomes more atrocious as he becomes seemingly more convinced of his own righteousness. It is as if he had to drown gnawing doubts in excessive bloodshed. We are not astonished, therefore, to see him blush and nervously fiddle with his helmet as he reads Luther's polemic mandate—a subtle artistic device for suggesting his inner disarray which Kleist makes more explicit when he quickly explains that Kohlhaas felt suddenly disarmed by a sense of total depravity. Kohlhaas is indeed "one of the most upright and at the same time one of the most terrible men of his day," as Kleist puts it in the famous opening phrase of the *Novelle*. And in moments of great stress Kohlhaas seems to be aware of the inner schism.

However, the ambiguities do not lie with Kohlhaas alone. They are found throughout the supposedly "objective" reality around him. This reality is neither unequivocally good nor bad. Kohlhaas's principal antagonist in the legal dispute over the horses, Junker von Tronka, is no melodramatic villain.

When, upon his first encounter with Kohlhaas, he lets his warden and steward do as they please with their quarry, he does not actively participate in their wrongdoing. He is rather inconvenienced by Kohlhaas's stubbornness. As he stands obliquely against the inclement weather and, shivering, wraps the skirts of his doublet around his frail body, he is more eager to regain the comfort of his private chambers than to solve a legal or moral problem. No doubt he is unprincipled but not actively villainous. He is rather the kind of weak and self-indulgent individual who may cause as much misery in the world as evangelic zealots or outright scoundrels. In his moral inertia he resembles the proverbial *Biedermann,* or Philistine, who is so effectively satirized in Max Frisch's *The Firebugs.* Even Tronka's wily cousins, Kunz and Hinz, show nothing but loathing for him, and Kleist takes care in removing the full burden of guilt from his person. When he is brought to reckoning at Dresden during the amnesty declared for Kohlhaas, we learn that the horses had been misused in the fields without his knowledge or express orders. Kleist withholds this information about the Junker's relative innocence deliberately, as though to suggest that the burden of responsibility rests as much on a series of unfortunate circumstances—the fragile constitution of the world—as on one man.

In fact, chance happenings play a considerable role in Kohlhaas's destiny. The riot on the public square in Dresden is a spontaneous expression of popular sentiment and in no way incited by Kohlhaas himself but comes to be linked with his name. Nagelschmidt, the knavish criminal, makes his move at a most dangerous moment. The stomach cramps which afflict his messenger, and subsequently allow Kohlhaas's enemies to discover and implicate him in Nagelschmidt's plot, are a somewhat theatrical contrivance to deliver the hero to the meanderings of an absurd fate, although the counterplot of the Dresden magistrates fails. The old woman singled out at random from an anonymous crowd by the Saxon Elector's emissary to act as a go-between for his master and Kohlhaas, turns out to be no other than the Gypsy woman—alias Lisbeth —herself. There are many other such seemingly negligible accidents which take on the aura of tragic incidents. The most portentous among them is, of course, the accidental, yet tragic, death of Kohlhaas's beloved wife. In Kleist's world, small causes may lead to dreadful consequences.

Worse still, absurdities of human fate reveal themselves not only in irrational chance happenings but even on the highest level of human reason. Symptomatic of the rational uncertainties which haunt human destiny are Kohlhaas's debate with Luther and the legal obfuscations perpetrated by the Dresden court. In no other work of Kleist is the way to truth or clarity so obstructed by juridical complexities as in "Michael Kohlhaas." Luther, the revered elder statesman of Kohlhaas's day, no doubt helps his cause gain respectability. Up to the point of his intervention, Kohlhaas had been largely dismissed by the authorities as a crank and mad dog. However, Luther's actions and reasoning in defense of Kohlhaas are fraught with ambiguities which do not solve but rather accentuate the motivational and circumstantial complexities of the case. In his proclamation, Luther argues that the ruler of the land is not to be blamed for any miscarriage of justice committed by his magistrates:

How can you say your rights have been denied you, whose savage breast, lusting for a base private revenge, gave up all attempts to find justice after your first thoughtless efforts came to nothing? Is a bench of constables and beadles who suppress a petition that has been presented to them or withhold a judgment it is their duty to deliver—is this your supreme authority? And need I tell you, impious man, that your sovereign knows nothing about your case: what am I saying?—the sovereign you are rebelling against does not even know your name, so that one day when you come before the throne of God thinking to accuse him, he will be able to say with a serene face, "I have done this man no wrong, Lord, for my soul is a stranger to his existence." [2]

It is, however, precisely the frustration over the impossibility of reaching the ruler himself which triggered Kohlhaas's revenge. Like Job, Kohlhaas yearned to prove his righteousness in the highest court only to fall prey, again not unlike his Biblical ancestor, to self-righteousness.

Even more symptomatic of the ambiguities lodged in the minds of the most astute men in Kohlhaas's world is his debate with Luther during the audience accorded him by the great reformer. Luther, the erstwhile firebrand, must feel a close kinship with the rebellious man of the people, but as a political conservative he is equally committed to the idea of the sovereignty of the State. Psychologically, this inner conflict of interests accounts partly for the equivocations in his thinking but also for his mercurial behavior during the interview, in contrast to Kohlhaas, who remains relatively calm and collected. The younger man points out that he had taken the law into his own hands because, in denying him his rights, the State had effectively expelled him from a lawful community of men, in fact made him an outlaw. Luther's angry retort to this interpretation of the natural law is an emphatic defense of the divine authority of kings, who are to be judged only by God. By implication, he seems to say that justice will be meted out only if God through his worldly ministers wills it. The ambiguous conclusion of *The Duel* comes to mind. Such a view can do little to restore Kohlhaas's faith in legal justice. But, finally, Luther concedes the legality of Kohlhaas's demands vis-à-vis von Tronka: punishment of the Junker, restoration of the horses to their former health, and modest indemnities for the losses suffered by Kohlhaas himself and his faithful servant, Herse, who, killed in battle, left behind a mother in need. However, when upon departing, Kohlhaas asks for the privilege of Holy Communion, Luther ostensibly reverses his stand. He will grant the request only if Kohlhaas desists from his demand for a lawsuit and agrees to forgive his enemy, which he refuses to do. The interview ends on a note of deep personal anguish for Kohlhaas. With an expression of "painful emotion," Kohlhaas presses both hands to his breast and takes leave in one of the most moving passages in the story. We can only guess from Kleist's laconic description of his deportment what thoughts must belabor his mind. While Luther's attitude augurs well for Kohlhaas's rehabilitation as a rightful member of the State, it effectively excludes him from the Christian community of believers. It is only before the execution in Berlin that Luther sends a special legate to Kohlhaas's prison cell to administer communion, thus allowing the condemned man to make his peace with the religious community.

We cannot necessarily accuse Luther of being muddle-headed [3] in his seemingly equivocal attitude, although in his replies to Kohlhaas he does not clearly formulate his insights. But as a man of God and of the world he is no doubt aware that the claims of religion and of worldly justice often pull in opposite directions. To forgive when one's legal demands have been met is a rather gratuitous, if not specious, virtue. The world will gain from the exercise of justice, but will Kohlhaas's character? Were he to forgive, Kohlhaas might conceivably be purged of the admixture of personal vanity and revenge which contaminates his quest for justice. There is little guarantee that this would happen through the mere application of the law. The inner magnanimity demanded by the religious virtue of forgiveness could effectively counteract the megalomania inherent in Kohlhaas's messianic pretense. Luther's seemingly equivocal posture not only reflects the conflicting springs of action in Kohlhaas's obdurate character, but it also highlights the human dilemma of knowing exactly what is right and what is wrong. Kohlhaas's case obviously transcends the confines of mere legal statutes. These may be the reasons why Luther is not particularly careful in observing the legal limits of the dispute. Yet in going beyond them he only creates a new set of juridical entanglements.

He says that he will plead for Kohlhaas's safe passage to the Dresden court, provided the Elector "will let mercy prevail over justice," as though safe-conduct were an act of mercy rather than a mere legal necessity to make the trial possible in the first place. Then, in his strongly worded letter to the Saxon ruler he insists not only on safe passage for Kohlhaas's person but amnesty for his past deeds. He exceeds Kohlhaas's own demands, though in more than one sense he is justified in doing so. For if Kohlhaas were brought to account for the murderous warfare he waged in the countryside, it would cloud the central legal issue revolving around the abuse of his horses and servant on von Tronka's estate. Luther has also enough political acumen to see that popular sentiment is on Kohlhaas's side and that the smoldering revolutionary feeling might erupt into a general uprising any day. Nevertheless, Luther's confusing the two concepts of "safe passage" and "amnesty" does not help to clarify the legal situation and is seized upon by the Dresden magistrates, some of whom have personal reasons to bring about Kohlhaas's demise. In one debate, Hinz von Tronka, who could not possibly have known what had been said between Luther and Kohlhaas, points out the confusion in the reformer's thinking. Maybe Kleist overlooked the fact of Hinz's relative ignorance. But it could also be a case of indirect author interference; Kleist ventriloquizes to draw our attention to a thorny legal problem:

As the Elector, with a perplexed look walked over to his desk, the Cupbearer, Sir Hinz von Tronka, began to speak in his turn: he could not understand how the right course for the state to follow in this matter had escaped men as wise as those assembled here. The horse dealer, as he understood it, had promised to disband his company in return for a simple safe-conduct to Dresden and the renewal of the inquiry into his case. But it did not follow from this that he must be granted an amnesty for criminally taking his revenge into his own hands: these were two entirely separate matters, which Dr. Luther as well as the Council of State seemed to have confounded.[4]

Even more symptomatic of the juridical morass in which Kohlhaas's sense of justice will become entrapped is the Elector's mandate. He promises safe passage if Kohlhaas disbands his marauders and then adds that amnesty will be granted him provided his suit or "complaint" concerning the black horses will not be "dismissed." It will most certainly not be "dismissed," but it could still be "lost," in which case we must assume that the promise of amnesty would be voided and Kohlhaas brought to justice for his reckless warfare. There is some craftiness in the Elector's mandate, but Kohlhaas, though seemingly wary, complies with the conditions set forth in it. However, we cannot categorically accuse the Elector of deception or obfuscation. Luther's demand for unconditional amnesty may have overshot the mark, for it is questionable whether any government could ignore the kind of violence that was perpetrated by Kohlhaas, in the event that the latter loses his suit. On the other hand, the Elector's mandate also demonstrates that no more than Kohlhaas is the State willing to "forgive" unconditionally. On both sides, forgiveness is made dependent on legal satisfaction.

From this point on, the law takes its tortuous course only to become further complicated by the incident of the public riot and by the Nagelschmidt plot. The Dresden magistrates exploit the latter so obviously as a plant to incriminate further the unsuspecting Kohlhaas that they must drop the charge upon Brandenburg's intervention in the case. Saxony does some legal juggling, and Kohlhaas is bound over to the Imperial Court in Berlin, which is empowered to overrule the vague promise of amnesty given by the Saxon Elector and consequently sentences Kohlhaas to death for having broken the public peace. On the other hand, it ratifies and enacts all his claims against Junker von Tronka. The solution is a strictly legal one. Von Tronka, in addition to paying indemnities and restoring the horses to their erstwhile state of health, will atone for his moral weakness with two years in prison, while Kohlhaas must pay for the unbridled excesses of his autonomous justice with his life. Posthumously, Kohlhaas's person will be vicariously honored in his two sons, who are to be elevated to knighthood.

The Imperial Court is mainly concerned with minimal peace-keeping through the application of the law. It will hear nothing of amnesty, though Kohlhaas wins his suit against von Tronka hands down. In this respect the Imperial Court, if less venal, is also more rigid than was the Saxon Elector. On the other hand, Brandenburg's action of conferring nobility on Kohlhaas's sons posthumously seems to lift his case out of the realm of mere legality. It is as if the Elector of Brandenburg meant to acknowledge a positive moral impulse in Kohlhaas's fight for justice, although the conciliatory gesture may be little else than a substitute for true forgiveness, which the Imperial Court could not extend to Kohlhaas in the form of amnesty.

Yet, it is primarily the Gypsy episode dominating the last portion of the *Novelle* which puts into relief the extralegal dimensions of Kohlhaas's case. In shifting the emphasis from the dispute between Kohlhaas and Tronka to the antagonism between Kohlhaas and the Saxon Elector, it accentuates the conflict between the individual and the State but also opens up a transcendental perspective on the problematic character of Kohlhaas's personal quest for justice. Structurally, the episode does not seem to be smoothly woven into the fabric of the plot. It is introduced suddenly and narrated primarily in flashbacks, as though Kleist felt he had some catching up to do. When it is first sprung on us, the element of surprise is great enough not to be readily absorbed. At first sight, it seems to introduce an incongruous supernatural ingredient into a plot which heretofore had revolved around a conflict of interests among men. It is not so unusual, however, that Kleist gives his story line a sudden new twist; witness the ring episode in "The Duel" or the discovery of the dead child's little finger in *The Schroffenstein Family*. The supernatural quality of the episode aligns the *Novelle* somewhat with the tales of such Romanticists as Tieck, Eichendorff, de la Motte-Fouqué, or Mörike. But more important, it is symptomatic of Kleist's constant tendency to cast a furtive glance at heaven even as he is deeply absorbed in describing the business of this world. The more than earthly dimensions of Kohlhaas's struggle are also hinted at earlier in the story in the strange ecstasy of his mind, the foreboding reactions of the heavens to his acts of violence, and perhaps even in the many chance happenings. The disclosure of the power he is able to wield over the Saxon Elector through the Gypsy woman also reanimates Kohlhaas's determination to continue his fight at a moment when he had all but given it up and had contemplated leaving the country. Symbolically, the episode makes eminent, though not unequivocal, sense. It is a kind of transcendental reflection on the ultimate meaning as well as the psychological complexities of Kohlhaas's pursuit of justice.

On the psychological level, the episode recapitulates the ambivalences in Kohlhaas's actions or motives and the choices he is given in the course of events. Although he himself cannot grasp its manifold implications, a closer analysis of the Gypsy woman's seemingly inconsistent attitudes yields insights into the complexities of Kohlhaas's motives. Kleist leaves little doubt that she is an incarnation of the dead Lisbeth. She acts like the dead woman, cherishes the children like a mother, has the same birthmark on the nape of her neck and, like Odysseus upon his homecoming, is recognized by the old family dog. But her admonitions to Kohlhaas are more equivocal. At first she predicts that the capsule will save Kohlhaas's life, which it does not, though it conceivably could. At her second appearance she exhorts Kohlhaas to moderation and

Christian forgiveness. Yet, immediately before Kohlhaas's execution she warns him of the Elector's designs on the capsule, thus abetting his personal revenge.

Upon reflection, however, it becomes clear that the Gypsy woman, far from being inconsistent, re-enacts the attitudes of the dead Lisbeth, who was torn between wifely loyalty and the injunctions of Christian charity. In her *démarche* at the Saxon court, Lisbeth obviously intended to help the cause of justice over the claims of forgiveness. On her deathbed, however, she counsels forgiveness rather than mere justice. She clearly perceives in Kohlhaas's quest an element of personal revenge, thus realizing that the moral issue is a complex, three-cornered problem. Justice versus forgiveness is an insoluble moral problem, while the moral superiority of forgiveness over revenge is a forgone conclusion. In reflecting back on Kohlhaas's actions we realize that he was never quite ready for true forgiveness. He is prepared to take a bow to charity either when justice has been done, as is made clear in his debate with Luther, or when he no longer is in a position to claim justice, as is the case in Dresden after the Nagelschmidt interlude. On the other hand, his need for revenge is pervasive. Lisbeth—alias the Gypsy woman—also clearly sees that a feeling of revenge born of undeserved suffering must have a visible object and become implacably fastened upon a person. As a matter of fact, to Kohlhaas himself the capsule containing the prophecy is no mysterious emblem of a lofty concept of justice. On the contrary, he sees in it a means of heaping a full measure of personal revenge upon the Saxon Elector, whose moral obtuseness he holds responsible for his dark fate, even the accidental death of his wife. He rejoices outright when he learns what psychological power is given him through the possession of the capsule. He asserts at one point that he would rather see his enemy plunged into an abyss of despair and die on the scaffold himself than surrender the capsule and preserve his own life.

Yet it is not only wifely loyalty which ultimately prompts the Gypsy woman to acquiesce in Kohlhaas's revenge. It may well be the realization that in the final analysis he fought for an ideal of personal dignity, though often with the wrong means. There are indeed a host of ancillary circumstances which suggest that the Gypsy episode is not merely a recapitulation of psychological ambiguities in a supernatural key but points toward the ultimate, existential meaning of Kohlhaas's struggle against the world. The people, for instance, do not believe that his death sentence will be carried out. Luther sends his emissary to grant him Holy Communion, although Kohlhaas has not really forgiven his adversary, von Tronka, in the legal dispute—a condition on which Luther had emphatically insisted in their meeting. Kohlhaas accepts the thought of his impending death in a cheerful mood, and we are expressly told that his sons are to be knighted. Finally, it is made amply clear at the end that the real antagonist of Kohlhaas is the Saxon Elector and not von Tronka. These developments are not merely fortuitous but are rather parts of a code that needs to be deciphered.

The people obviously feel that Kohlhaas's person embodies a value that would compensate for his guilt. Luther's concession, though seemingly inconsistent with his earlier stand, suggests that he acknowledges a heightened self-awareness in Kohlhaas, who as a result of his trials has been able to sort out his motives of personal revenge from his claims on universal justice. His new sense of personal authenticity may account for his equanimity in facing death. Even his revenge, Kohlhaas must feel, is not all reprehensible, for it was largely born of a lacerated sense of personal dignity.

The Saxon Elector's role in his life accentuates this theme. He first chose to ignore Kohlhaas's case altogether—to be ignored is manifestly a greater offense to personal dignity than to be heard and hurt in the process—and he became interested in Kohlhaas's person only from self-centered motives. For, ultimately, he is more absorbed in the pursuit of the capsule than in the enactment of justice. No more than Tronka is he actively villainous. In his promise of conditional amnesty he may even have shown a measure of good will toward Kohlhaas, though it may have largely been dictated by political expediency. In the early stages of the court proceedings he also demonstrated a measure of good sense in listening to reasoned counsel. But eventually he obliquely acquiesced in the legal maneuvering of the Dresden Court to inculpate Kohlhaas and let himself be carried along by intrigues instead of thwarting them. Although the vast accumulation of legal and circumstantial detail seems to diffuse responsibility for Kohlhaas's demise among a large number of persons, the Saxon Elector is nevertheless derelict in his duty as a ruler through a lack of personal strength. This Kleist seems to suggest in the strange and languorous sickness which befalls him recurrently as he vainly attempts to get possession of the mysterious capsule. By contrast with the Elector's inner weakness the innate strength and dignity of Kohlhaas's own character become manifest.

Spiritually and existentially, the Saxon prince is indeed Kohlhaas's antagonist, and his psychological defeat constitutes a triumph for the principle of individual dignity for which Kohlhaas dies. Seen from this vantage point, the Gypsy episode helps shed light on Kohlhaas's ultimate purpose. A progressive clarification of his motives seems to have taken place in his own mind which, as already suggested, may be responsible for the mood of cheerfulness he experiences before his death. The feud with Tronka was soon overshadowed by his megalomaniac pretense to restore justice in the world at large. As a result of his debate with Luther and the degradations he suffered at Dresden he seemed to become subtly aware that he was really defending his dignity as a person, which, as much as an abstract notion of justice, represents a universal value and may explain the charisma he exerts on the populace. Through error a subtle reorientation has been effected in his life. The value of the *persona* for which he fought and the courage with which he followed his existential summons attenuate the motive of revenge in his last dramatic gesture under the Saxon Elector's eyes. He fought for the right ideal with the wrong means. But then, the world could be awakened from its moral slumber only through the excesses of his autonomous justice. This central paradox explains many of Kohlhaas's earlier conflicting emotions.

Despite the psychological complexities it reflects, the Gypsy episode, then, helps vindicate Kohlhaas's sense of justice, connected as it is with his feeling for the worth of the individual. It does not thereby exonerate the perversions and excess of his sense of righteousness but it draws at least greater attention to its very presence in his life. It is as though Kleist intended to say that no strong positive feeling as such can be ignored by higher powers, no matter how it may err in the empirical world. Kleist obviously could not indict such a feeling but he grieves over its inevitable corruption in an imperfect world. With a sure dramatic sense and a realistic awareness bordering on existentialist toughness, he shows how any principle, no matter how lofty, becomes inexorably tainted with ambiguities as soon as it is enacted in a dualistic world. The ending of "Michael Kohlhaas" is no synthesis of conflicting forces. The hero is only partially reconciled with the world and the world with him. He has won his legal battle, affirmed his personality, and intuitively suggested to his generation a principle of justice centered in the individual's worth. But a note of disharmony is still sounded in the fervor with which he exults in his revenge and its destructive effect on his antagonist. The redemptive quality of a moral will, operative in a world sensitive to the claims of individuality, is depicted more fully in *The Prince of Homburg*, though only as an evanescent dream.

NOTES

[1] Sembd., Vol. 4, p. 34; Greenberg, p. 121.

[2] Sembd., Vol. 4, p. 36; Greenberg, p. 122.

[3] It is especially Walter Silz who argues eloquently for the inconsistencies in Luther's thinking as well as the craftiness in the subsequent mandate of the Elector. R. S. Lucas ("Studies in Kleist: 'Michael Kohlhaas,'" in *Deutsche Vierteljahresschrift*, 44. Jahrgang, 1970, Heft 1, März) tries to attenuate this view by insisting on Luther's divided allegiances as a man of God who must extol the religious virtue of forgiveness and as a statesman who cannot ignore the demands of legal justice. The complex problem obviously has both legal and religious aspects.

[4] Sembd., Vol. 4, p. 44; Greenberg, p. 132.

The Dream of Reason Produces Illusions

"The Prince of Homburg"

Although Kleist's reticence in giving information about his writings is particularly striking in the case of his last drama, there are enough indications to suggest that he first conceived of it at the beginning of 1809 and finished it perhaps as early as March 1810, most certainly by the summer of 1811. This final period in his life is marked by the vain hopes for national liberation stirred up in the wake of the Archduke Charles's victory over Napoleon at Aspern in May 1809 and the despair caused by his subsequent defeat at Wagram. As to Kleist himself we only have scant information about some hectic journeys he allegedly undertook through Germany and possibly Austria, apparently in search of his own role in the fight against the French, and some vague allusions to a nervous collapse he suffered while sojourning in Prague. In early 1810 he seemed to appear from nowhere in Berlin, there to stage his last battle with his fate, especially his losing fight with the Prussian censors over the publication of his *Berliner Abendblätter*.

Although the play reflects Kleist's concern with the destiny of the nation, the patriotic sentiment is but a surface gloss. The focus of the drama is rather on the individual's peremptory demands for self-fulfillment and the rival claims made on him by the State, a conflict which under Kleist's pen opens up vistas on a lofty concept of inner freedom but also on the psychological ambivalences which seem to detract from it. The collapse of the Austrian resistance to Napoleon's aggression in 1809–10 and his own emotional involvement in the events of the day apparently led Kleist to re-evaluate the viability of a subjectivistic mode of existence in a world in which individual destiny is inescapably linked with that of the nation.

The subject matter of the play he found in the not too distant Prussian past, namely in the battle of Fehrbellin of June 18, 1675, between the armies of the Great Elector Frederick Wilhelm of Prussia and the Swedes under Field Marshal Wrangel, which ended in a partial victory for the Prussian forces. According to partly legendary accounts, an impetuous officer, the Landgrave of Homburg, attacked the Swedish vanguard against orders, and though successful in his premature action, lightheartedly endangered the fate of the whole State. Nonetheless, after due admonishments to be more careful next time, the Elector pardoned his impulsive and all too devoted officer.

In the treatment of this topic Kleist's concern with the individual's answerability to the State and the common good of the nation is very much apparent. In contrast to most earlier works, the hero is personally responsible for his error as well as his subsequent rehabilitation. His first inner certainties are morally and legally fallible, and he is given a real choice between life and death and is not merely defeated by a deceptive world. The reality with which he must contend is, at the surface at least, a rational, though by no means perfect, world of law and order represented by his antagonist, the Elector, who must counteract the extreme behavior of the hero. In the process, both learn a lesson, the Prince *what* he must do, the Elector *how* he should do what he must. The result is a dialectic interplay of forces which culminates in a moral ideal of inner freedom and personal responsibility. Seen from this vantage point, Kleist's last play seems to be his "idealistic" legacy to the world. On another plane, however, the drama also sounds out the psychological premises of the characters' conscious actions and thus may put into question the very ideal it advocates. The play contains many puzzling features which make of it both more *and* less than a Schillerian or Kantian praise of duty. In writing *The Prince of Homburg* Kleist's psychological penetration of his characters rivaled his understanding of a moral ideal.

In a park at Fehrbellin, the Elector's residence, the Prince of Homburg, seated under an oak tree, dreams in a trance-like state how he will cover himself with glory in the impending battle with the Swedish army. His friend Hohenzollern lures the Elector and his retinue into the park to observe the strange spectacle. As though to test Homburg's self-absorption, the Elector takes the laurel wreath which Homburg holds in his hands, puts a golden chain around it, and hands it to Princess Natalia, his niece. Still dreaming, Homburg jumps up to seize the wreath and crown himself with it but succeeds only in snatching a glove of Natalia's, who retreats with the others in utter amazement at the scene. The Elector rebukes the Prince with the ominous words: "Back into the dark and nothingness!" [1]

At next day's war council, Homburg is distracted and can think of nothing else but the strange glove in his possession, which seems to lend reality to his dream. When he discovers that it belongs to Natalia, he is filled with excitement and gains only a confused notion of the battle plan. The Elector admonishes him to do his job this time, while chastising him for having spoiled two earlier battles with his erratic actions. During the new battle, Homburg is so filled with eager anticipation of his own glory that he launches his cavalry charge prematurely, routing the right wing of the Swedish army but perhaps preventing a complete victory over the enemy. Believing his troops to have carried the day for the Brandenburg colors he rejoins Natalia and the Electress. As rumors of the Elector's death in battle reach them, Homburg, though saddened, is more visibly elated at the thought of his own glory and his future union with Natalia, to whom he declares his love. When the rumor of the Elector's death proves false and it is learned how he was saved by the sacrifice of his equerry Froben, Homburg shares the general feeling of gratitude but expresses some envy of Froben's glorious death in battle.

Arriving in Berlin for the victory celebration, clutching conquered Swedish pennants in his arms and fully expecting to be praised, Homburg is summarily arrested at the Elector's behest. He is dazed, but manages to jeer at the Elector's archaic concept of justice just as Froben's body is carried into the castle church for the funeral services. A contrast of great dramatic effectiveness: Homburg's self-glorification pitted against Froben's self-sacrifice.

Sentenced to death by a military court, Homburg is still confident that the Elector will follow his heart's impulse and pardon him, now that the letter of the law has been satisfied and especially since his cavalry charge had been crowned with success. But when Hohenzollern intimates that the Elector may have a political motive not to relent—a marriage alliance between Natalia and the Swedish King—Homburg is quick to impute base machinations to his antagonist. In despair he decides to implore the Electress to plead his cause. As he passes the grave which is to receive his body, a paralyzing fear of death seizes him. He declares his willingness to give up everything that is dear to him, honor and love, if only his life be spared:

> The most lowly mortal is to me
> A god! Oh! I could hang myself upon the neck
> Of your most humble stableman,
> Imploring him to save me. Save me!
> On the whole of God's wide earth,
> Only I am helpless, abandoned, and can do
> Nothing, nothing.
> . . . .
> Don't forget to tell him [the Elector] also
> That I no longer wish to take Natalia in marriage.
> Every spark of feeling for her now has vanished from my heart.
> She is free again, free as the wild deer in the heathered hills,
> . . . .
> I only want to go back to my own estate.
> There I shall build, pull down, and build again,
> And sow my fields, and reap them till the sweat
> Pours down my breast, and labour hard,

> As if for wife and child: but I shall be alone there.
> And when I have reaped, then I shall sow again,
> Turning calmly in the year's great circle, that is life's
> Until, at close of day, life sinks and dies.[2]

Natalia, disturbed by Homburg's loss of selfhood, appeals to the Elector's clemency. When he hears of Homburg's condition, he is "confused." On a sudden impulse, he promises to free him and hands Natalia a sealed note she is to deliver to Homburg. On her way she learns of a petition drawn up by Colonel Kottwitz and the other officers of the regiment of which she is titular commander asking the Elector to pardon the Prince. Intuitively knowing that Homburg has gained enough strength to reject too easy a pardon, she makes preparations to summon her regiment to Fehrbellin to plead for Homburg's life. As Homburg reads the Elector's note in Natalia's presence, he becomes increasingly thoughtful and hesitant. The Elector's message states that Homburg is to be freed if in his own judgment he did no wrong. To Natalia's dismay and pride, he resolutely indicts himself and his selfish motives!

> Let him [the Elector] do as he likes
> I know now that I am doing as I should!
> ....
> I will not appear despicable and weak
> Before a man who treats me with such great nobility.[3]

As he thus regains his dignity, Natalia moves swiftly to save his life by asking Kottwitz to come to Homburg's rescue.

The fifth act brings about the dramatic confrontation of the Elector with his army officers over Homburg's life. Kottwitz and Hohenzollern offer impassioned and eloquent pleas in Homburg's defense. The Elector, who knows of Homburg's decision, pays no heed to their entreaties but lets Homburg talk for himself. Homburg declares that it is not personal success over an external enemy which is of ultimate value but the conquest of the enemy within. The officers can only listen in stunned silence at Homburg's lofty exposition of inner freedom and responsibility. Returned to his cell, Homburg is overawed by reverence for the moral principle he has discovered within himself. In an operatic final scene, he is led blindfolded through a gate, anticipating death. But instead, Natalia puts a laurel wreath on his brow. Overwhelmed with emotion, he faints. As he comes to, he asks incredulously: "Tell me: is this a dream?" [4] But his anxiety is drowned in the wild cheers going up around him: "Death to all the enemies of Brandenburg!" [5]

Before entering upon a discussion of the thematic and linguistic complexities of the play, several dramatic elements should be noted that give the drama a characteristically Kleistian note. Most obvious are the eloquent object—Natalia's glove—and a number of fainting spells but also the self-absorbed, even daydreaming, stance of the principals which distinguishes them from Schiller's vocal reasoners. The climactic idea of inner freedom emerges from the spontaneous interaction of their feelings almost in spite of them. Equally noteworthy is the evidence of Kleist's skill in handling irony and paradox, though in keeping with the ideological element in the play, ironic reversals of the action leading to paradoxical situations are due more to human agency than the caprice of an extraneous fate. The whole structure of the drama seems to rest on a "law of opposites." [6] The precise instructions given at the war council are counterbalanced by the Prince's distraction. His expansive mood after the battle is cut short by the Elector's brusque order for his arrest. The seriousness of the death sentence elicits at first Homburg's glibness; Hohenzollern's political fancies, his abject despair. The seeming leniency shown in the Elector's choice given to the Prince is counteracted by the latter's severity with himself. The Elector's impulsive act of mercy generates Homburg's deliberate thought in making his fateful decision—a vivid contrast to his blustering attack during the battle. Finally, Homburg's newly found redemptive wisdom furnishes the occasion for an ambiguous celebration saved by a thunderous call to arms as the Prince recovers from his faint. Even the discreet Natalia becomes involved in the interplay of force and counterforce. As the Prince reaches his nadir of despair, she reveals an unsuspected strength of will and independence of mind. When the Elector entrusts her with his message to the Prince, she makes furtive preparations to outmaneuver the Elector. Intuitively she knows that the Elector's offer of liberation will induce Homburg to accept his fatal responsibility and that his life can only be saved by those who live in constant proximity to death.

But the play's rhythmic pattern cannot fully account for its philosophic, psychological, and existential ingredients or yield a satisfactory explanation for some crucial episodes, such as the dream scene at the beginning.

At its most obvious, the dream scene is an expression of Kleist's continual fascination with the problem of appearance and reality, truth and illusion. But within the play, its function is both expository and psychological. Kleist can literally turn his hero inside out and expose him to our analytic gaze and at the same time introduce the eloquent object—Natalia's glove—which seems to vest Homburg's dream with reality. Finally, the scene and its immediate sequel allow him to disclose the ambiguity and furtiveness of human motives, which he does with a combination of boldness and subtlety rarely found in dramatic literature. For he not only shows us the actual circumstances of Homburg's dream—his encounter with the Elector and his retinue in the garden of Fehrbellin —but also has the Prince give us his own recollection of it (scene four). We are thus afforded a view of how things happened and what Homburg's psyche makes of them. The discrepancies are revealing. In reality he wound the laurel wreath himself and snatched at it after the Elector had twisted a golden chain about it and handed it to Natalia, only to come away from the comic attempt at reappropriation with Natalia's glove in his possession. In his own retelling of the dream, the wreath appeared from nowhere in the Elector's hands. Further, in his trance, he calls Natalia not only by her first name but also "My love! My bride!" [7] Afterward, he cannot immediately recall her name and when he finally does, he refers to her stiffly as the "charming Princess of Orange," [8] and then only outside the context of the dream. The process of repression has done its work. Finally, in his dream vision, the company moving down the ramp resembles an exalted, celestial procession approaching him.

Obviously, the juxtaposition of Homburg's actions in his trance and his view of them in the waking state unveils the wish-fulfillment role of his dreams as well as his tendency toward mindless self-exaltation. At the same time, the episode gives a first subtle glimpse of the Elector's personality and the emerging tension, perhaps even rivalry, between himself and Homburg. At first approaching the daydreaming Prince with fatherly benevolence, he reacts vehemently to the latter's pursuit of Natalia holding the wreath: "Back into the dark and nothingness!" Like Homburg, he seems prone to act on impulse, though he immediately regrets his uncontrolled outburst of anger. For he sends a messenger to Hohenzollern ordering him not to breathe a word to Homburg ". . . about the little trick / He played on him just now." [9] His recognition of guilt may be due as much to his undignified role in the event as to a disturbing feeling of jealousy that he would much rather keep hidden. He must also sense that Homburg has an exalted notion of him as his protector. Indeed, in his dream vision, Homburg sees the Elector with "his forehead high as Zeus upon Olympus." [10] When he is ultimately forced to view him as a fallible human being, the props are knocked out from under him. In this respect, the dream scene makes Homburg's later collapse at the sight of his grave psychologically more plausible. The dream episode is also the model for the controversial final scene, when the Elector once more plays a trick on Homburg—having him blindfolded for execution only to release him to freedom—as though he meant to affirm again his own power against the younger man's challenge.

There is no doubt that the dream scene suggests in a subtle way the incipient tension between the two principals and not only puts into focus the character of the Prince but also gives us a quick flash of the Elector's ambiguous feelings. Much more so than in such earlier works as *Amphitryon,* "The Marquise of O——," and *Penthesilea,* Kleist creates in his last drama an antagonist who has an absorbing life of his own and must pass through an inner catharsis. The latter is only intimated, for the Elector's character is not turned inside out as is Homburg's. Thus a kind of mystery surrounds his person, and for a while his omnipresence looms in the unregenerate Prince's life like that malevolent, a-human fate which overwhelms Kleist's earlier characters. But not only in the sequel to the dream scene but in a number of other episodes it becomes clear—at times through Kleist's stage directions—that the Elector is subject to unsettling inner experiences. In two or three instances he is visibly shaken.

It would be a travesty of the obvious authenticity of his emotions if he were merely play acting in a pedagogic scheme of his own making, whose outcome is clear to him from the outset. He seems to give the impression of having foreknowledge and omniscience. But this is due to Kleist's stagecraft. We do not see and hear the Elector very often, he simply makes revelatory appearances at key points in the action, thus making his presence felt throughout the play even if he is absent from the stage.

He is also more self-contained than the Prince. When overwhelmed by the turn of events and the necessity to absorb new realities, he remains practically silent—with the exception of one beautiful soliloquy when he is confronted with the danger of a military uprising:

> Strange! If I were the Dey of Tunis,
> I should sound the alarm at such a mysterious conspiracy.
> The streets would be strewn with the bodies of my janizaries,
> And at the doors of my seraglio
> I should deploy a ring of cannon! [11]

Conversely, the Prince, at least in the beginning, tends to confront reality with flat statements or garrulousness. The Elector's relative taciturnity seems at times more germane to the character of a Kleistian hero than the Prince's more loquacious temper. Kleist's discreet portrayal of the Elector's person and the ensuing aura of mystery surrounding him have induced interpreters to see him as a symbol of divine wisdom or an embodiment of a philosophic idea. Admittedly, he represents the State and its laws—a kind of "objective" world —which he must defend against the rival claims of Homburg's subjectivity. But he is not thereby a mere allegoric personage. He is rather an intensely human person caught between his duties as head of State and his private feelings, which Kleist suggests in the opening and subsequent episodes, especially when he describes him as "confused" upon hearing Natalia's plea for clemency toward Homburg.

Nevertheless, in the conflict and reconciliation between the Elector and Homburg, a moral ideal transpires which lends the drama an abstract quality, although the humanity of its principals—the ambiguity of their feelings—continues undiminished throughout the action. On that abstract level, the dialectic of the play suggests an ideological element that has surprising affinities with Kantian ethics and the concept of a future rational State embodied in the philosophy of history of German idealism. This element, then, is contained in the action itself and not incarnate in one personage—the Elector—as has often been maintained.

From this vantage point the opening scene may well be Kleist's final reckoning with a subjectivistic mode of existence that can find an outlet only in the isolated world of personal dreams. For Kleist portrays Homburg's narcissistic self-absorption with a subtle comic touch that implies ironic distance. The fumbling actions of the sleepwalker hardly suggest that inner serenity we could observe in the Kaethchen of Heilbronn. Kleist even intones ominous notes when he has the Elector repudiate the Prince with the cruel words: "Back into . . . nothingness," as though to intimate that Homburg's dream illusions cannot possibly fill him with "being" but will rather make him come face to face with a dreadful inner void. Even in the midst of his somnambulist fit Homburg attempts to break out of his inner isolation by making reality comply with his dream of personal glory. Hence the strange episode of his snatching at the laurel wreath in Natalia's hands, only to be left with her glove. From the outset the realization of Homburg's dream is quite other than he dreamed.

During the battle, Homburg's untimely cavalry charge makes him obviously answerable to the law of the State. But throughout the play Kleist makes it amply clear that Homburg's *Versehen* or error consists less of his disregard of military orders than the basic disposition of his character. He is possessed of heedless pride—the classical form of *hybris*—which he recognizes only after he has gone through his inner catharsis:

> Oh, my brothers-in-arms, what is a victory worth
> That I perhaps might gain against the Swedish general
> Beside the victory we shall gloriously win to-morrow
> Over the most pernicious enemies we know,
> The enemies within ourselves; defiance, arrogance? [12]

However, as long as he is under the spell of self-love rather than self-possession he does not question the underlying maxim of his action and is little affected by the Elector's rumored death but rather glories in the seemingly impending realization of his dreams—military honors and Natalia's hand. His decision in battle was obviously a result of his freedom of choice, but he has used the latter only toward his own ends. In acting *willkürlich,* to use rather freely a Kantian term—i.e., "capriciously"—he applies a standard of behavior to himself which he could not possibly will to be a general rule or, by extension, a "universal law." Thus he becomes alienated from the world and ultimately from his own personality.

Strategic considerations have little significance in the ensuing conflict between the Prince's self-will and the legalism of the State. It is left an open question whether Homburg's premature attack saved the day for the Brandenburg colors or prevented the Elector from winning a more decisive victory. Although the Elector inclines toward the latter view, he does not make it the central issue. What is at stake for him at this point is the sanctity of the law. At this stage of development, he cannot be much concerned with Homburg's inner disposition but with the problem of maintaining law and order, the lifeblood of the legalistic State. But as Homburg will subsequently be led from mere willfulness to a recognition of the responsibilities residing in freedom, the Elector will be made to understand the difference between mere legality and the "moral law within."

The dialectic development of these themes moves along with cogency and force. Homburg's alienation from the world is drastically apparent at the beginning of the second phase of the drama. When arrested, he looks in vain for support. "Help me, friends! Help me! I'm going mad!" [13] It is now, when confronted with an inescapable reality that he imagines that he is dreaming. "It this a dream? Do I wake or sleep? Am I still in my right mind?" [14] This stands in marked contrast to the beginning of the drama when Homburg, his feelings buoyed up by the possession of Natalia's glove, thought to have glimpsed reality in the midst of his dreams. His excessive egotism is matched by the Elector's aloofness in ordering his arrest. The scene dramatizes in muffled tones not only the violent clash between two rivals but also the contending claims of individuality and the demands of the law. As he recovers from his daze, Homburg does not suffer in eloquent silence as would Kleist's pure heroes. He launches into a petulant diatribe against the Elector's Roman concept of justice:

> It seems my cousin Frederick will play the part of Brutus
> And sees himself in some official portrait sitting
> In a lofty seat, wearing the imperial toga,
> The articles of war held in a magisterial hand.[15]

Even in prison, when left to his own thoughts Homburg feels that the relative success of his action will in due time exonerate him. He does not realize that he might owe his Pyrrhic victory to mere luck or chance rather than his own courage. He is stupefied to learn that during the victory Mass he has been hailed as the day's hero, while the Elector's court-martial has sentenced him to death. At this point, the State's jurisdiction seems to be one step ahead of Homburg in its conception of wrongdoing. It can at least distinguish between the favorable chance results of an action and the overt deed itself. It must acknowledge the one and punish the other. But Homburg feels that the death sentence is only a formality, a bow the Elector must make to the law. If at this stage of development Homburg showed contrition and were to admit that the overt deed and its legalistic import are at least as significant as the chance results of his action, an uneasy balance between individual caprice and legality might be established. But it testifies to Kleist's dramatic talent and perhaps also to his understanding of inner freedom and its functioning in the Ideal State that he drives the conflict to a point where Homburg must take stock of his whole personality or character rather than a mere isolated deed. Concurrently, the State will be forced to subject its principle of legality to a closer scrutiny, for what matters in the Ideal State is the spirit, not the letter, of the law. The concept of right will have to undergo a progressive clarification. Ideally, the State must be based on an internal harmony of individual wills, which will occur when the inwardness or intentionality of the moral law has been clearly recognized by rulers and ruled alike, rather in keeping with Kant's moral philosophy, which is essentially an ethics of intention. What must ultimately be at stake is Homburg's inward personality, not merely his physical existence.

Quite cogently, the third act moves quickly toward the annihilation of Homburg's "romantic" personality, while the first steps are undertaken to save his empirical person from death. In counterpoint fashion, the fourth act brings about the resurrection of Homburg's inward personality and his acceptance of physical death, while the last act culminates in the reconciliation of the rival claims of individual and State but not before the State has undergone an inner purification paralleling Homburg's.

In the third act a breach is made in Homburg's illusive inner certainty. When Hohenzollern intimates that ignoble political motives may prompt the Elector to carry out the death sentence, Homburg makes for the first time a conscious attempt to relate himself to reality, although in the wrong direction. Instead of turning his gaze toward his own will, he turns it toward the world of sense and seeks the explanation for his pathetic fate in a vicious concatenation of events:

HOHENZOLLERN ....
It is said that the Swedish envoy, Count Horn,
Has come to negotiate the marriage of
Princess Natalia of Orange with his master,
King Carolus Gustavus,
And that the Elector has been bitterly offended
By something that his wife revealed to him;
The Princess has already set her heart on someone.
Have you had anything to do with this?

PRINCE. Why?

HOHENZOLLERN. Have you?

PRINCE. My friend, I have. Now all is clear to me.
The proposal sets the seal upon my luckless fate.
It is I who am the cause of her refusal,
For she is betrothed to me.[16]

This scene may be symptomatic of Kleist's long-standing distrust of human reason, the merely intellectual capacities embedded in the mind. "Understanding" cannot go beyond grasping a mere causal, perhaps deceptive, sequence of events. To activate the moral will, another capacity is needed, a direct insight of Reason which the Prince is still lacking. When Homburg fully grasps the breach opening up between his "feeling" and reality, the inner collapse is inevitable. The widening gulf between inner and outer world is symbolized in the open grave. The fear of death which grips Homburg is the very opposite of Penthesilea's self-willed death and Kohlhaas's equanimity at his execution. They retain a measure of faith in the absoluteness of their inner feeling. Homburg has lost all such hope. His courage will resurge only after he has found the strength to judge himself.

The fourth act brings into focus the person of the Elector, who so far has largely remained in the background. Through Natalia's intervention he is made to see the potential fallibility of his legalistic position. Natalia argues ingenuously for a principle of action that would reconcile law with feeling, the impersonal demands of the world with the sanctity of the human person. It is as though the "Cunning of Reason" [17] were speaking through her in order to urge the protagonists on toward the realization of an Ideal State in which harmony would prevail on the basis of the individual's self-determination. The news of Homburg's collapse introduces a new factor and elicits in the Elector a corresponding reaction—an act of seeming leniency. But the free choice given to the Prince embodies its own ironic dialectic of opposites. It will free Homburg from the tyranny of the outer world but will subject him to the inescapable demands of his own inner world. Though "confused," [18] the Elector makes the right move instinctively. If Homburg were made to accept his fate merely in passive resignation or soldierly courage but were not given a chance to judge himself, the essential demands of morality might not be met. The moral imperative demands unequivocally the active participation of the individual in adopting maxims of behavior. Only thus may he implement his autonomous will and become a truly self-legislating member in a "Kingdom of Ends." The conflict of individual and State must therefore be driven one revolution higher on the dialectic spiral, which is done precisely through the choice given to the Prince.

Before receiving the Elector's letter, Homburg expresses in a short monologue a feeling of utter hopelessness. Musing about the passing and irretrievably lost beauty of life, he has reached a point of resignation which contrasts vividly with the elevation of thought and feeling that overcomes him after he has made his decision:

> "Life," says the dervish, "is a journey, and a short one."
> How true! The furthest we ever get
> Is five or six feet above the earth,
> And the same distance underneath it!
>
> (*Lying almost full-length.*)
>
> Well, now I'm halfway between the two! One day
> A man can bear his head up proudly on his shoulders;
> The next it's hanging low with fear;
> And the next day it's lying at his feet.
> Ah, well, they say the sun shines up there too
> And over brighter fields than we have here.
> I believe that's true: a pity that the eye should rot
> Before it can glimpse those wonders— 19

Though at this moment he seems to have made his peace with the inevitable, he is still far from an active and positive acceptance of responsibility for his inner personality. When Natalia arrives and hands him the Elector's message, the critical point of the action has been reached. Kleist's treatment of the dramatic impact of the letter on the Prince is characteristic of his "psychology" and stagecraft. No grandiloquent speeches, no open effusion of feeling, but a constrained inner tension, a silent battle with thought and language mark the scene. The inner turmoil is only suggested in the playful struggle between the two lovers over the possession of the letter. Behind the chaste love-play looms a portentous obligation, no less than a choice between life and death. In ironic contrast, the triviality of the dialogue underscores the seriousness of the situation:

> PRINCE, *reading.* "Your Highness, the Prince of Homburg,
> When I consigned you, on account of your premature attack,
> To prison, I believed I was doing my duty.
> And I counted on your recognition of this fact.
> But if you are of the opinion
> That I have done you an injustice,
> Then will you kindly send me word—

A single line will do—
And at once I shall restore to you
Your sword and your command."

NATALIA *grows pale. A silence. The* PRINCE *gives
her a questioning look.*

NATALIA, *with a look of sudden joy.* There, you see!
A line, that's all he wants!
Oh, my dear friend, you are free!

She presses his hand.

PRINCE. My angel!

NATALIA. Oh, happy, happy moment! Look,
Here is the pen. Take it and write!

PRINCE. What signature is this?

NATALIA. That is "F," his sign for Frederick.
That is how he always signs himself.
Oh, Bork! You must be happy for me!
You must be happy too!
Oh, I knew his kindness is as infinite as the sea.
Bring a chair for His Highness, he must write at once!

PRINCE. He says: If I am of the opinion—

NATALIA, *interrupting.* Of course! Hurry, now. Sit down.
I shall dictate your reply to you.

She sets a chair for him.

PRINCE. I'll just read the letter over once again.

NATALIA, *snatching the letter from him.* What good will that do?
Did you not see, in the courtyard of the church,
The grave yawn up to you with open jaws?
Time is short. Sit down and write!

PRINCE, *smiling.* Really you're acting now as if the grave
Were set to pounce upon me like a panther.

*He sits down and takes up the pen. She turns away
to weep.*

NATALIA. Now write, if you do not want to make me
angry with you!

The PRINCE *rings for a* SERVANT, *who enters.*

PRINCE. Paper and ink! Some sealing-wax! A seal!

The SERVANT, *after having brought these things,
goes off again. The* PRINCE *writes. Silence. He
tears up the letter he has started and throws it
under the table.*

A bad beginning.

He takes another sheet of paper.

NATALIA *picks up the letter.* Why? What did you say?
But that is very good! That's excellent!

PRINCE, *muttering.* Pooh! It might have been written by a
cobbler,
Not by a Prince. I must turn it more gracefully.

A silence. He tries to snatch the ELECTOR'S *letter
again, which* NATALIA *still holds in her hand.*

What did he really say in the letter?

NATALIA, *refusing to give it to him.* Nothing! Nothing at all!

PRINCE, *insisting.* Give it to me!

NATALIA. But you've read it!

PRINCE, *tearing it from her grasp.* What if I have?
I must see what terms to use in my reply.

He opens the letter and reads it again.

NATALIA, *aside.* Oh, God! Now all is lost again!

PRINCE, *perplexed.* Look here! How very curious! Did you miss
this part?

NATALIA. No. Which part?

PRINCE. He leaves the decision to myself!

NATALIA. Oh, that! Yes, he does.[20]

Homburg's thought crystallizes only in fits and starts expressed in fragmentary phrases. He is comparable to the
Mirabeau of Kleist's essay whose thought after a struggle with
language suddenly erupts with pith and incisiveness: "Let him
[the Elector] do as he likes. I know now that I am doing as
I should." We can only guess what went on in his mind before
he reached this insight. At critical moments, Kleist's style
is akin to that of the Elohim writer of the Old Testament.

According to Erich Auerbach in *Mimesis,* in this style of writing

> . . . the decisive points of the narrative alone are emphasized, what lies between is nonexistent . . . thoughts and feelings remain unexpressed, are only suggested by the silence and the fragmentary speeches; the whole, permeated with the most unrelieved suspense and directed toward a single goal . . . remains mysterious and fraught with background.[21]

Certainly Homburg "gets a hold of himself." In so doing, he may realize that he is free to choose but that a will without a law may really not be free but subject to mere outer chance. In Kantian terms, he "is free but has no choice" if he is to become a self-legislating member of a rational community of men, at least "worthy," if not in actual possession, of happiness. "Fate" in its most esoteric meaning becomes thus identified with man's autonomous will, his moral or "intelligible" personality, for in recognizing the law within he becomes at least master of his soul or inner disposition. Through Kleist's dramatic skill, the locus of Homburg's "guilt" has been subtly shifted from an infraction of the rules of war—an isolated deed—to his character as such. And in confronting himself he must admit his innate debility—in almost Protestant fashion.

Meanwhile, the State, though taking the strategic consequences of Homburg's action out of the debate and resting its case on his disobedience of orders—his overt deed—has not yet come to terms with the moral aspect of the case. In the impending confrontation between the Elector, his officers, and the Prince, the ethics of personality involved in the case as it stands now will come into full view, but not before Kottwitz and Hohenzollern have spent considerable energy on forensic arguments. Kottwitz's rhetoric is beguiling but does not deceive the Elector, although some Kleist scholars profess to see in it the thematic solution of the drama. He first insists that tactical considerations prompted the Prince's premature attack, on which count he is easily refuted. Shifting to the consequences of Homburg's action, he alleges that the cavalry charge proved the Brandenburgers' mettle and inspired them with confidence for a decisive victory. But had the attack failed, what then?, the Elector asks. The security of the State should not have to depend on personal caprice and shifty fortunes of battle. "The only and the highest rule is conquest!" [22] is Kottwitz's Machiavellian retort, which also forms the basis of his impassioned plea for a patriarchal sort of government. The concern for the welfare of the State and the stern demands of the law are synthesized, he maintains, in the notion of the "Fatherland" or the "Crown" worn by the enlightened ruler whose personal judgment is the last court of appeal. Such ideas can be traced to cherished political theories expounded by Adam Müller, Kleist's erstwhile collaborator on the *Phoebus* journal, in his writings. But they are mere echoes in the drama, not its thematic substance. Kottwitz must finally admit that, given an opportunity to defeat the enemy, he would seize it even against express orders and then put his life confidently in the ruler's hands. In the final analysis, Kottwitz's defense rests on little else than the ethics of success which prompted Homburg's impulsive action in the first place, provided, of course, that such personal opportunism is beneficial to the State.

Kottwitz's patriotic utilitarianism emphasizes by contrast the inner change Homburg has experienced in his prison cell. Judging one's personality may well lie beyond the ken of worldly jurisdiction, Kleist seems to suggest, but in confronting himself and in his more metaphysical moments of inner experience, the individual may be able to do so. This existential insight, tortuously expressed in Kant's ethics, seems to be an important element in Homburg's regeneration.

In order to contrast the inwardness of the moral law with mere empirical considerations, Kleist introduces with a sure dramatic touch Hohenzollern's speech just before Homburg makes his entry. On the surface, Hohenzollern's attempt to exonerate the Prince abounds with specious reasoning. He maintains that the Elector himself could be made responsible for Homburg's infraction, since in the garden of Fehrbellin he stirred up the Prince's dream vision by entwining his own necklace around the laurel wreath in Homburg's hands. The Elector has no trouble in showing him that by carrying the argument a step further, the responsibility could easily be turned back on Hohenzollern himself, who called the

Elector's party into the garden in the first place. Unless one assigns an arbitrary beginning to the chain of empirical causes of an action, Hohenzollern's argument would lead to an infinite regression and away from the autonomy of the moral agent to a compelling external force. According to Kant, there must be a spontaneous power in man which enables him to initiate on his own a whole new causal series. But, of course, Hohenzollern's argument could also be intended subtly to urge the Elector to fathom his own inner disposition—in the garden scene he played, after all, a rather distasteful joke on the Prince, which he immediately tried to cover up. If the Elector turns away from Hohenzollern in open disgust, it may as much be from displeasure over having been reminded of an unpleasant truth as from impatience with faulty logic.

Nevertheless, when Homburg appears and makes his impassioned self-accusation, he does start a new causal series, as it were, by giving the action a new ironic turn. Having found the locus of guilt in his inner disposition, he has invalidated his friends' arguments in his defense, who must now plead with him, not with the Elector, for his life. And the Elector, who has neither accepted Kottwitz's utilitarian ethic of success nor Hohenzollern's seeming casuistry, thereby focusing attention on the intentional aspect of the Prince's behavior, finds himself in the ironic position of having to punish for his intentions and thus his character a man whose inner life has already been chastened. Through his freely willed adherence to the inward summons to personal responsibility, the external, legalistic exigencies of Homburg's "social contract" with the State have become superfluous. The spirit which animates his character transcends the letter of the law. Though not invalidating the law, it shows the law's limitations in the formation of human personality. If the irrational or psychological side of the drama is ignored, Homburg's inner experience leads to a hypostasis of the will, not the law, thereby reflecting the "ethical voluntarism" that pervades much of Kantian and Idealistic philosophy. And one could conceivably maintain that Homburg represents now the "advanced individual" of Fichte's philosophy of history, who disavows egocentrism and rises above the State without transgressing its law, in this sense becoming the harbinger of a new historic era.

When the Prince reaches his cell again, he is overawed by reverence for the unexpected force he has discovered in his own autonomous personality. His stirring hymn to immortality is a fitting parallel to Kant's praise of "duty" contained in *The Critique of Practical Reason:*

> Now, Immortality, you are entirely mine!
> You shine, with the radiance of a thousand suns,
> Through my eyes' dark bandages into my very soul!
> My arms feel like a pair of slowly spreading wings
> That bear my spirit through the quiet lofts of air;
> And as a ship whose sail fills with the evening wind
> Sees the lighted harbour sink along the rising waves,
> So, like the happy shore, my dying life
> Drowns slowly in the dusk of death:
> Now I can distinguish only forms and colours,
> And under my weightless feet
> Drift only clouds and those ethereal vapours
> That are the mists of time.[23]

The elevation of Homburg's soul to almost mystic heights stands in obvious contrast to the nihilistic despair that befell him after the breakdown of his self-centered personality. In his inner experience Homburg has gone farther than Penthesilea, as Hebbel pointed out. He has not only accepted death but in a sense conquered it within. The State may now pardon him and restore him to life.

If the drama ended in a lofty peroration by the Elector, it would indeed be a beautiful moral tale not devoid of tragic accents. But it ends in an ostentatious display of the Elector's mercy, Homburg's dazed question, "Tell me, is this a dream?" and Kottwitz's cryptic retort "A dream, what else," [24] followed by an incongruous patriotic call to arms. This and many other enigmatic episodes suggest that below the surface of a rational ideal the drama touches on motivational forces that barely cross the threshold of the principal characters' awareness.

Dramaturgically, the coexistence of two levels of inner experience is suggested in the striking contrast between the day scenes, where conscious values and ideas clash, and the night scenes in the garden at Fehrbellin at the beginning and end, which enshroud the drama in mystery. A case can be made for the critical viewpoint that the very theme of the drama consists in the opposition between conscious and unconscious motives.[25] Undoubtedly, Kleist knew from his own experience the Pascalian truth that the heart has reasons of which reason knows not. He was not so naïve as to believe that a philosophic ideal can easily be converted into a motive of action without an admixture of personal feeling or self-interest. Nor was Kant, for that matter. Therefore, below the surface of a moral ideal Kleist probes the wellsprings of psychological undercurrents.

The psychological profiles of the major characters are suggested in the drama primarily in enigmatic episodes which cry out for interpretation but can be sketched here only in rough outlines.

The Elector often acts and responds to his own actions and those of others in ways that may suggest a suppressed jealousy and guarded fear of the younger man's brash intrusions into his own domain of influence. His angry response to Homburg's dream vision of impending personal glory is out of keeping with the occasion. He quickly realizes his *faux pas* and tries to cover it up. Later he arranges for the Electress and Natalia to be present at the war council—a rather unusual role for women—thereby providing the source for Homburg's distraction. In the battle plan he assigns a waiting role to the Prince quite unsuited to his impulsive nature. It is questionable whether he does it for pedagogic reasons, especially since he himself assumes the active hero role in the midst of battle, though he is subsequently brought back to his natural position as strategist by his equerry Froben, who pays with his life for his master's "thoughtless" action. The role of strategist mapping out a battle plan in the background is obviously less visible and glorious than that of the dashing field commander. This may be the reason why he invited the two women to the war council in the first place, namely to make them fully aware of the decisive role played by the master strategist in military action. Upon departing from the council he chides the Prince for having spoiled complete victory through his untimely cavalry charges in two recent encounters with the enemy, although Field Marshal Dörfling rather ambiguously refers to Homburg's role in the recent battles as "glorious." (We are left in the dark whether he has in mind the assignment as such or its execution!) Yet, despite the Prince's purported unreliability the Elector entrusts him with a key role in the upcoming battle, a role, however, which accords ill with Homburg's impetuousness. It is as if the Elector were unconsciously bent on destroying the Prince's image as a hero and superseding him in this role.

Other episodes are equally puzzling. When the Elector learns from Natalia of Homburg's inner collapse and that he even wishes to renounce his love if only his life be spared, he quickly seizes the opportunity to annihilate his opponent as a hero figure by pointing out to Natalia that ". . . he can thank you (a woman!) for his life." [26] And to make sure that through his kindness he has again brought her over to his side: "My dear child! Do you forgive me?" [27] Seen from the Elector's private sphere, the "free" choice he gives to the Prince is no great gamble and might conceivably enhance his stature. For if Homburg chooses life he must do so at the cost of appearing unheroic and ready to shun the law. If, on the other hand, he chooses to accept death he will implicitly exonerate the Elector's judgment and at the same time provide him with an opportunity to show magnanimity in pardoning him. Homburg seems to be fully aware of the psychological dilemma into which the Elector's appeal to his own judgment has led him:

> If his pardon must depend
> Only upon my own impertinent objections
> Then I do not merit and do not want forgiveness [28]

When, finally, the Prince upstages him with his heroic acceptance of a "free death"—an act of inner self-confrontation that goes considerably beyond the mere admission of disobedience—the Elector makes a public spectacle of his pardon as though to outshine Homburg with his own nobility.[29]

As to Homburg, his erstwhile longing for self-fulfillment through a heroic deed is obviously tinged with an element of self-aggrandizement which implicitly challenges the Elector's authority. His offensive egocentrism is especially apparent in his strange reactions to the rumor of the Elector's death. Rather frigidly expressing some grief, he shows an ignoble haste in assuming a protector's stance toward Natalia and the Electress, precipitously makes his joyous marriage proposal, and is stunned upon learning that the Elector is alive. Addressing the messenger, he says rather cryptically:

> Speak! Each word you utter
> Hangs on my mind as heavily as gold! [30]

This is certainly an ambiguous way of expressing joyful relief. Though the sheen of gold may suggest the happiness of the occasion, in Kleist's metaphor it is rather the metal's heaviness that is stressed. The Prince is hardly buoyed up by the news. One must not necessarily go so far as to say that he is disappointed at being deprived of the chance to fill the older man's place in the lives of those dear to him. The episode rather subtly reveals the flaw in his character. If his heart is heavy at the happy news of the Elector's survival, it may be due to a sudden insight into his own frightful egocentrism. It is especially in this episode that Kleist's masterful verbal and dramatic strategy succeeds in interiorizing Homburg's *hybris* from mere disobedience of battle orders to real debility of character. Therefore, the Prince's later admission of guilt focuses on "The enemies within ourselves: defiance, arrogance . . ." and no longer on his infraction of the rules of war.

But for the moment he brushes off the challenge of self-encounter and relies on the Elector to sanction whatever he does and "is." When, however, that emotional prop is removed from his existence he suffers that monumental collapse of his being which is the prelude to his regeneration. In declaring his readiness to give up Natalia he is not necessarily cowardly but instinctively feels that his inner *hybris* has stripped him of his right to happiness and that he must atone for it by abandoning the very thing he loves. Yet, right to the end, he has a lingering suspicion that his claim on Natalia may not only contravene the Elector's alleged plan to marry her off to the Swedish king but also intrude on the older man's jealously guarded private sphere of influence. When he pleads with the Elector to desist from carrying out his plan, does he also suggest that the Elector not exploit her as a political weapon as he may have used her as a psychological ploy, or does he merely express his own feeling of responsibility toward her?

> Sire, do not purchase with your niece's hand
> The peace that you must win from Sweden.
> Dismiss from your camp the go-between
> Who made you such an ignominious proposal!
> Give him his answer in a round of shot! [31]

We cannot be sure. Again, Kleist leaves us guessing. And he places the *dramatis personae* who can directly observe the clash between the Elector and Homburg in the same position.

The spectators of the conflict are puzzled by what they see but seem to feel instinctively that it has deep roots that had better be left undisturbed. Especially in the beginning they envelop themselves in silence only sporadically interrupted by a knowing remark or an ambiguous action. Rittmeister Golz, a witness of the sleepwalking scene and other key episodes, as well as a stand-in for Colonel Kottwitz at the war council, staunchly promises to relay to the latter the Field Marshal's intent to see Kottwitz personally in order to warn him of Homburg's unreliability. But upon encountering Kottwitz in the battle zone Golz only meekly remarks that "It seems/He [the Field Marshal] had something important to tell you." [32] Subsequently, he only offers weak resistance to Homburg's disregard of battle orders and in the end utters mere trivialities in defense of the Prince. Golz, though timid if not cowardly, seems to know that, psychologically, the Elector's and Homburg's personal obligations are about to lead to a clash and that he had better not become involved in such a touchy issue. Field Marshal Dörfling, knowing of the weakness in the Elector's battle plan (the assignment of wrong battle roles to Homburg and himself) and fully aware that it has not been clearly transmitted to Kottwitz, a key figure in the impending encounter, does nothing to remedy the situation. Later on, he expresses amazement at Homburg's arrest but toward the end repeats vague rumors to the Elector about the army's plot to free Homburg by force. He obviously vacillates between sympathy for the Prince and obsequious loyalty toward the Elector. Fear of his superior may be a motivating force in Dörfling's behavior, but perhaps there is also a dim realization that the military strategy is contaminated by a complex private issue which is none of his business to solve.

Hohenzollern is not necessarily Homburg's evil genius who revels in sowing distrust between the Prince and the Elector. When he visits Homburg in his cell and asks him: "Could you perhaps, *unconsciously or not,*/Have committed some folly that offended him?" [33] he merely articulates in cautious terms the possible unconscious rivalry between the two men hidden behind their overt mutual admiration and respect. As early as in the immediate sequel to the dream scene he gives evidence not only of understanding the Prince's strange behavior but also of "seeing through" the Elector. When the messenger arrives enjoining him to "breathe no word" to the Prince of the Elector's part in the garden episode, he brusquely, and rather ambiguously, remarks: "I knew all that before." [34] And in his defense of Homburg's actions in the confrontation scene with the Elector he may be subtly reminding the latter of unavowed motives in his own behavior rather than merely intending to score a rhetorical point. Hohenzollern, more than the others, comes close to expressing his psychological guesses, although they remain couched in the terms of an argument dealing with logic.

Before they take a more active part in Homburg's rehabilitation, the two women, Natalia and the Electress, also display strangely ambiguous behavior patterns. Upon first hearing of the Elector's death, they do not hesitate to accept Homburg's hasty offers of protection, but when the rumor proves false they quickly withdraw from the Prince, as though they had been accessories to his *hybris*. In rushing away with her niece, the Electress pretends not to grasp Homburg's allusions to his impending betrothal to Natalia, and when pressed to give her consent, answers evasively:

> It doesn't matter. To-day there is no one in the world
> I would say "No" to, whatever he asked me.
> And to you, the victor in battle, least of all.
> Come! We must away! [35]

At this moment, the Elector has again assumed the dominant role in the two women's lives and removed Homburg from the center stage. These scenes and a number of others suggest the complex entanglement of private motives with public interests in the conflict between the Prince and his alleged protector, the Elector.

The drama has long been noted for the richness of its imagery and the boldness of its metaphors. But not until recently have they been plausibly interrelated with the thematic fabric of the play.[36] Particularly striking is the frequent use of horticultural images—plants, fields, and estates. The Elector is cast in the role of a gardener who plans and jealously guards the growth of the vegetation on his estate but cannot completely control the quirks of nature. The Prince is a plant that has grown out of control, which Homburg expresses himself thus:

> Do I not owe everything to him?
> And now, after having raised me with his own
> Devoted hands, you think he'll trample down into the dust
> So ruthlessly his favourite plant
> Merely because it put out rather too
> Abundantly and hastily its buds and flowers? [37]

When in the first scene the Elector asks where the Prince obtained the laurel for his wreath (he first thought it was a willow branch), he is astonished to discover that such a foreign plant could flourish on "my Prussian soil." Since a number of other images suggest an association of human beings with plants, an analogue between the encroachment of a foreign plant on his estate and the Prince's intrusion on his sphere of influence is implied. This impression is reinforced later in the play when Homburg, facing death, offers to withdraw to his own estate, there to "sow and reap." When Natalia pleads with the Elector for Homburg's life she compares him to a flower that should be allowed to ". . . live upon the earth/ Independent, free, and unrestrained." [38]

Such sequences of images can be observed throughout the play. At times they are arranged in striking parallelism. In the opening scene, the image of death and mourning—the willow branch which the Elector imagines to see in Homburg's hands—is immediately replaced by the image of the laurel, a symbol of triumphant victory. At the end, when the blindfolded Prince, expecting to meet his death, praises the scent of the "midnight violet"—its deep purple color suggesting sadness and mourning—he is quickly made aware that the plants are actually bright gilly flowers and pinks, images of light and life. Strangely enough, he is also told that ". . . a maiden/Planted them there," [39] no longer a "gardener." Does Kleist suggest that Homburg has been freed from the Elector's direct control and is about to enter Natalia's world of light? Plausibly.

Other images are used with equal suggestiveness. In the battle the Elector must exchange his white horse for a brown one, and before the encounter Homburg was seen riding a black stallion, only to refer after the battle to his "sorrel." [40] This sequence seems to suggest the nature and outcome of the conflict, namely a development from extreme positions—black and white—to a conciliatory ending. Quite obvious is the concordance between Homburg's appearance in the opening scene—his shirt wide open—and the Elector's at the beginning of act five, when he is stirred up from his sleep by the rumors of the army's sedition and enters upon the stage in a night robe. As the Field Marshal rushes in, the Elector rebukes him: "You know how I detest it when/People enter my apartments unannounced!" [41] In both cases, the protagonists' appearance suggests that they have exposed themselves to the spectators' view. But while the Prince wears his heart on his sleeve, the Elector resents the intrusion on his private world. The imagery effectively underlines the contrast in their characters.

In *The Prince of Homburg* the metaphoric richness of Kleist's style is no unchecked linguistic growth. It is rather an instrument finely attuned to the complexity of the theme.

However, in the final analysis it remains an open question whether the drama stresses the irreconcilability of conscious and unconscious levels of behavior or shows instead that a moral ideal, if not a psychological motivating force itself, can be a fragile product of inner, albeit only temporary, victories over self.

That "victory over self" in Kleist's last work means affirmation—not abnegation—of one's inward personality, an insistence on the inviolable nature of one's being, precisely at moments when the reality of death threatens to erode the unity of self. Penthesilea finds her self in conjuring up a powerful "feeling" that both kills and redeems her. Kohlhaas ascends the scaffold in cheerful self-possession. Homburg journeys from the threat of inner dissolution at the sight of his grave to inner integrity when he opens himself up to his own being in his determination to accept death.

In fact, the psychological mode of interpretation of *The Prince of Homburg*, from which the shades of the Oedipus complex are never far removed, tends to overlook the importance of the protagonists' individual struggle for inner coherence and self-realization. It sees their private battles with themselves and the personal anxieties caused by the uncertainties of the future—emblematically expressed in the unpredictable fortunes of war—as essentially a power struggle *against* each other, a covert tug of war for the "possession" of a beloved object, in this case Natalia. But they may rather be fighting *for* their "selves" with the absolutist urge that we have come to expect of the Kleistian character. What they seek is not the psychological *defeat of the other* but rather the *recognition by the other* of the ontological integrity of their own subjective being. This they are able to do *for* each other once they have come face to face with themselves in confronting the threat of death and disintegration. For the shadow of dissolution falls not only across Homburg's life but also across the Elector's existence as the embodiment of a world of rule and law in the near-sedition of his troops. But once they have gained their inner composure they find no difficulty in acknowledging the other's right and courage "to be." Kleist seems to express the existential insight that the acceptance of the other as an autonomous person is possible only after one has been able to accept oneself.

In contrast to Homburg's dramatic experience, the Elector's parallel journey toward selfhood is barely audible in the play. But it is there, nevertheless. His attempt to conceal from Homburg his rather ignoble role in the dream scene reveals a certain inauthenticity of behavior. His foolhardy attempt to lead his troops into battle conspicuously on his white horse repeats in a minor key Homburg's untimely cavalry charge (and is reminiscent, ever so slightly, of Penthesilea's mad rushes on horseback!). It is questionable whether in doing so he is more bent upon "showing up" the younger man than affirming his own person. Even an older man, Kleist knows, is never "complete," but forever in search of his own being in thought and action. And in Froben's sacrificial death Kleist may not merely celebrate a heroic feat but give a hint of the *hybris* of egocentrism in the Elector's own impetuous attempt at self-affirmation. When he is "confused" upon hearing of Homburg's collapse, he may dimly realize that his own inner world is not built upon the firmest of foundations. And if he leaves the decision about the justice of his legalistic position up to Homburg, he may not be trying to "outmaneuver" the younger man but to find support for his own being in the other's judgment. By all means, it is possible to see in the tension between the Elector and Homburg an existential search for mutual self-confirmation rather than a subterranean rivalry for glory and dominion over others. It would seem highly improbable that a man could serenely accept death merely because it affords him an opportunity to carry off a psychological victory over his rival and thus bind anew the object of their common affection—Natalia—to his own person. Conversely, it is more plausible that the recognition of his dignity as a person, evinced in the Elector's decision to let him decide his own fate, may provide Homburg with the needed strength to face death.

That Homburg and the Elector finally accept each other's right to be as they now are after having gone in their own way through a process of inner clarification is made amply clear in the text itself, unless the critic is inclined to read mere sarcastic irony into such statements as:

HOMBURG. How noble of him, and how dignified!
This is the way a great man should behave! [42]

ELECTOR. Now that he [Homburg] *has graduated from these trials,*
Can you entrust yourselves to him again? [43]

Certainly, both the Elector and the Prince as a result of their experience have learned something about themselves and have arrived at greater self-possession, especially the Prince, who in wishing to die a "free death" shows that he is no longer a bondslave to earlier dependencies. What the substance of Homburg's inner conquest is, still remains a matter of controversy among critics of Kleist. Referring to the author's own death, some tend to believe that Homburg submitted to the law only after he recognized in himself an irresistible suicidal urge. The inner freedom he discovered would then not be the freedom of the self-willed law but the freedom of self-willed death. Further, Homburg's statement: "Death now will wash away my sin" [44] would be a rather blasphemous declaration of absolute independence from all earthly jurisdiction. However, it may express nothing more than the realization that the strength he has finally discovered within himself amply compensates for his earlier weakness in the face of death. This would be especially true if the actor puts the rhetorical stress on *"now."* Fundamentally it remains questionable whether an inner preparedness for death should be equated with a suicidal urge. To lift the thought of death from an abstract mathematical certainty to a lived inner reality may be more a matter of existential authenticity than a syndrome of suicidal pathology, as is shown in some of Heidegger's and Camus' writings. This existential dimension can only deepen the moral problem which invariably ensues when the individual seeks to affirm his own being against the rival claims of the world.

At any rate, both the Elector and the Prince will have to reorient themselves within a new set of circumstances. But as in all his other works, Kleist leaves us guessing how they will cope with new inner and outer realities. The Prince's dazed question ". . . is this a dream?" may well express his dim awareness that he has entered into a new world requiring a radical readjustment. Whether his dream will turn into another nightmare, only the future will tell. But despite the lack of sensitivity manifest in the Elector's ostentatious way of pardoning him, an element of hopeful expectation and obvious surprise vibrates in Homburg's question rather than a sour note of regret at not being able to upstage the Elector one last time with an act of heroic martyrdom. The festive occasion can hardly be turned into a scene of resentment over the loss of opportunity to die a hero's death. And Kottwitz, though never showing much intellectual perspicacity and easily swayed by the enthusiasms of the moment, certainly interprets the Prince's question in a positive way: "Yes, your dream has come true. You are exonerated and celebrated as the hero of the day." The patriotic sentiment which played a part in Kleist's writing of *The Prince of Homburg* cannot be entirely ignored in speculating on the meaning of the last scene. Though it has the earmarks of an expedient and may gloss over new inner challenges in his hero's destiny, the scene still suggests an elevation of collective feeling.

In Kleist's own life, however, such patriotic fervor could never eclipse the urgency of his personal problems. But we must concede that in his last and perhaps most mature dramatic work he gained enough distance from himself to illustrate the truth of T. S. Eliot's statement: "The more perfect the artist, the more completely separate in him will be the man who suffers and the mind which creates." [45] Taken out of the drama's context and directly applied to Kleist, Homburg's final question suggests the artist's own skepticism about the possibility of reconciling private with public concerns. Seen from the vantage point of Kleist's own inner experience, the ideal moral State in which the claims of personality are harmonized with those of the world is but an evanescent dream of reason producing its own illusions.

NOTES

[1] (Quotes from *The Prince of Homburg* are taken from James Kirkup's translation of the play contained in *The Classic Theatre*, ed. Eric Bentley, Vol. II, Doubleday Anchor, 1959. Another, slightly less poetic but at times more accurate translation of the drama, is Charles Passage's, published by Liberal Arts Press, Inc., in 1956.) Sembd., Vol. 3, p. 218, ll. 74–77; Kirkup, pp. 426–27, act one, scene one.

[2] Sembd., Vol. 3, pp. 257–58, ll. 978–79; 1022–27; 1030–37; Kirkup, pp. 470–71, act three, scene five.

[3] Sembd., Vol. 3, p. 271, ll. 1374–75, 1380–81; Kirkup, p. 486, act four, scene four.

[4] Sembd., Vol. 3, p. 289, l. 1856; Kirkup, p. 507, act five, scene two.

[5] Sembd., Vol. 3, p. 289, l. 1860; Kirkup, *loc cit.*

[6] Kleist's propensity to introduce ironic reversals may have been reinforced by his increasing fascination with the phenomena of oppositions in the world. In his later epistolary and aesthetic

writings, this notion becomes almost as prominent as his preoccupation with "feeling" and "trust." About the time of his writing *The Prince of Homburg,* it may have become crystallized in his mind through Adam Müller's philosophic and political treatises. In the essay "On the Gradual Formation of Thought in Speaking," Kleist explains how an electrified body of matter when coming into the atmosphere of another nonelectrified body will induce in the latter the opposite current. In other occasional writings, he expatiates on this idea in similar ways. But it is his friend Adam Müller who in his influential *Lehre vom Gegensatze* ("Theory of Opposites") elaborated the idea into a political and historistic theory which became the forerunner of dialectic idealism and exerted no mean influence on Kleist and his contemporaries. The "law of opposites" has undoubtedly a natural affinity with the artistic canons of peripety and irony which play a role in most dramatic literature. But under the influence of Adam Müller, Kleist seems to have become more acutely conscious of this kinship. This awareness may have prompted him to compare *Penthesilea* and *The Kaethchen of Heilbronn* with the + and – in algebra.

7 Sembd., Vol. 3, p. 218, l. 65; Kirkup, p. 426, act one, scene two.

8 Sembd., Vol. 3, p. 223, l. 208; Kirkup, p. 433, act one, scene four.

9 Sembd., Vol. 3, p. 219, ll. 83–84; Kirkup, p. 427, act one, scene three.

10 Sembd., Vol. 3, p. 222, l. 158; Kirkup, p. 431, act one, scene four.

11 Sembd., Vol. 3, p. 273, ll. 1412–16; Kirkup, p. 489, act five, scene two.

12 Sembd., Vol. 3, p. 284, ll. 1753–58; Kirkup, pp. 501–2, act five, scene seven.

13 Sembd., Vol. 3, p. 248, l. 772; Kirkup, p. 460, act five, scene ten.

14 Sembd., *loc cit.,* l. 765; Kirkup, *loc. cit.*

15 Sembd., Vol. 3, ll. 777–79; Kirkup, p. 461, act two, scene ten.

16 Sembd., Vol. 3, p. 254, ll. 917–28; Kirkup, p. 467, act three, scene one.

17 In Hegel's philosophy the "Cunning of Reason" depicts the early stages of historic development in which Reason expresses itself as mere "instinct."

18 Sembd., Vol. 3, p. 263, l. 1175; Kirkup, p. 447, act four, scene one. (Kirkup, unaccountably, omits the translation of the German *"verwirrt"* altogether. Passage translates "in confusion.")

19 Sembd., Vol. 3, p.267, ll. 1286–96; Kirkup, p. 482, act four, scene three.

20 Sembd., Vol. 3, pp. 268–69, ll. 1307–42; Kirkup, pp. 483–84, act two, scene four.

21 Erich Auerbach, *Mimesis,* Willard Trask, trans., New York, Doubleday Anchor, 1957, p. 9. Original U.S. edition, 1953, Princeton University Press.

22 Sembd., Vol. 3, p. 278, l. 1578; Kirkup, p. 495, act five, scene five.

23 Sembd., Vol. 3, p. 287, ll. 1830–37; Kirkup, p. 585, act five, scene ten.

24 Sembd., Vol. 3, p. 289, l. 1857; Kirkup, p. 507, act five, scene eleven.

25 This is the viewpoint of Professor J. M. Ellis in his very perceptive study, *Kleist's "Prinz Friedrich von Homburg,"* University of California Press, 1970. The psychological profiles which follow are to a great extent influenced by his monograph but also by Heinz Politzer's "Kleists Trauerspiel vom Traum: Prinz Friedrich von Homburg," in *Euphorion,* 64, Band, 3/4, Heft, 1970.

26 Sembd., Vol. 3, p. 263, l. 1198; Kirkup, p. 478, act four, scene one.

27 Sembd., Vol. 3, l. 1199; Kirkup, *loc. cit.*

28 Sembd., Vol. 3, p. 271, ll. 1383–85; Kirkup, p. 486, act four, scene four.

29 Psychoanalytic critics insist that Homburg and the Elector continually strive to outdo each other, first through military feats, then through acts of nobility. They further maintain that the two are basically contending for Natalia's affection. The whole drama can thus be presented as a sublime expression of an Oedipal struggle.

30 Sembd., Vol. 3, p. 244, ll. 637–38; Kirkup, p. 454, act two, scene eight.

31 Sembd., Vol. 3, p. 285, ll. 1779–83; Kirkup, p. 502, act five, scene seven.

32 Sembd., Vol. 3, p. 232, ll. 398–99; Kirkup, p. 443, act two, scene one.

33 Sembd., Vol. 3, p. 253, ll. 911–13; Kirkup, p. 466, act three, scene one. (Italics mine.—R.E.H.)

34 Sembd., Vol. 3, p. 219, l. 86; Kirkup, p. 427. (Passage's accurate translation, Kirkup freely renders: "He might have known I would not do that," which somehow misses the point.)

35 Sembd., Vol. 3, p. 245, ll. 707–10; Kirkup, p. 457, act two, scene nine.

36 This has been done in great detail in J. M. Ellis's above-mentioned monograph. The examples given here have been suggested by his study as well as by Mary Garland's *Kleist's "Prinz Friedrich von Homburg,"* *An Interpretation through Word Pattern,* The Hague, Mouton, 1968.

37 Sembd., Vol. 3, p. 251, ll. 833–39; Kirkup, p. 464, act three, scene one.

[38] Sembd., Vol. 3, p. 260, ll. 1097–98; Kirkup, p. 475, act four, scene one.

[39] Sembd., Vol. 3, p. 288, l. 1843; Kirkup, p. 505, act five, scene ten.

[40] Kirkup pays no attention to this subtlety and translates "*goldfuchs*" or "sorrel" in Sembd., Vol. 3, p. 246, l. 744, merely as "horse"; p. 459, act two, scene ten.

[41] Sembd., Vol. 3, p. 273, ll. 1429–30; Kirkup, p. 490, act five, scene three.

[42] Sembd., Vol. 3, p. 269, ll. 1343–44; Kirkup, p. 485, act four, scene four.

[43] Sembd., Vol 3, p. 286, ll. 1822–23; Kirkup, p. 504, act five, scene nine. (I have slightly altered this translation to adapt it better to the original.—R.E.H.)

[44] Sembd., Vol. 3, p. 284, l. 1770; Kirkup, p. 502, act five, scene seven.

[45] T. S. Eliot, "Tradition and the Individual Talent," first published in 1917, included in *Selected Essays, 1917–1932*, New York, Harcourt Brace Jovanovich, Inc. and, London, Faber & Faber Ltd., 1932.

Epilogue: The Sense of the Grotesque

"The Beggarwoman of Locarno" and "St. Cecilia, or The Power of Music"

Despite its conciliatory ending, Kleist's last drama contains many jarring notes of disquietude. The suggestion of the disturbing rupture between conscious actions and unconscious motives as well as Homburg's final expression of disbelief cast a pall of doubt on the ideal which the play depicts. In quick, furtive flashes Kleist bares the make-believe character of an idealistic philosophy. Its notion of a Rational State ensuing from the individual's enactment of moral freedom is at best a beautiful dream. But for a fleeting moment in his career as a writer Kleist acted as though the dream of Reason were valid. In one sense, his Idealistic legacy to the world shares the "as if" nature of Kant's moral philosophy. The notion of a Kingdom of Ends is viable only if it is assumed that nature itself is a kingdom governed by a teleological law and is so constituted as to guarantee and even promote man's moral activities. The Kantian moral faith makes some sense if one embraces the corollary belief in universal teleology. But Kant asserted emphatically that the idea of purpose can never be a constitutive principle of knowledge and therefore does not properly belong to the realm of "nature." He points the way to an existential view: against the uncooperativeness of nature to reveal its purposes, practical reason must stress the need for self-determination in accord with a normative and faintly teleological law. And although Kant attached to the exercise of the purposive faculty of the will the promise of a future world and the existence of God, what remains prominent in his view of moral action is man's autonomy, his self-dependence, the human predicament of having to make choices in an ostensibly purposeless and impassive universe. The moral law is ultimately something quite apart from being. In Kant's ethical voluntarism, one can detect the germs of existential anguish.

In his last two stories, "The Beggarwoman of Locarno" and "St. Cecilia, or the Power of Music," [1] Kleist reverts again to the anguished mood of his earlier works. They depict a world which, far from rational, is not only impassive to the purposive drive of man, but alien, absurd, even grotesque and strangely dualistic. "The Beggarwoman . . . ," little more than a brief anecdote, is literally a ghost story portraying the irruption of an incomprehensible, destructive force in human life. A marquis who had indirectly caused the death of an old beggarwoman finds a miserable end in his burning castle, which he had set afire himself, "weary of life," after he had vainly attempted to exorcize the spirit of the dead woman. Although there is a hint of moral justice in the story, the maniacal frenzy of the nobleman and other narrative elements create an atmosphere of unrelieved anguish. In this sense the anecdote is a transposition of Kleist's predominant inner mood into a succinct artistic metaphor.

"St. Cecilia, or the Power of Music" is a more complex and grotesque tale of an event taking place in the (imaginary) Cloister of St. Cecilia near Aachen during the time of the religious wars. Four brothers, iconoclasts, plan to destroy the cloister but are diverted from their intent by a strange miracle. Sister Antonia, believed to be seriously ill, suddenly appears, wan but healthy, and leads the congregation in an oratorio whose musical splendor forces the four marauders to their knees in reverent prayer. It turns out that Sister Antonia had laid unconscious in her cell the whole time, while St. Cecilia herself must have conducted the oratorio, a conjecture later sanctioned by the Pope. But it is the aftermath to the oratorio that is most puzzling. The miracle conjures up in the four brothers a state of mind that can only be described as religious hysteria. They spend the rest of their lives observing silence, fasting, worshiping the crucifix, and singing at regular intervals the *gloria in excelsis*. At a ripe old age, they die, a seemingly happy lot, but not before having sung once more the *gloria* with booming voices that reverberate grotesquely through the insane asylum to which they had been committed.

In his last two stories, Kleist depicts a world in which good and evil, the heavenly and diabolic, the fearful and exalted, live in confusing proximity, a stark contrast to Homburg's ideal world of moral purposiveness. Yet, when he finally made his choice to commit suicide, Kleist seemed to have regained a measure of confidence in the ultimate goodness of the world and the eternal purpose of the soul. His last letters, no doubt written in a state of euphoria, abound with metaphysical hopes and a joyous anticipation of happiness and the discovery of life's meaning in a blessed hereafter. If he did not possess it in this life, Kleist seems to have taken a certain faith in a Kingdom of Ends into his voluntary death. But one cannot help overhearing in his death litany some of the hysterical accents of the *gloria in excelsis* sung by the four brothers in "St. Cecilia, or the Power of Music."

NOTES

[1] The time of writing of the two tales coincides roughly with the late stages in Kleist's work on *The Prince of Homburg* (from the end of 1810 to the beginning of 1811).

Bibliographical Notes

I. A sketch of Kleist criticism in the nineteenth and twentieth centuries up to 1945:

In his lifetime, Kleist received mild approval for his *Schroffen-stein* and *Amphitryon* and puzzled reactions to the *Kaethchen.* Conversely, Goethe was repelled by *Penthesilea,* made a censorious remark about the "confusion of feeling" of Alkmene in *Amphitryon,* and showed little understanding for the dynamics of *The Broken Pitcher.* In general, he considered Kleist's temperament and art to suffer from unfortunate pathological excesses, a judgment which showed surprising tenacity for almost a hundred years.

Johann Ludwig Tieck, in his introduction to the first edition of Kleist's works (1821), made some concessions to the alleged "mental illness" of the author but singled out *Homburg* as being unmarred by Kleist's psychological problems and categorized him as a "mannerist" (in a typifying rather than evaluative sense). Tieck's second edition (1826) was reviewed by Heinrich Gustav Hotho, a disciple of

Hegel. On a high intellectual *niveau*, the review postulates a three-fold development in Kleist's art: one, erroneous actions prompted by inner states of mind; two, manifestations of the divine will in a world of chance; three, human consciousness confronting the historic world. The first complete critical biography was done by Alfred Wilbrandt (*Heinrich von Kleist*, 1863), who could still draw on the personal reminiscences of Kleist's friend, Ernst von Pfuel. Wilbrandt claims that Kleist's prepoetic period was under the influence of Shaftesbury's and Goethe's ideal of the "aesthetic" man and sees in Kleist's style a development from an artistic climax in *Penthesilea* toward deterioration in "St. Cecilia," "The Duel," and "The Beggarwoman."

Scholarly research into Kleist's life and epistolary writings began with Eduard von Bülow's edition of *Kleist's Leben und Briefe* (1848) and continued in Rudolf Köpke's edition of some political tracts from the *Abendblätter* (1862), Theophil Zolling's study of Kleist's sojourn in Switzerland (1882), and the complete edition of Kleist's letters by Georg Minde-Pouet (1905). Since then, thirty more letters have been discovered and incorporated into newer editions, especially Sembdner's.

The period of positivism (from *c.* 1880 on) gave impetus to Kleist studies. It shows a tendency toward critical biography, the exploration of biographical documents, the tracing of literary and other sources of the works combined with some stylistic anaylsis. Otto Brahms in his *Das Leben Heinrichs von Kleist* (first edition, 1884) stressed the influence of the "milieu" on Kleist, his emancipation from the "Prussian spirit," and the development in his outlook, especially from 1808 on. He also advanced the still controversial theory of Adam Müller as Kleist's "evil genius." However, he opposed the theory of Kleist's "pathological" character. The notion of Kleist as a pathological talent, underpinned gradually by Freudian theories, was also opposed by Sigismund Rahmer, an M.D., in two separate studies (1903 and 1909). The stylistic research of Richard Weissenfels (*Vergleichende Studien zu Heinrich von Kleist*, 1887–88) focused on Kleist's supposed poetic eccentricities culminating in *Penthesilea*, while generally characterizing his style as vacillating between "unbridled naturalness" and "unprosaic artificiality." Others, such as Minde-Pouet (*Heinrich von Kleist, Seine Sprache und sein Stil*, 1897) and August Sauer (*Kleists Todeslitanei*, 1907), tried to capture with more or less success the essence of Kleist's style.

A spinoff of positivistic research is the clarification of Kleist's political attitudes, primarily in his Berlin (*Abendblätter*) period.

Reinhold Steig (*Heinrich von Kleists Berliner Kämpfe*, 1901) assembled valuable material on this period but made the error of attributing to Kleist the reactionary, royalist, and anti-Semitic attitudes of the conservative nobility. Later research, contained primarily in dissertations, rather conclusively disproved this theory (see, for instance, Richard Samuel's Cambridge dissertation of 1938, "Heinrich von Kleist's Participation in the Political Movements of the Years 1805 to 1809 and Helmut Sembdner's "Die Berliner Abendblätter Heinrichs von Kleist," in *Schriften der Kleistgesellschaft*, 1939).

The centennial year of Kleist's death, 1911, saw an efflorescence of Kleist studies: Julius Hart, *Das Kleist-Buch*, 1912; Wilhelm Herzog, *Heinrich von Kleist. Sein Leben und sein Werk*, 1911; Heinrich Meyer-Benfey, *Das Drama Heinrich von Kleists*, 2 vols., 1911–13, and a revised edition of Brahms's book. These works show a tendency to enshrine Kleist as a "classical" dramatic genius, i.e., an "original" dramatist untouched by abstract ideas or ideals such as Schiller. Hart maps out a development in Kleist's works centering on the notion that he never quite abandoned his pre-Kantian views and sought to overcome "tragedy," which he almost succeeded in doing in his last dramas. Meyer-Benfey presents Kleist wrestling with a "new form of drama," but supports his views unconvincingly —Kleist is credited with rather trivial "innovations." In the second volume he maintains that Kleist's increased concern with political problems was due to his waning interest in creating new literary forms.

In the twenties and thirties of this century, Kleist scholarship took a marked turn toward research into the intellectual content of his works, at times at the expense of methodology and stylistic analysis. Rudolf Unger (*Herder, Novalis und Kleist*, 1922) gave a sensitive portrayal of the problem of death in Kleist's major dramas, especially *Penthesilea* and *Homburg*, while stressing a development from aesthetic to ethical concerns. Philipp Witkop (*Heinrich von Kleist*, 1922), rather than seeing "development" in Kleist's works, emphasizes variations on the same underlying "tragic-Dionysian" theme. Friedrich Gundolf (*Heinrich von Kleist*, 1922), a member of the Stefan George circle, shows Kleist's affinities with modern expressionism which, in Gundolf's doctrinaire classicist views, leads to many artistic and stylistic aberrations. According to Walter Muschg (*Kleist*, 1923), Kleist's life and works express a certain pessimism which ensued from the encounter of his basically tormented psyche with Kant's criticism. Friedrich Braig (*Heinrich von Kleist*, 1925) gives a lengthy Catholic analysis of Kleist's works, which are seen sweeping out a development from the pagan idea of "fate" in *Schroffenstein* to the Christian idea of "providence" in *Kaethchen*. The notions of "original sin" and "redemption" are said to play a major role in all works.

The most influential critic of the twenties and thirties has been Gerhard Fricke, with his *Gefühl und Schicksal bei Heinrich von Kleist*, 1929. Starting from Kierkegaardian categories, he defined the notion of "feeling" in Kleist as an intense experience of the integrity of the self which manifests itself increasingly in his works from *Amphitryon* on. His prepoetic stage is seen merely as a rationalistic pseudomorphosis of his existential concern with his own inner being or "vocation." In the works, there is a discernible development from the confrontation of the "I" with the "Thou" to the conflict between the integrity of the "I" and the claims of society, leading to a hypostasis of the feeling of self in *Homburg*. Fricke's influence on succeeding Kleist scholars has been great, although his views have come under increasing criticism, especially by more psychologically or linguistically oriented interpreters.

Besides presentations of Kleist's life and works under one aegis or another, the twenties and thirties produced a number of studies on specific aspects of Kleist:

a. His Kant crisis, above all Ernst Cassirer's thesis in *Heinrich von Kleist und die Kantische Philosophie,* 1919, which purports that Kleist's crisis was triggered by Fichte's *The Vocation of Man* rather than a work by Kant. Cassirer's "Fichte-Thesis" has had few followers other than Braig and Unger.

b. Kleist's relation to music and its influence in his works. This theme has led to speculative comparisons with Wagnerian music drama and equally unsatisfactory essays on the supposed affinities between Kleist's drama and the form of Baroque music. However, in the last two decades several of Kleist's works have been successfully turned into operas.

c. The importance of the essay "On the Marionette Theater" as a kind of mystic cipher for the exegesis of all of Kleist's works. Expounded in Hanna Hellmann's brief essay *Heinrich von Kleist. Darstellung des Problems,* 1911, the idea was championed and refined by Paul Böckmann ("Kleists Aufsatz über das Marionettentheater," *Euphorion,* 28, 1927) but rejected by Karl Schultze-Jahde ("Kleists Gestaltentyp," *Zeitschrift für deutsche Philologie,* 60, 1935), who feels that Kleist's mildly philosophical and speculative writings are an insufficient basis for the interpretation of his literary works.

d. Rousseau's influence on Kleist. Cassirer denies such influence. Roger Ayrault (*La Légende de Heinrich von Kleist*, 1934) limits it to the time of Kleist's Würzburg journey, while Oskar von Xylander (*Heinrich von Kleist und J. J. Rousseau*, 1937) sees it pervading all of Kleist's works and as the very basis of his relentless fight against rationalism.

e. Kleist's relation to Adam Müller. So far this topic has produced unsatisfactory investigations. It is indeed very questionable whether Kleist espoused to any appreciable degree Müller's theories, although the two men collaborated on the *Phoebus*.

A remarkable attempt made outside of Germany in the thirties to interpret Kleist's works *in toto* is Roger Ayrault's above-mentioned book, in which he traces Kleist's search for an ideal form of drama all the way from the "education" by Molière (*Amphitryon*) and the creative imitation of Greek drama (*Penthesilea, The Broken Pitcher*) to *Arminius* and *Kaethchen*, which attain unity through their chief characters, and finally to *Homburg*, where near-perfection is attained.

The philological problem of the chronology of Kleist's works, especially the *Novellen*, has given rise to many treatises and dissertations in the pre-War period and is still under debate at this moment. To trace the many theories advanced so far would go beyond the intentions and confines of this book.

II. In the post-War period Kleist scholarship received much impetus again in Germany as well as abroad. In England and the United States, psychoanalytic interpretations and structural analyses with some attention paid to symbols and imagery are especially prominent. In Germany, an increasing number of studies deal with style, rhythm, linguistic structure, and textual analysis, without displacing, however, larger works concerned with the essence of Kleist's *Weltanschauung*, especially on the basis of a conflict between individual "consciousness" and "reality," a topic which still owes much to Fricke's seminal work.

The following critical bibliography is an attempt to list and abstract the most important books and monographs of the post-War period that might be of particular interest to the American or British student of German literature.

Blankenagel, John C. *The Dramas of Heinrich von Kleist. A Biographical and Critical Study*. Chapel Hill: The University of North Carolina Press, 1931. (Mentioned here because it is the first complete critical study of the dramas to appear in print in the United States and is still quite useful as an introduction to Kleist.) An exegesis based on the notion of a conflict between "reason" and "emotion" as the central theme of all the dramas.

Blöcker, Günter. *Heinrich von Kleist oder Das Absolute Ich*. Berlin: Argon Verlag, 1960. Sees Kleist's life and works as an intransigent search of the individual for his being which transcends ideational or ideological categories and is essentially a quest for a kind of "absolute ego." Contains a perceptive analysis of the idiosyncracies of Kleist's language.

Dürst, Rolf. *Heinrich von Kleist. Dichter zwischen Ursprung und Endzeit. Kleists Werk im Licht idealistischer Eschatologie*. Bern: Francke Verlag, 1965. An interpretation of Kleist's works on the basis of the chiliastic ideas contained in the *Marionettentheater*, with emphasis on their affinity with Hegel's philosophy of history. A typical example of *Geistesgeschichte*.

Ellis, J. M. *Kleist's "Prinz Friedrich von Homburg." A Critical Study*. (University of California Publications in Modern Philology, 97) Berkeley: University of California Press, 1970. A very perceptive and original analysis of the structure and imagery of *Homburg* guided by the thesis that the play portrays the irreconcilability of conscious actions and unconscious motives.

Garland, Mary. *Kleist's "Prinz Friedrich von Homburg": An Interpretation Through Word Pattern*. The Hague: Mouton, 1968. An attempt to arrive at new insights through textual criticism concentrating on word patterns, at times marred by esoteric cabalistic speculations. Subtle interpretative arguments try to disentangle the complexity of Homburg's feelings toward the Elector as a relative, a father-figure, and the symbolic embodiment of the Christian God-Father.

Gearey, John. *Heinrich von Kleist. A Study in Tragedy and Anxiety*. Philadelphia: University of Pennsylvania Press, 1968. An ingenious attempt to show that the central problem in Kleist's works and literary character is a fascination with the phenomena of opposition *per se* rather than with a conflict between definable entities such as "feeling" and "reason" or "consciousness" and "reality."

Hafner, Franz. *Heinrich von Kleists "Prinz Friedrich von Homburg."* Zürich: Atlantis Verlag, 1952. The drama of Homburg's inner experience reflects the triad of human development suggested in the *Marionettentheater* from original unity of "feeling" over "discursive conflict" with the world to the conquest of reality through the revelation of the "absolute" in a moral ideal. The Elector: an incarnation of divine wisdom. Kleist's hyperbolic, allegoric language, the syntax and rhythm of the drama are perfectly adapted to the theme.

Hoffmeister, Elmar. *Täuschung und Wirklichkeit bei Heinrich von Kleist.* Bonn: H. Bouvier & Co., 1968. A (quite successful) attempt to establish a typology of the various forms of deception, including self-deception and illusion, in all of Kleist's works.

Hohoff, Curt. *Heinrich von Kleist in Selbstzeugnissen und Bilddokumenten.* ("rowohlts monographien") Hamburg: Rowohlt Taschenbuch Verlag, 1958. A readable and popular critical biography containing many illustrations and endeavoring to show that Kleist was the "first modern man" in German literature.

Holz, Hans Heinz. *Macht und Ohnmacht der Sprache. Untersuchungen zum Sprachverständnis und Stil Heinrich von Kleists.* Frankfurt a.M.: Athenäum Verlag, 1962. An interpretation of Kleist's works on the basis of his skeptical attitude toward the communicative ability of language. Shows the psychological connections between the sobriety of the *Novellenstil* and the subjectivity of the *Dramenstil* and attributes tragedy to the confusions created by language.

Ibel, Rudolf. *Heinrich von Kleist. Schicksal und Botschaft.* Hamburg: Holstein Verlag, 1961. A compact critical biography and readable guide for the semi-initiates to Kleist's world with some attention given to the "Prussian" or "German" elements in his character and literary work.

Ide, Heinz. *Der junge Kleist. ". . . in dieser wandelbaren Zeit . . ."* Würzburg: Holzner Verlag, 1961. An exhaustive analysis of Kleist's letters, written prior to and immediately after the Kant crisis, on the basis of existentialist theories, attempting to prove that he experienced the world in his very own (existential) way but had to express himself in the prevailing and inadequate matrices of thought of the "popular philosophy."

Koch, Friedrich. *Heinrich von Kleist. Bewusstsein und Wirklichkeit.* Stuttgart: J. B. Metzlersche Verlagsbuchhandlung, 1958. In Kleist's portrayal of the clash between man's subjective "consciousness" and "reality," Koch detects three major phases: one, despair over the absurdity of the world and man's helplessness in the clutches of fate; two, revolt against this absurdity and frenetic strive to realize one's goal; three, recognition of the invincibility of "reality" and retrenchment into inner "feeling" as an effective counterforce.

Kohrs, Ingrid. *Das Wesen des Tragischen im Drama Heinrichs von*

Kleist. Marburg/Lahn: Simons Verlag, 1951. An interpretation of the tragic element in Kleist's dramas based on existentialist notions of man's "engagement" in the world.

Kommerell, Max. "Die Sprache und das Unaussprechliche. Eine Betrachtung über Heinrich von Kleist," *Geist und Buchstabe der Dichtung. Goethe, Schiller, Kleist, Hölderlin*. Frankfurt a.M.: V. Klostermann, 1956 (first published in 1937). A classic treatise on the verbal and extraverbal means used by Kleist to portray his central concern: the preservation of the individual's enigmatic but deeply felt inner substance, his self.

Kreutzer, Hans Joachim. *Die dichterische Entwicklung Heinrichs von Kleist. Untersuchungen zu seinen Briefen und zu Chronologie und Aufbau seiner Werke*. Berlin: Erich Schmidt Verlag, 1968. A thorough philological investigation of the sources and genesis of Kleist's works and their chronology, preceded by a survey of Kleist criticism from its beginnings to the present, and followed by a discussion of Kleist's development as a writer on the basis of all his works. The book does not propound an overall concept but generally insists that an existentialist notion of man's "feeling of self" only explains one (among many) elements in Kleist's literary character. The book is highly recommended by the *Kleist-Gesellschaft* (the Kleist Society).

Lukács. Georg. "Die Tragödie Heinrich von Kleists," *Deutsche Realisten des 19. Jahrhunderts*. Bern: A. Francke, 1951 (an essay first published in 1936). A Marxist critique and interpretation of Kleist's life and work. His tragedy reflects the general tragedy of man living in a capitalistic society: individual isolation and inner solitude. Society cannot mediate between the individual and his destiny. The portrayal of monomaniacal feelings as in *Amphitryon, Penthesilea* and *Kaethchen* or the exaggerated importance of "chance" in most other works does not produce genuine tragedy. Kleist remains outside the lineage of high tragedy reaching from Shakespeare over Goethe and Schiller to Pushkin. In Kleist's "political" dramas nationalistic concerns quell the demands of personal feeling. From a sociological standpoint, only *The Broken Pitcher* and *Kohlhaas* are devoid of pathological traits (!).

Maass, Joachim. *Kleist, die Fackel Preussens. Eine Lebensgeschichte*. Wien: K. Desch, 1957. An informed and comprehensive biography leading to the rather gratuitous conclusion that in Kleist the "Prussian" spirit transcended itself and found its most ethereal expression.

March, Richard. *Heinrich von Kleist*. ("Studies in Modern European Literature and Thought") New Haven: Yale University Press,

1954. A very brief and useful critical biography stressing Rousseau's influence on Kleist and his own psychological problems as a basis for his works, especially *Penthesilea*.

Mayer, Hans. *Heinrich von Kleist. Der geschichtliche Augenblick.* Pfullingen: Verlag Günther Neske, 1962. Tries to connect the crises in Kleist's life with the crises in the "bourgeois" culture of his time. Only if one understands these "historic moments" can one supposedly grasp the tragedy of Kleist's life and the nature of his works.

Michaelis, Rolf. *Kleist.* ("Friedrichs Dramatiker des Welttheaters," 5) Velber b. Hannover: Erhard Friedrich Verlage, 1965. A cursory, journalistic account of Kleist's life and his dramas.

Müller-Seidel, Walter. *Versehen und Erkennen. Eine Studie über Heinrich von Kleist.* Köln: Böhlau Verlag, 1961. A discursive analysis of many formalistic and ideational aspects of Kleist's works centering on the notion—only peripherally expressed—that in seeking to preserve his self-identity the Kleistian character misapprehends reality and faces the danger of self-alienation but through error arrives at greater self-possession.

Muth, Ludwig. *Kleist and Kant. Versuch einer neuen Interpretation.* Köln: Kölner Universitäts-Verlag, 1954. A cogent and almost convincing argument for the theory that Kleist's Kant crisis was triggered by the *Critique of [Teleological] Judgment.*

Prang, Helmut. *Irrtum und Missverständnis in den Dichtungen Heinrich von Kleists.* Erlangen: Universitätsbund Erlangen, 1955. A brief monograph tracing the role of error and misunderstanding as the source of tragedy through the bulk of Kleist's works.

Reske, Hermann. *Traum und Wirklichkeit im Werk Heinrich von Kleists.* Stuttgart: Kohlhammer, 1969. A relatively short general presentation of Kleist's major works based on prevailing scholarly opinions but specifically trying to illustrate that Kleist should not be associated with German Romanticism and rather be seen as a peculiarly modernistic talent.

Reusner, Ernst von. *Satz-Gestalt-Schicksal. Untersuchungen über die Struktur in der Dichtung Kleists.* Berlin: Walter de Gruyter & Co., 1961. A highly theoretical and abstract discussion of the relationship between structure and meaning in Kleist's works.

Richardson, F. C. *Kleist in France.* Chapel Hill: The University of North Carolina Press, 1962. An exhaustive survey and discussion of Kleist's relationship to France and the reception of his works in that country from the early nineteenth century to *c.* 1960, containing a list of all French translations of Kleist's works up to that time.

Schlagdenhauffen, Alfred. *L'univers existentiel de Kleist dans le*

"*Prince de Hombourg.*" Paris: Société d'Edition Les Belles Lettres, 1953. An existentialist analysis of *Homburg* leading to the pessimistic conclusion that the Prince's absolutistic urge can never lead to a viable compromise with an absurd world, much less to personal fulfillment.

Silz, Walter. *Heinrich von Kleist. Studies in His Works and Literary Character.* Philadelphia: University of Pennsylvania Press, 1961. A collection of essays on various facets of Kleist's works by the doyen of contemporary American Kleist critics. Especially noteworthy are Silz's unorthodox and somewhat censorious interpretation of the essay "On the Marionette Theater" and his readings of *Kohlhaas* and *Homburg.* A useful and exhaustive chapter deals with recurrent linguistic motifs in all of Kleist's writings.

Stahl, Ernst Leopold. *Heinrich von Kleist's Dramas.* (Modern Language Studies, 4) Oxford: B. Blackwell, 1948. A terse discussion of Kleist's intellectual and artistic development from the metaphysical pessimism of the early period, through the mild optimism of the *Kaethchen,* to a concern with more practical, thisworldly problems in *Arminius* and *Homburg.* Contains many valuable observations on structure, technique, and style and attempts to prove that *Guiscard* was Kleist's first work.

Streller, Siegfried. *Das dramatische Werk Heinrich von Kleists.* Berlin: Rütten and Loening, 1966. An assessment of Kleist's dramas and of *Kohlhaas* by a critic from the Democratic Republic of Germany stressing the importance of the clash between Kleist's inner experiences and the social developments of his time, which supposedly led to his alienation from the bourgeois class.

Turk, Horst. *Dramensprache als gesprochene Sprache. Untersuchungen zu Kleists "Penthesilea."* Bonn: H. Bouvier & Co., 1965. A detailed linguistic analysis of *Penthesilea* showing how the subjectivist drive for "self"-expression of the Kleistian individual affects syntax and imagery.

Wiese, Benno von. "Der Tragiker Heinrich von Kleist und sein Jahrhundert," *Die deutsche Tragödie von Lessing bis Hebbel. II. Teil. Tragödie und Nihilismus.* Hamburg: Hoffmann und Campe, 1964 (6th edition), pp. 275–344. Comparison of the tragic in Schiller, Goethe and Kleist, followed by a discussion of various themes in Kleist, such as "illusion" and "reality"; the tragic and the transfigured existence; Penthesilea as the marionette and the tragic being; tragedy, death, and history in Kleist. A perceptive, if somewhat wordy, study.

Wolff, Hans M. *Heinrich von Kleist. Die Geschichte seines Schaffens.* Bern: Francke Verlag, 1949. A critical biography postulating a highly controversial chronology of Kleist's works and stressing the importance of political theory in their interpretation, such as Rousseau's ideal state in *Penthesilea* or Adam Müller's political philosophy in *Homburg*.

III. The articles and essays listed below have been of particular aid to this study:

Baumgärtel, Gerhard. "Zur Frage der Wandlung in Kleists *Prinz Friedrich von Homburg*," *Germanisch-Romanische Monatsschrift*, New Series, XVI/3 (July 1966), 264–77.

Burckhardt, Sigurd. "Kleist's *Hermannsschlacht:* The Lock and the Key," *The Drama of Language. Essays on Goethe and Kleist*. Baltimore: The Johns Hopkins Press, 1970.

Crosby, Donald H. "Heinrich von Kleist's 'Der Zweikampf,'" *Monatshefte*, LVI (1964), 191–201.

Dyer, D. G. "Plus und Minus in Kleist," *Oxford German Studies*, 2 (1967), 75–86.

Dyer, Denys. "The Imagery in Kleist's *Penthesilea*," *Publications of the English Goethe Society*, 31 (1961), 1–23.

Fricke, Gerhard. "Kleists *Prinz Friedrich von Homburg*," *Germanisch-Romanische Monatsschrift*, N.S., II (1951/52), 189–208.

Friedrich, Heinz. "Heinrich von Kleist und Franz Kafka," *Berliner Hefte*, 4/11 (1949), 440–48.

Gausewitz, Walter. "Kleists 'Erdbeben in Chili,'" *Monatshefte*, 55 (1963), 188–94.

Gray, Ronald. "Jenseits von Sinn und Unsinn. Kleist's *Penthesilea* and its Critics," *Publications of the English Goethe Society*, 37 (166/67), 57–82.

Henschel, Arnold J. "The Primacy of Free Will in the Mind of Kleist and in the 'Prince of Homburg,'" *German Life and Letters*, 17 (1963/64), 97–115.

Hubbs, V. C. "The Concept of Fate in Kleist's '*Schroffenstein*,'" *Monatshefte*, LVI (1964), 339–45.

Kunz, Josef. "Das Phänomen der tragischen Blindheit im Werke Kleists," *Germanisch-Romanische Monatsschrift*, N.S., XIII (1963), 180–93.

———. "Die Tragik der Penthesilea," *Literatur- und Geistesgeschichte. Festgabe für Heinz Otto Burger*. Edited by Reinhold Grimm and Conrad Wiedemann. Berlin: Erich Schmidt Verlag, 1968, 208–24.

Lepper, K. H. "Zur Polarität der Weltsicht in Kleists Novellen," *Trivium*, II (1967), 95–119.

Lucas, R. S. "Studies in Kleist. I. Problems in 'Michael Kohlhaas' II.

'Das Erdbeben in Chili.' " *Deutsche Vierteljahrsschrift,* 44/1 (March 1970), 120–50.

Mann, Thomas. "Kleists *Amphitryon:* Eine Wiedereroberung," *Thomas Mann. Gesammelte Werke,* Vol. 9 ("Reden und Aufsätze"), 187–228. Berlin: S. Fischer, 1960.

Martini, Fritz. "Kleists 'Der zerbrochene Krug,' Bauformen des Lustspiels," *Jahrbuch der Deutschen Schillergesellschaft,* 9 (1965), 373–419.

Müller, Richard Matthias. "Kleists 'Michael Kohlhaas,' " *Deutsche Vierteljahrsschrift,* 44/1 (March 1970), 101–19.

Nordmeyer, Henry Waldemar. "Kleists *Amphitryon,*" *Monatshefte,* 38/1, 3, 5, 6 (1946); 39/2 (1947).

Peters, F. G. "Kafka and Kleist: A Literary Relationship," *Oxford German Studies,* I (1966), 114–62.

Politzer, Heinz. "Kleists Trauerspiel vom Traum: *Prinz Friedrich von Homburg,*" *Euphorion,* 64/2 (1970), 200–20.

Reske, Hermann. "Die Kleistische Sprache," *The German Quarterly,* 36 (1963), 219–35.

Schadewaldt, Wolfgang. "Der 'Zerbrochene Krug' von Heinrich von Kleist und Sophokles' 'König Oedipus,' " *Schweizer Monatshefte,* 37/4 (July 1957), 311–18.

Scherer, Michael. "Die Heilige Caecilie oder die Gewalt der Musik," *Monatshefte,* 56 (1964), 97–102.

Schrimpf, Hans Joachim. "Tragedy and Comedy in the Works of Heinrich von Kleist," *Monatshefte,* 58 (1966), 193–208.

Schunicht, Manfred. "Heinrich von Kleist: 'Der Zerbrochene Krug,' " *Zeitschrift für deutsche Philologie,* 84/4 (November 1965), 550–62.

Seeba, Hinrich C. "Der Sündenfall des Verdachts. Identitätskrise und Sprachskepsis in Kleists 'Familie Schroffenstein,' " *Deutsche Vierteljahrsschrift,* 44/1 (March 1970), 64–100.

Sembdner, Helmut. "Neues zu Kleist," Sonderdruck aus dem *Jahrbuch der deutschen Schillergesellschaft,* VII (1963) Stuttgart: Alfred Kröner Verlag.

Sokel, Walter. "Kleist's Marquise of O . . . , Kierkegaard's Abraham and Musil's Tonka," *Wisconsin Studies in Contemporary Literature,* 8 (1967), 505–16.

Stahl, Ernest L. "Guiscard and Oedipus," *Tulane Drama Review,* 6/3 (1962), 172–77.

Staiger, Emil. "Kleist: Das Bettelweib von Locarno," *Meisterwerke deutscher Sprache.* Zürich: Atlantis Verlag, 1957, 100–17.

Szondi, Peter. "Amphitryon," *Euphorion,* 55/4 (1961), 249–59.

Tatar, Maria M. "Psychology and Poetics: J. C. Reil and Kleist's 'Prinz Friedrich von Homburg,' " *The Germanic Review,* XLVIII/1 (January 1973), 21–34.

Thomas, Ursula. "Heinrich von Kleist and Gotthilf Heinrich Schubert," *Monatshefte*, 51 (1959), 249–61.
Wittkowski, Wolfgang. "Skepsis, Noblesse, Ironie. Formen des Als-Ob in Kleists 'Erdbeben,' " *Euphorion*, 63/3 (1969), 247–83.
——. "Absolutes Gefühl und Absolute Kunst in Kleists 'Prinz Friedrich von Homburg,' " *Der Deutschunterricht*, 13/2 (June 1961), 27–71.

Note: The *Jahrbuch der Kleist-Gesellschaft*, 1937, contains a complete Kleist bibliography up to 1938. Subsequent bibliographies that might be consulted are: Paul Kluckhohn, "Kleist-Forschung 1926–43," *Deutsche Vierteljahrsschrift*, 1943, and Eva Rothe, "Kleist-Bibliographie 1945–60," *Jahrbuch der deutschen Schillergesellschaft*, 1961. The annual bibliography of the *Publications of the Modern Language Association* and the serviceable *Bibliographie der deutschen Literaturwissenschaft*, 1945 following, by Eppelsheimer-Köttelwesch will provide up-to-date information.

IV. The following are the most important critical editions of Kleist's works published from 1900 on:

Schmidt, Erich, ed. *Heinrich von Kleists Werke* in cooperation with Georg Minde-Pouet and Reinhold Steig, 5 vols. Leipzig and Wien: Bibliographisches Institut, 1904–5. Revised and expanded edition, by Georg Minde-Pouet. 7 vols. Leipzig: Bibliographisches Institut, 1936–38.
Sembdner, Helmut, ed. *Heinrich von Kleist. Sämtliche Werke und Briefe*. 2 vols. München: Carl Hanser Verlag, 1952. Revised and expanded edition of the above. 2 vols. 1961.
Sembdner, Helmut, ed. *Heinrich von Kleist. dtv Gesamtausgabe*. Based on Sembdner's 1961 edition, with some additions and revisions. 8 vols. München: Deutscher Taschenbuch Verlag, 1964 (first 7 vols.), 1969 (8th vol.).

Usable editions are the following:

Laaths, Erwin, ed. *Heinrich von Kleist. Sämtliche Werke*. München, Zürich: Droemersche Verlagsanstalt Th. Knaur Nachf., 1 vol., 1962 (?). (Contains Kleist's dramas, *Novellen*, poems, and prose writings but not the letters, with an introduction by the editor.)

Stenzel, Gerhard, ed. *Heinrich von Kleist. Werke.* ("Die Bergland Buch Klassiker") Salzburg, Stuttgart: Verlag "Das Bergland Buch," 1 vol. (no date). (Contains the dramas, *Novellen,* some poems and prose writings, a few letters, some illustrations and commentaries, and a biographical study of Kleist written by the editor.)

V. The following publications are helpful for purposes of biographical research:

Sembdner, Helmut, ed. *Heinrich von Kleists Lebensspuren. Dokumente und Berichte der Zeitgenossen.* ("Sammlung Dieterich") Bremen: Carl Schünemann Verlag, 1964 (revised 2nd edition). (Letters and commentaries by Kleist's contemporaries.)
——. *Heinrich von Kleist. Geschichte meiner Seele. Ideenmagazin.* ("Sammlung Dieterich") Bremen: Carl Schünemann Verlag, 1959. (An attempt to extrapolate from Kleist's letters those passages which might express the essence of his "Geschichte meiner Seele" and "Ideenmagazin," two lost autobiographical treatises.)

VI. Very absorbing and elucidating is Sembdner's collection of judgments pronounced on Kleist by well-known writers, thinkers, and critics in the nineteenth and twentieth centuries:

Sembdner, Helmut, ed. *Heinrich von Kleists Nachruhm.* ("Sammlung Dieterich.") Bremen: Carl Schünemann Verlag, 1967. Sembdner has also edited Kleist's *Berliner Abendblätter* (Stuttgart, 1959) and *Phoebus* (Darmstadt, 1961).

VII. The Kleist Society ("Heinrich-von-Kleist-Gesellschaft"), revived after World War II, publishes an annual or biannual monograph or collection of essays on some facet of Kleist scholarship. The following have been of particular interest to this study:

1964. *Kleist und die Gesellschaft. Eine Diskussion.* (Essays by E. Catholy, K. O. Conrady, H. Ide, W. Müller-Seidel.) Berlin: Erich Schmidt Verlag, 1965.
1965–66. *Kleists Aufsatz über das Marionettentheater. Studien und Interpretationen.* (Containing ten essays.) Berlin: Erich Schmidt Verlag, 1967.
1968. *Kleist und Frankreich.* (Essays by C. David, W. Wittkowski, L. Ryan.) Berlin: Erich Schmidt Verlag, 1969.

VIII. The following existing translations of Kleist's works have been used:

DRAMAS

Kirkup, James. *The Prince of Homburg.* (*The Classic Theatre.* Edited by Eric Bentley. Vol. II.) New York: Doubleday Anchor, 1959.

Morgan, Bayard Quincy. *The Broken Pitcher.* (University of North Carolina Studies in the Germanic Languages and Literatures, 31) New York: AMS Press Inc., 1966.

Pierce, F. E. *The Kaethchen of Heilbronn. Fiction and Fantasy of German Romance. Selections from the German Romantic Authors, 1790–1830, in English Translation.* (Copyright © 1927 by Carl F. Schreiber). New York: Oxford University Press, 1927.

Price, Mary J., and Lawrence M. *The Feud of the Schroffensteins.* ("Poet Lore," XXVII) Boston, 1916.

Scheuer, L. R. "Robert Guiscard," *Tulane Drama Review,* Vol. 6, No. 3 (March, 1962).

Sommerfeld (*sic.*) = Sonnenfeld, Marion. *Amphitryon.* Ungar Paperbacks, 1962.

Trevelyan, Humphrey. *Penthesilea.* (*The Classic Theatre.* Edited by Eric Bentley. Vol. II.) New York: Doubleday Anchor, 1959.

Note: There is no complete translation of *The Battle of Arminius* (*Die Hermannsschlacht*). The translations of the few passages cited in the respective chapters are my own. All the translations of the dramas used in this study have been slightly modified by replacing "thou," "thee," "thy," and similar forms with their more modern equivalents.—R.E.H.

NOVELLEN

Greenberg, Martin. *The Marquise of O—— and Other Stories.* New York: Criterion Books, 1960. Reissued, Ungar Paperbacks, 1974.

ESSAYS

Murray, Cherna. "About the Marionette Theater," *Life and Letters Today,* Vol. 16, No. 8 (Summer 1957).

Note: The translations from Kleist's other essays and his letters are my own.—R.E.H.

Index